W9-CGN-856

ANXIOUS PLEASURES

Thomas Gregor

ANXIOUS PLEASURES

The Sexual Lives of an Amazonian People

The University of Chicago Press
Chicago and London

Thomas Gregor is director of the Program in Anthropology at Vanderbilt University. He is the author of *Mehinaku: The Drama of Daily Life in a Brazilian Indian Village* and is one of the filmmakers of "We are Mehinaku."

THE UNIVERSITY OF CHICAGO PRESS, CHICAGO 60637
THE UNIVERSITY OF CHICAGO PRESS, LTD., LONDON

Printed in the United States of America

94 93 92 91 90 89 88 87 86 85 54321

Library of Congress Cataloging in Publication Data
Gregor, Thomas.
Anxious pleasures—the sexual lives of an Amazonian people.

Bibliography: p.
Includes index.
1. Mehinaku Indians—Social life and customs.
2. Indians of South America—Brazil—Social life and customs. 3. Sex role—Brazil. I. Title.
F2520.1.M44G725 1985 306.7'08998081 84-23938
ISBN 0-226-30742-5

For
Robert F. Murphy

Contents

Illustrations

Tables

Acknowledgments

IT HAS BEEN SEVENTEEN YEARS SINCE I FIRST VISITED THE MEHINAKU Indians of Central Brazil, who are the subjects of this book. Looking back over these many years, it is difficult to separate my own efforts from those who assisted me. Most influential of all has been Robert F. Murphy, my dissertation advisor at Columbia University in the 1960s. Long before research on gender was fashionable, he encouraged his students to study this vital dimension of human life. His own work on the Mundurucu Indians of Brazil has served as a model for me in the analysis of Mehinaku sexuality.

Field work in tribal societies is of necessity a cooperative endeavor, demanding major commitments of funds and assistance from granting agencies and colleagues. My work in Brazil has been generously supported by grants from the National Science Foundation, the National Institutes of Health and the University Research Council of Vanderbilt University. In the field, my work was formally sponsored by the Museu Nacional of Rio de Janeiro and the Fundação Nacional do Índio. I benefited from the hospitality and assistance of the Indian post (Posto Leonardo Villas Boas) and its capable administrators, Orlando Villas Boas and Olimpio Serra. The Mehinaku themselves, during my more than a year and a half of research, have always been gracious hosts and patient teachers.

In writing this book, I owe much to my colleagues. I am especially grateful to Kenneth Kensinger, Bernd Lambert, and Waud Kracke for their careful reading of the manuscript and helpful criticisms. Some of my interpretations of Mehinaku myths and dreams owe much to Professor Kracke's suggestions. His own pioneering research in the dreams of South American Indians has demonstrated the potential of this kind of inquiry and stimulated my own efforts among the Mehinaku. I also gratefully acknowledge the invaluable and generous assistance of Emilienne Ireland. She has conducted research among the Waura Indians, a tribe whose language and culture are similar to those of the Mehinaku. Ms. Ireland's comments and corrections have enriched this study in many areas, but I have especially benefited from her rapport with and knowledge of Waura and Mehinaku women.

I also must acknowledge the assistance and encouragement of my family and friends. George Guilfoyle's and Michael Shodell's reading of the manuscript has enhanced the final product. Arthur S. Gregor's world-class editing rounded the corners of my prose and sharpened the logic of my discussion.

To all of these friends, kin, and colleagues, my gratitude and appreciation.

Author's Note

The translations of Mehinaku words and text are free ones, intended to render the sense of what is said rather than its literal meaning. Mehinaku words are transcribed with phonetic symbols that have rough equivalents in English: *a* as in f*a*ther, *e* as in b*e*t, *i* as in mach*i*ne, *o* as in n*o*te, and *u* as in r*u*le. Among the dipthongs, *ai* as in *ai*sle, *au* as in h*ou*se and *ei* as in v*ei*l. One vowel, *ɨ*, has no near equivalent in English. It is a high, central, unrounded vowel somewhat like the vowel sound in the French *seule*.

To protect the privacy of individuals, all of the Mehinaku names other than those crediting art work are pseudonyms.

Introduction: Sexuality, the Mehinaku, and Ourselves

Good fish get dull, but sex is always fun.
—Ketepe, a Mehinaku villager

WE AMERICANS LIVE IN AN EROTICIZED ENVIRONMENT. SEX INFUSES OUR media, advertising, popular culture, and arts. At least fifteen regularly published scientific journals in English are devoted to sex research, and a major advance in our knowledge about sex, such as those achieved by Kinsey or Masters and Johnson, receives national attention.[1] Surprisingly, however, we know little about sexual behavior beyond the boundaries of Western society. With the exception of Bronislaw Malinowski's pioneering research (1929) and a few more recent studies (such as Ortner and Whitehead 1975), our knowledge of human sexuality (as opposed to Western sexuality) is focused on relatively mechanical accounts of the who, what, where, and how of sexual activity. Ford and Beach's classic study, *Patterns of Sexual Behavior,* is a compendium of this kind of anthropological exotica. Tables and charts summarize the preferred locations for coitus (indoors, outdoors, private family dwellings, unpartitioned multiple family dwellings), standards of female beauty (small ankles, shapely and fleshy calves, long and pendulous breasts), positions of intercourse, and much more. From the text, we learn that upon "returning

1. The following titles are derived from a perusal of Ulrich's *International Periodicals Directory* (1982) under several index subheadings: *Journal of Sex Research, Journal of Homosexuality, Archives of Sexual Behavior, Medical Aspects of Human Sexuality, Sexual Medicine Today, Sexuality and Disability, Journal of Sex and Marital Therapy, Journal of Sex Education and Therapy, Journal of Sex, Sexology, Sessuality/Sexuality, Sexology Today, Sex Education Today, SIECUS Report,* and *Sex News.* There are undoubtedly other titles as well.

from a head-hunting raid, the Lhota Naga hang up the heads, fingers and toes of their victims and then sleep apart from their wives for six nights" (1951, 77).

Patterns of Sexual Behavior was a path-breaking work in the comparative study of sexual conduct and deserves an eminent status. Lost in the often intriguing accounts, however, are the meaning and context of sexuality. What are the explanations of the people themselves for their sexual behavior? How do they conceive the sexual relationship of male and female, the nature of libido, and the act of conception? What is the relationship of their sexual conduct to other aspects of gender, such as work and kinship? The answers to such questions make behavior meaningful, place it in a cultural context, and give a new dimension to the comparative study of sexuality. Moreover, they open unexpected vistas on other areas of culture since sexual ideas invariably spill over into and infuse apparently sex-neutral spheres of daily life. We are aware of this pattern in our own society, where sex and eroticism appear in what are objectively outlandish contexts, such as promotional pitches for automobiles and toothpaste. In many non-Western cultures, sexuality is even more pervasive, constituting an organizing model for social life. Although it has been many years, I still recall the beginning of my own education on this point.

In November of 1967, I arrived in Jalapapuh, "Place of the Ant," the Mehinaku village in Central Brazil where I was to spend the next year gathering data for my doctoral dissertation. The women had carried my duffle bags and trunks into the house of the chief, and I was escorted into the men's house, a small building in the center of the village. Inside the windowless temple and clubhouse, the men worked on baskets, arrows, and other crafts. A few men, in pairs, rubbed red and black pigment in ornamental designs upon each others' bodies. The mood was warm and rowdy. A shouted joke occasioned a chorus of laughter and playful banter. Suddenly, one of the older men gestured to a set of three bassoon-sized musical instruments in the corner of the building and began to lecture to me in Mehinaku. The laughter died down, and the other men listened attentively. Not having understood a word, I turned to a villager who spoke some Portuguese. He translated: "You are in the house of the spirit Kauka. Those are his sacred flutes. Women may not see anything in here. If a woman comes in, then all the men take her into the woods and she is raped. It has always been that way."

Although I did not fully understand it at the time, this brief speech was an introduction to some of the facts of Mehinaku male-female relations. Here, the men in effect told me, is a society in which sex determines the use of public space, the organization of religion, and the politics of village life. The system is maintained by the threat of phallic aggression. Sex is an overwhelming basis for relationships that permeates and deflects virtually every other social bond.

Living in this "genderized" society, the Mehinaku villagers are consciously aware of sex as a fascinating human activity. Like us, they are self-reflective and inquiring. Lacking journals and laboratories, however, they look back to mythical times for explanations of today's behavior. The legends of the past account for the differences between male and female, the origins of sexual desire, the invention of sex, the mechanics of procreation, and the nature of sexual jealousy. Ultimately, sex is an organizing metaphor for the villagers that structures their understanding of the cosmos and the world of men and spirits. A description of Mehinaku sexuality is also an account of their culture. One aim of this book is to explain who the Mehinaku are by examining their sexual nature. Beyond this goal, a richly textured account of a foreign culture's sexuality provides a basis for comparing ourselves to others, for sorting out the biological and cultural determinants of sexuality, and for testing theories of sexual behavior. This study is intended as a step beyond the limits of our own society's mores toward a greater knowledge of human sexuality.

Human Sexuality

The anthropology of sexual behavior has established that sexuality is astonishingly plastic and variable in its expression from culture to culture. No purported universals of sexual behavior are unquestioned, and only a few seem reasonably well documented. Among the best established of these is that males have a higher level of sexual interest than do females. Evidence in favor of this proposition includes men's higher levels of androgens, which are connected to the sexual drive in both male and female; the suppressibility of the orgasm in many sexually dysfunctional women; and the lower level of sexual stimulation required for male arousal.[2]

The cultural evidence in favor of higher levels of male libido is also persuasive. Societies differ in the relative sexual freedom they accord men and women, but everywhere men are freer than women. Men are the ones who pursue women, who initiate sexual relations, and who

2. Only the latter point is seriously contended by a few experiments showing that women may be as easily aroused as men by erotic materials (see Hoyenga and Hoyenga 1979, 329–31, for a review of the literature). The most thorough-going statement of the more persuasive case for substantial biological differences between men and women in sexual arousal is Donald Symons's *The Evolution of Human Sexuality*, which will be frequently cited during the course of our discussion.

pay for sexual services with goods, services, and tokens of commitment. As Peter Blau puts it in describing the pattern in our own society, "courting is . . . a series of strategies and counter strategies with sex and commitment as the principal commodities" (1964, 88). Cross-cultural studies of gift giving in sexual relationships show that the American pattern is widespread. Where gifts are given in the context of sexual relationships, women do not reciprocate, or they reciprocate with gifts of lesser value (Symons 1979, 257–58). The reasons for greater male interest in sex may be primarily biological, but the evidence is clear that the pattern is substantially reinforced by culture. Practices such as female infanticide, polygyny, and a double standard of sexual behavior reduce the availability of female sexual services and make them scarce relative to male demand. It seems that everywhere in the world of sex we find a seller's market.

Among the Mehinaku, we shall see that high male libido, even in a society of relatively abundant female sexuality, has a profound impact on the villagers' culture. The imbalance of desire and gratification leads men to compete with other men for the favors of attractive women. It encourages them to produce the kinds of goods—notably fish—that women accept as a currency for sexual favors. The vacuum of unmet needs generates a culture of intrigue, jealousy, and humor. Mehinaku culture, in many ways like our own, is an eroticized culture. Sex, as the villagers like to say, is the pepper that gives life and verve.

VARIATIONS

Cultures differ in the amount of sex they permit, in the sexual orientation they promote, and in the details of courtship and sexual conduct. In an effort to classify the overall tone of these variations, George Becker (1984) usefully distinguishes between "sex-positive" and "sex-negative" orientations. The classic example of the former are the Polynesian islanders, among whom the sexual behavior of the Mangaians is especially well described. Here we learn that sex approaches a national pastime in which both men and women are enthusiastic participants. A general belief that abstinence from sex causes physical harm plus a sense of competition encourages a remarkable amount of sexual activity. Thus Donald Marshall notes, "Some of the strongest contestants in the 'race' (those who have a penis tattooed on their thigh or a vagina tattooed on their penis) will have tested up to sixty or seventy" lovers before they are twenty. The term for "orgasmic experience is the same as that for the achievement of perfection" (1972, 126, 162).

On the opposite end of the sexual spectrum are the sex-negative Irish of Inis Beag, as described by John Messenger (1972). In Inis Beag, sex is shrouded with feelings of guilt and sinfulness. Sexual activity is limited to the marital relationship, but even there occasions little joy. Intercourse takes place "with underclothes not removed," with a minimum of foreplay, and in an atmosphere of tension and guilt. For the women, sex is regarded as a kind of abuse that they must endure in the interest of procreation.

Despite their differences in the evaluation of sex, the people of Inis Beag and the Mangaia show a number of points of agreement. Among the Mangaians, men are more sexually motivated than women. Thus a man must please a woman by prolonging the act of intercourse and engaging in a variety of sexual techniques designed to gratify her. Such is the market in sexuality, however, that women need not perform to retain a man's interest. Among the sexually anxious Irish, the equation seems to balance in the same way. Hence Messenger learns from a local woman that "men can wait a long time for 'it,' but we can wait a lot longer" (ibid., 109). A second point of agreement between the two cultures is that although one is sex-positive and the other sex-negative, both are sex-oriented. Despite all appearances to the contrary, the inhabitants of Inis Baeg devote substantial energy to sex: repressing it, feeling guilty about it, denying it. A thoroughgoing sex-neutral orientation remains only a theoretical possibility, although there are a few candidates for this designation.[3]

Statistical research on sexuality in large samples of societies has tentatively established that sex-negative and sex-positive orientations are traceable to social complexity and, more directly, to socialization practices. Sex-positive societies like the Mangaians' tend to be those with small-scale communities where sexuality is free from the entanglements of arranged marriage, centralized religion, property rights, and political control (Murdock 1964; Prescott 1975; Stephens 1972). Sexual freedom is also associated with an introduction to sex in childhood that leaves the individual relatively

3. The Dani of the New Guinea Highlands may qualify. Karl Heider (1976) reports that the Dani are a low-energy people. Their expressions of emotion are muted, their intellectual life is minimal, and even their attitude toward death is casual. According to Heider, they honor a four-to-six-year taboo on sexual relations after the birth of a child. So scrupulously is this custom followed that no Dani siblings are less than five years apart. Moreover, the Dani have no alternate sexual outlets such as masturbation or homosexuality. The Dani are candidates for the sex-neutral designation because, unlike the Irish of Inis Beag, their low levels of sexuality are maintained without visible evidence of repression. Abstinence, Heider tells us, is so easily achieved that for the Dani it is a nonissue. The jury is still out on a final verdict of sex neutrality for the Dani, however, owing to Pontius's criticism of Heider's data (1977) and the possibility that their low levels of sexuality may have a simple biological cause, such as an inadequate diet and the use of a pubic garment that places continual pressure on the *vas deferens.*

free from anxiety about his sexual feelings. Punishment for sexual activity in early years apparently represses adult sexual behavior and is associated with cultural practices that suggest sexual anxiety, such as beliefs that illness is caused by sex, taboos surrounding menstruation, and severe restrictions on sexual expression (Munroe and Munroe 1975, 107).

These associations are suggestive, but they may imply more knowledge than we actually have. In an article reviewing the many correlations between cultural practices and sexual permissiveness, Gwen Broude notes that the studies "provide an embarrassment of hypotheses with very little synthesis of theoretical positions and propositions from one investigation to the next" (1981, 646). Moreover, statistical correlations have only limited explanatory power when our focus moves from a large sample of cultures to a particular society. In the Victorian era, for example, America was largely a sex-negative culture.[4] During the nineteenth century, "excessive" sexuality was regarded as a cause of illness and insanity. Men were advised to "avoid marrying widows who may have had one or more husbands whose premature deaths were caused other than by accident . . . for they are likely to possess qualities in them that in their exercise, use up their husbands' stock of vitality, rapidly weakening the system and so causing them premature death" (Cowan 1980, 18). During this period, the language was dissected to remove sexual referents. Our speech still bears the scars. "Cock" became "rooster," "haycocks" became "haystacks," and "breasts" became "bosoms" (except on poultry, where they were referred to as "white meat"). In middle-class drawing rooms, piano legs were decorously dressed in ruffles, and the word "leg" itself gave way to the more antiseptic "limb."

By World War I, Victorian sexual morality was in decline, and today, after the sexual revolution of the last two decades, it persists only in isolated backwaters of our heterogeneous society. We can point to a variety of explanations for its demise, including the emergence of a benign scientific view of sexuality, the development of contraception, and the effect of the inclusion of women in the work force. But relative to the differences between most sex-positive and sex-negative societies, these are minor changes. The fundamental rhythms of American kinship, marriage, and socialization would not

4. Peter Gay (1984) presents a revisionist perspective of the lives of Victorians. His examination of diaries and other life history materials shows that some individuals managed to lead sexually fulfilling lives despite the antisexual culture of the period. Although Gay makes a strong case for sexual liberalism among some individuals, it is difficult to judge how typical these persons were.

seem to have shifted sufficiently to account for the sea change in sexual morality.

The American experience suggests that tracing the links between sexual expression and other facets of culture is not simple. The virtue of a case study rather than a statistical approach is that we can take account of the complexity of a system and present it in its full richness. Among the Mehinaku, for example, we shall see conduct that clearly appears to be sex-positive. By the time children enter early adolescence, they already have had sexual experience. As adults, they will participate in a system of extramarital sexuality that defies even the Mangaians' for comparison. Yet the villagers' pleasure is tempered by anxious feelings about the consequences of sexuality. Women are attractive and sex is pleasurable, yet men fear that intercourse will make them ill, stunt their growth, sap their vitality as wrestlers, attract dangerous spirits, and impair their skill as hunters and fishermen. The clash of desire and fear affects each man differently. A few are severely limited in their sexual behavior. A larger group participate in the system but make uneasy compromises in honoring taboos and otherwise evading the consequences of sex. And a few throw caution to the winds, maximize all their sexual opportunities, and worry little about the consequences. One of the goals of this book is to document the coexistence of a seemingly permissive pattern of sexual socialization with early experiences that may make sex seem dangerous as well as desirable. We shall follow the tensions generated by desire and fear as they are played out in masculine psychology, religion, and folk belief. Mehinaku culture is a sexualized culture that owes its energy as much to anxiety as to libido.

SEXUAL ORIENTATION

Among the strongest evidence for the plasticity of the sex drive is variation in sexual orientation. It is well known that some cultures foster homosexual experimentation (for example, ancient Greece), but recent evidence from New Guinea shows that with sufficient cultural pressure, the male sexual orientation can be alternately heterosexual and homosexual. The most comprehensive report is that of Gilbert Herdt, who describes a people of the Eastern Highlands who are pseudonymously named the "Sambia." After five months of working in a small Sambia village, Herdt unexpectedly learned of "secret institutionalized homosexual practices between youths and initiates." If a Sambia were to tell women or outsiders of these practices, he would be castrated or killed. "Even today," writes Herdt, "homosexuality remains hidden from women, children and outsiders" (1981, xv).

At age seven or eight, Sambia boys are taken from their mothers for initiation. They are told that semen is the source of life and growth. Semen makes babies. Semen is like mothers' milk. To grow up into men, they must consume semen by having oral sex with older boys. Initially the children are repelled by this prospect and are more or less forced into oral intercourse with adolescent boys. Eventually, however, they come to enjoy it and seek to multiply their sexual contacts so that they will rapidly grow to be manly warriors. At adolescence, the boys' role changes, and they now provide semen to the new generation of children. At first they are anxious about losing their own semen, but after instruction on how to magically replace it by consuming tree sap, they accept and enjoy this new form of homosexual relations. The next phase of Sambia sexuality is bisexual, and begins with betrothal to a preadolescent girl. When she is mature, the husband gives up his homosexual contacts and devotes himself exclusively to heterosexual relations. Only five percent of the men, according to Herdt, have serious difficulty in following the twisting trail of Sambia sexual orientation (ibid., 252 n. 60).

Herdt's work, as well as data from other societies (c.f. Ford and Beach 1951) further establishes the thesis first stated by Freud, that as a species we are "polymorphous perverse," capable of acting out virtually any sexual inclination. Among the Mehinaku, however, there are pressures and constraints that exclude homosexuality and restrict the choice of sexual object and behavior. The target of an individual's sexual overtures must fall within a narrow range of a continuum whose extremes are "self" and "nonhuman." Thus at one end, autoeroticism, incest, and homosexuality are ruled out. At the other, relations with Brazilians, culturally different Indians, and animals are also forbidden. The only proper sexual object is a cross-cousin of the opposite sex. Although a villager is occasionally able to negotiate exceptions and amendments to these rules, their existence makes sex a social activity that interwines with kinship, tribal identity, and the Mehinaku sense of what it means to be human.

We shall see, however, that the decisions the villagers make about sexual orientation are close calls. In mythology and ritual, the Mehinaku fantasize about an altogether different sexual world. In this world, humans engage in autoeroticism and copulate with close kin, with others of the same sex, with animals, and even with plants. In the most evolved of the fantasies, the villagers tell of an ancient matriarchy in which women occupied the men's house and men nursed babies. These tales are partly enacted in rituals of role reversal during which the men symbolically menstruate and imitate women.

Taken together, the myths and rituals suggest that there is a feminine core to the male personality that is in normal times shouted down by the aggressive bravado of Mehinaku men's culture. We shall see that ambiguity in male sexual identity is built into the process of socialization. Becoming a Mehinaku man is a painful process fraught with tension and insecurity. Dreams and other psychological data show that even as adults many of the village men continue to struggle with problems of masculine self-definition and separation from women. Ultimately, these conflicts penetrate every level of Mehinaku culture and show up in such apparently sex-neutral areas as folk medicine, blood kinship, and religion. Sex thereby brings a supreme ambiguity to Mehinaku life. It provides a basis for connectedness and warmth between men and women, but at the same time it generates fear, antagonism, and insecurity. The bittersweetness of sexuality makes the topic compellingly fascinating for the villagers and an object of intense speculation and interest. The Mehinaku culture of sexuality is dense and richly textured.

The purpose of this book is to explore Mehinaku sexual culture, to make it intelligible, and to cast it within a wider context of theory and data. There is much about the pattern that is exotic and even bizarre by our standards. American men are not as sexually free as the Mehinaku, they do not institutionalize rape, nor do they symbolically menstruate. Yet there are many points of correspondence, some appearing just where the two cultures seem to be farthest apart. One of the contentions of this study is that there are universalities in the male experience, and even a common symbolic vocabulary for its expression. If we look carefully, we will see reflections of our own sexual nature in the life ways of an Amazonian people.

ONE

The Mehinaku and the Sexual Data

> In ancient times, the Sun created man and woman. . . . He created the tribes of humankind. And to each he gave a place and a way to live.
>
> —from a Mehinaku myth

IN 1887, THE GERMAN EXPLORER KARL VON DEN STEINEN SET OUT WITH A pack train of oxen and mules to explore the headwaters of the Xingu River. After crossing nearly 350 miles of arid plains and scrub forest, he reached the vast and well-watered basin of the Xingu and its tributaries. Leaving the pack animals behind and hiring Indian guides and boatmen, he made his way down the Culiseu River. On 12 October 1887, he became the first recorded visitor to a Mehinaku village.

To von den Steinen, the villagers were savages. He cowed them into submission with shouts, gestures, and on one occasion, by shooting a bullet into a housepost (1940, 136–7). To the Mehinaku, von den Steinen was an apparition, a spirit visitor from another world who, like all spirits, was malevolent and unpredictable. Eighty years later, the villagers described their ancestor's reactions to this first visit: "When the white man came, everyone was very frightened and fled to the forest, leaving only the best bowmen in the village. . . . the young girls covered their bodies with ashes so they would be so unattractive that they would not be carried off. The people were given knives by the visitor but did not understand them, and they cut their arms and legs just trying to see what these new things were for." Today, the Mehinaku are easier to reach and more accustomed to visitors. They live on a vast government-secured reservation, the Xingu National

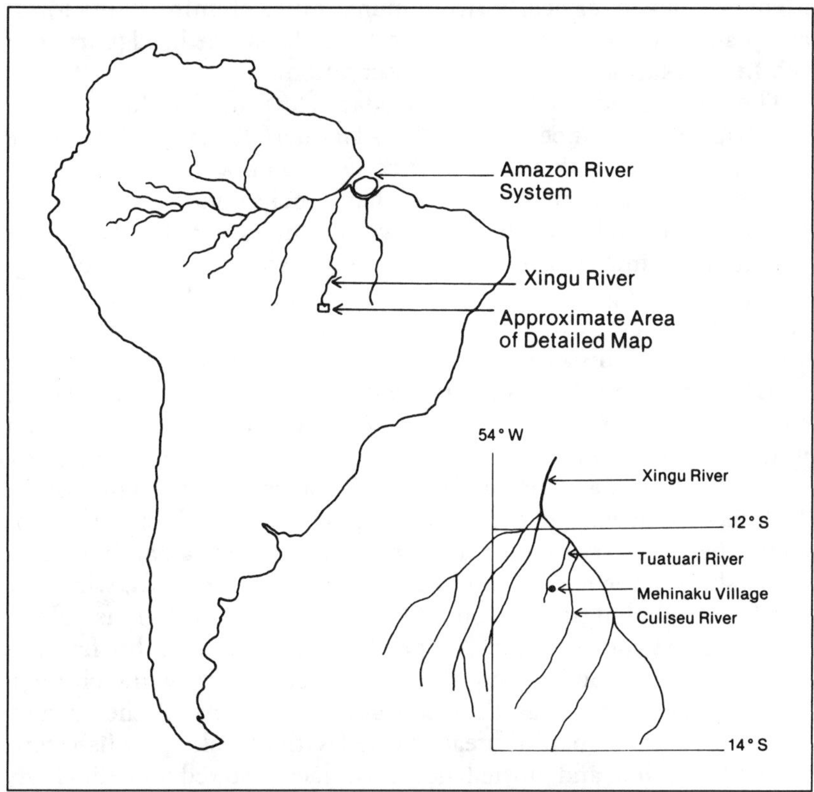

Location of the Xingu National Park and the Mehinaku Village.

Park (see map), whose headquarters are linked to the Brazilian Indian Agency in São Paulo by daily shortwave transmission. Yet the culture of the tribes of the region remains surprisingly similar to what von den Steinen described. The visitor still senses that he has left a familiar world and stepped into a distant time and place.

My wife and I first arrived in the Mehinaku village in 1967 when I was a graduate student of anthropology. We had begun our trip from Rio de Janeiro on a government plane, an ancient C-47 that had been used in World War II for paratroop missions. We sat with the other passengers on the long narrow metal benches on either side of the plane; the central aisle was reserved for cargo bound for airforce outposts—huge sacks of rice and beans, carcasses of beef—and for injured or sick persons on stretchers being carried to distant hospitals. In Xavantina, an all-but-inaccessible village on the "River of the Dead," we were stranded for five days awaiting a spare part that had to be flown in by the next plane from São Paulo. On the last leg of our flight, we flew over nearly two hundred miles of uninhabited forest and plain to land at Posto Leonardo Villas Boas, the headquarters of the Xingu National Park Indian reservation.

The post looked much as it does today: a few small buildings, a dirt air strip, and a canoe port on the Tuatuari River. Visitors were provided with a breakfast of sweet coffee and milk, two meals of rice and beans, and a space to hang their hammocks under a large thatch-roofed verandah. It was there that we first met the tribesmen of the region, who came to take a close look at the Americans and their bags of supplies and gifts. Among the visitors were the Mehinaku, who arrived in several canoes in the hope of bringing us back to their village. "We Mehinaku dance a lot," volunteered one of the young men who had an inkling of our interests. "We sing a lot too. And we speak a lot of Portuguese." The Mehinaku also claimed that their village was free from biting insects and near a beautiful stream. These were strong selling points, and so the following day, we set out for the Mehinaku village. The trip from the post was three hours by canoe along the Tuatuari River, and then a little more than an hour over land. The women carried our heaviest gear on their heads, while the chief walked alongside us, shouldering only my prestigious rifle.

Arriving at the community, the chief escorted us to his family's house. Our hammocks were tied to the house poles while children raced about to bring us firewood and water. One of the women presented us with manioc bread covered with a thick, spicy fish stew. Little boys tied and untied our shoe laces, stared unbelievingly through my eyeglasses, and peered into my mouth to marvel at my gold fillings. Later in the evening, the men of the village carried small benches sculpted in the shape of birds out to the center of the circular plaza, where a small fire was burning. The chief, who had assumed the role of my host, brought me with him. After being presented with a long cigar, I was asked a series of questions about why I had come and how long I intended to stay. I was closely interrogated about my relatives. Were my mother and father living? Was my sister married? Why did I have no children? What of my uncles and aunts?

As a beginning anthropologist, I understood that among the Mehinaku, a tribal community of only eighty-five persons, kinship was the basis of social life. The villagers' inquiry was an effort to bridge the cultural gulf between themselves and the strange outsiders. But I was not prepared for the next line of questions, which were initiated by the chief. "We have heard of Americans," he assured me. "They are white men like Brazilians, though they are taller than Brazilians and other white men. Is it true that Americans eat babies?" I told him that was not true, and that Americans would be as horrified as Mehinaku at such a practice. The chief was apparently willing to accept my

Fig. 1. The world beyond the village. Our interest in the Mehinaku is matched by their curiosity about us. A book of photographs will circulate from house to house, and the visitor is closely questioned about the meaning of each picture. Where do the people who are illustrated live? How long would it take to get there? Are they warlike? Are they related to the visitor and his tribe? Do they make machines or buy them from Brazilians?

reassurances, yet the possibility of Americans' eating babies was within the realm of belief. I had entered a world astonishingly different from my own, so remote and parochial that my humanity was open to question. Yet in the days and months ahead, I came to appreciate that the Mehinaku world seemed isolated and remote only from my own perspective.

The villagers and the eight other similar tribes of the region had lived for hundreds of years in the vastness of the Upper Xingu Basin where they created a rich and complex culture. They surmounted the barriers of their different languages and developed a peaceful system of trade, intermarriage, and participation in each others' ceremonies. Today the invitations to these rituals are issued by ceremonial ambassadors who exchange gifts with the men of the neighboring tribes and address them with long speeches in an archaic tongue.

All of the tribes who participate in this system are called *putaka* by the Mehinaku, a term linguistically linked to the word for village and connoting a civilized and hospitable way of life. The term for "guest," by which I was referred to, is also putaka. In reality, however, my status as a putaka was at best honorary. Like all other white and Brazilian visitors, I was a *kajaiba,* a term that is tinged with ambivalent emotions of respect, fear, and uncertainty, even though the kajaiba, are regarded as humans (*neunei*). Both races were made in ancient times by the Sun, who sat the tribal chiefs about a fire in the center of his village. He then passed gifts around the circle, presenting to the kajaiba milk, machines, cars, and planes, and to the Xinguanos, manioc, bows and arrows, and clay bowls. Despite their different life ways, putaka and kajaiba are children of the Sun. Not so the non-Xingu Indians surrounding the putaka tribes, who in the past have raided the area, kidnapping women and children. These Indians are called *wajaiyu,* a term that is seldom uttered without a tone of contempt for their reputed filth and barbarism. Unlike the peaceful, civilized putaka, the wajaiyu "kill you in the forest. They sit on the prows of their canoes and defecate into the water. They eat frogs and snakes and mice. They rub their bodies with pig fat and sleep on the ground."

Gradually, as I came to appreciate the complex world the Xinguanos had created, I began to see the Mehinaku village, not as remote, but as a center of life. Each morning I was awakened by the rhythmic whistling of the young men as they went to bathe and the bustle of activity as the villagers left to tend their gardens or go fishing. Later, the women returned, carrying baskets of manioc tubers to begin the long process of reducing them to flour. At all times, the children played about the village. They played "plaza games," in which they imitated the men's wrestling in front of the men's house. By the river, they sculpted turtles, alligators, and forest animals from clay and ambushed one another in games of "jaguar."

Toward afternoon, the men returned from fishing trips, and the villagers whooped as they came into view along the straight paths that radiated from the village. Later in the men's house, after the heat of the midday sun had begun to subside, the fishermen worked on crafts and decorated their bodies in preparation for "wrestling time." Close by the wrestling matches, several of the men, dressed in feather headdresses and fiber skirts, danced and sang for the spirit Kaiyapa, who must be periodically appeased to ward off illness. After "wrestling time" families took their meals together. The returning fishermen shared their catch, so that there was something to eat in every house. As the sky darkened, the women and children got into their hammocks, and the men gathered around the small fire in the center of the village. Behind them was the wall of houses that surrounded the plaza, then the dark rampart of forest that encircled the now quiet village; overhead, a dome of stars, brilliant beyond the experience of city dwellers. Only during those quiet moments, when the hum and bustle of human activities had subsided, did my feeling of remoteness and isolation return.

The Nature of the Sexual Data

I had not intended to study sexuality when I first began to work with the Mehinaku. After my first field trip, however, I became convinced that a full understanding of the culture demanded it. Community organization, religion, the division of labor, and even the village ground plan reflected the importance of sex and gender. The villagers themselves seemed to have drawn the same conclusions. Their explanations of the conduct of their fellows emphasized erotic motivation and the idealized images of masculinity and femininity. But the Mehinaku did not clearly formulate a philosophy of gender and sex. A question such as "What does it mean to be a man or a woman?" inspired incomprehension in my informants. To approach the topic as an ethnographer, I found that I needed what has been called a "sociology of the obvious" in order to discern the assumptions and logic that the villagers took for granted. The data that inform this book therefore come from a variety of sources that include but go beyond the Mehinaku's own formulations about their society. Much of this material is the basic data of social anthropology, including ritual, kinship practices, dress, concepts of development, and the life cycle. Some of the evidence, however, is more personal in nature and requires a special introduction.

MEHINAKU SEXUAL BEHAVIOR AND ATTITUDES

Like many of the Indians of the Upper Xingu, the Mehinaku are open about sex (cf. Carniero 1958; Zarur 1975). There is little shame about sexual desire, and children will tick off the names of their parents' many extramarital lovers. Coming from a culture where such topics are approached delicately did not prepare me for the villagers' candor and unembarrassed accounts of sexual conduct. In retrospect, as I go over my taped interviews and other data on Mehinaku sexuality, I find that some of my uncertainties and gaps in knowledge are due more to my own occasional reticience than to my informants' unwillingness to respond. My material on female sexuality, for example, seems limited in light of the villagers' openness about sexual intimacies. Much of my information on this topic was elicited by my wife on our first field trip. This material was later supplemented by my own interviews and by indirect information such as biographies, dreams, and drawings.

My data on male sexual conduct is fuller and more intimate than my information on the women. The best of this material has come from my most recent trips to the Mehinaku (especially during the summer of 1977) because I had already acquired some knowledge of the topic and built relationships of trust and confidence with the villagers. The richest information of this period is included in some fifty hours of recorded interviews with four of the village men, the youngest a boy of twenty years, the oldest, a famous myth teller and village elder in his late sixties, the oldest man in the village. These interviews, conducted in the Mehinaku language, range from biographical information, dreams, and personal experiences to directed discussions of sexual attitudes and conduct. Interspersed throughout the interviews are a remarkable series of sexally oriented myths, which the men frequently offered as illustrations and evidence for their ideas about sexuality. Since these myths form some of the essential data in the study, we need some preparation for their logical structure and significance.

SEXUAL MYTHS

History for the Mehinaku has relatively little depth. Ask a villager about his ancestors, and he quickly moves back through the four or five generations of known genealogy and community history. In the minds of the villagers, this historical time was preceded by a period of time, perhaps equally long, in which events are uncertain and ancestors unknown. No matter how murky this time may have been, however, the life of the Mehinaku then is assumed to have been very much like that of the villagers of today, albeit idealized. Chiefs were said to be less prone to invidious oratory, and virtually everyone was taller, stronger, and better than they are today. Nonetheless, the descriptions of this period are plausible and may be based on fact. Both of these periods of historical time are designated "the past" (*ekwimya*).

Moving still further back in time, beyond the boundaries of the known or the possible, we come to the distant past, a period designated as *ekwimyatipa*, which I gloss as "ancient" or "mythic" time. During this period, the Sun shaped the geography of the Xingu and created the culture of its people. Breaking a great cauldron of water along the headwaters of the Xingu Basin, he fashioned the network of interlacing rivers and streams that crisscross the Xinguanos' territory. Then he shot arrows into the ground, creating the various tribes of humankind, and gave them their speech, dress, rituals, and technology. So rich is the oral tradition describing this period that there are few institutions that do not have a charter from mythic times. Religion, the relationships between the tribes of the region, geography, and cosmology all receive detailed treatment in these origin myths.

Within the body of myths, we find a set of stories that directly probe the nature of masculinity and femininity. These tales are not linguistically differentiated from others, though they occasionally may be jokingly referred to as *itsi aunaki*, "genital myths," as opposed to simply *aunaki*, "myths." With any encouragement from the listener, some of the stories are told in succession, for they are informally regarded as forming a group (*teupa*), in contrast to the remainder of the Mehinaku mythic heritage. Moreover, unlike other Mehinaku myths, these sexually related stories are usually told in the men's house rather than in the residences. The women are aware of the tales and even tell them themselves, but the stories are more properly a part of male culture.

Since the myths are a fundamental source of data for our study, it is critical to understand what they mean to the Mehinaku and what uses we can make of them. Clearly few, if any, of the stories can be read as literal history. Many of the events they describe are impossible (such as the creation of the Xingu River) or improbable (the belief that Mehinaku society was once matriarchal). The villagers themselves recognize the implausibility of the legends, at least for present times. Question an informant about the truth of the story, and he is likely to say: "In mythic time, mythic time, these things took place—not today." By the concept of ekwimyatipa, the Mehinaku create a second world where the laws of day-to-day living do not apply. In the curiously frozen world of the mythic past, events may occur out of sequence or be in total contradiction to one another. Thus we learn that the Sun, who created all men, was himself born at a time when men already seemed to exist, and that women, who were created to meet men's sexual needs, were sculpted out of wood prior to the creation of men. The Mehinaku are not overly preoccupied with such contradictions. They implicitly recognize that the myths are ahistorical and stand apart from the mundane world, where the limitations of reality can be ignored only at one's peril. As in the world of dreams, mythic events may occur with little relevance to the laws of space or time.

MYTHS AND DREAMS

The similarity of myth and dream, first proposed by Freud and subsequently developed by Jung, Roheim, and others, is perceived by the Mehinaku. As one informant speculatively remarked, "A myth is a dream that many have begun to tell." For our purposes, the comparison is particularly apt. Both myth and dream are fantasies whose content is minimally constrained by the checks and balances demanded by action in the real world. Thus the myth reveals emotional truths even when the plot is outlandish or impossible. Our search for these truths is facilitated by the special circumstances of the Mehinaku and their mythology. The Mehinaku are a small, homogeneous tribe whose mythology reflects a common heritage and a shared emotional life. Moreover, many Mehinaku tales are unabashedly rooted in the sexual wishes, fears, and conflicts that psychoanalysis tells us are at the core of our innermost selves. The stories are redolent with emotionally loaded sexual themes. Staple fare in Mehinaku mythology is incest, bestiality, and castration.

The style of the myths also encourages us to view them as personal fantasies. The tales often have an eerie, dreamlike quality suffused with elements of the mysterious and the uncanny. Scenes shift without explanation from earth to air and water. Symbols are condensed, so that the protagonists are simultaneously animal and human or are transformed from one to the other without preparation or explanation by the narrator. Events occur without finality; a death may be undone and persons brought back to life. The emotional emphasis is displaced, and what appears to be detail emerges as the myth's central meaning.

To the analyst of the dream, these distortions are commonplace. They are what Freud called "the dream work," the dreamer's effort to conceal unacceptable wishes or conflicts and still discharge their energy. The major difference between the dream and the myth is that the mechanism of the dream work is only rarely successful in making the dream entirely palatable. As a result, recollection of the dream rapidly disappears in the cloud of amnesia that fogs our waking moments. In the words of the psychoanalyst Jacob Arlow, dreams "are made to be forgotten" (1951, 379). Myths, on the other hand, are made to be remembered and repeated. They express "communally acceptable versions of wishes," which are so well dressed up in the esthetics and drama of narrative art that they are not only acceptable but even fun. As J. S. Bruner states, the myth "makes possible the containment of terror and impulses by the decorum of art and symbolism" (1960, 227).

Among the Mehinaku, myth telling is an especially relished art. The master of the myth (*aunaki wekehe*), as the accomplished raconteur is called, creates an atmosphere of enchantment that holds his audience spellbound. In our textual versions of the myths, I will only be able to do partial justice to this art form, since we will miss the rhetorical devices and sense of timing by which the narrator gives meaning to the story. We lose onomatopoeic vocabulary: the *puh-puh-puh* slap of the canoe paddle against the water, the *tek-tek-tek* of feet along a path, or the *tssyu* of a knife cutting a cord. In making the transition to written form, however, I have tried to present the myths as they were actually told, making only minor editorial changes, such as the elimination of extensive repetition. Even without the presence of a narrator, the stories are a delight.

But our pleasure in the Mehinaku tales of ancient times should not obscure the fact that the myth, like the dream, has a serious meaning. My approach to this meaning is eclectic. At times, as is increasingly true of contemporary psychological analysis of dreams, I focus on the "manifest content" of the myth, seeing it as a cautionary tale, a reflection of relationships between men and women, or a justification for an institution that governs the conduct of males and females. On occasion, however, I go further, examining the myth as a reflection of unconscious wishes or deep-seated conflicts. In support of such interpretations, I offer the villagers' personal fantasies, such as dreams or other life-history material, as well as additional cultural evidence. The myth thereby becomes one of a number of windows through which we view the Mehinaku personality.

MYTH, METAPHOR, AND LOGIC

Throughout the discussion of Mehinaku masculinity and femininity, I offer many of the villagers' own explanations of their institutions and customs. My interest in these beliefs derives from a conviction that unless native ideas about causality and motivation are understood, the data is threadbare. We may have the stuff of which the material is made, but not the weave that holds it together. Consider the following myth, which is similar in its underlying logic to many others we shall examine.

> A man learned that another villager was having sexual relations with his wife. Late one night, while the lover was asleep, he crept over to his house and slipped a loop of string over his penis. Pulling the string tight, he severed the penis and left the lover to bleed to death in his hammock. The next day, after returning from a successful fishing trip, he hid the penis in a fish and gave it to his wife. No sooner did she eat the fish than her tongue became immensely long and stretched to the ground. "Ahaaa!" she cried, and choked to death.

This myth can be properly approached as a cautionary tale about the hazards of extramarital adventures or as a myth reflecting castration fears. But what are the connecting links that hold the tale together? The first problem is that of motivation. I asked my informant why the husband castrated his wife's lover. Not surprisingly, the answer is sexual jealousy. The informant explains that the husband was angry because he did not wish to share his wife. In the picturesque Mehinaku vernacular, he "prized her genitals highly."

But how did the penis, once introduced into the wife's food, have its devastating effect? Here the answer is far from obvious, and it brings us directly to questions of logic and understanding. When pressed for an explanation, the informant seemed to feel that the connection of tongue and penis was intuitively clear. After some reflection, however, he said that the penis "got into" the tongue or that it "took" the tongue. But why the tongue and not some other part of the body? "Because," came the reply, "the tongue is like the penis" in that it is long, wet, sensual, and "eats its food."

The relationship of tongue and penis is based on analogy. The tongue is like a penis in that there are resemblances in appearance and activity. Some of the analogies, such as that of sex and eating, need to be explored further (see chapter 3), but the informant sees them as a sufficient explanation in themselves. Because the penis is like the tongue, the spatial differences between them collapse, the two organs merge, and the tongue-phallus chokes the woman to death. The analogy thereby establishes a bridge between things and concepts and makes possible leaps in thought that are unrestrained by either reality or logic.

To a large extent, thinking by analogy seems to lie behind many of the villagers' explanations of their culture. One would do well to avoid eating fish before wrestling, for example, because fish bones (like human bones) are easily broken. Similarly, a wrestler, by rubbing his body with rendered anaconda fat, can acquire the strength of the giant snake. Although it is no longer fashionable to ascribe such prelogical thought patterns to "primitive" people, there is no doubt that they are prevalent in the magical beliefs of many tribal groups. Sigmund Freud, in a still vital essay on the subject, "Magic and the Omnipotence of Thought", argued that metaphoric thinking, which he described as the overvaluation of thought, was characteristic of primitive peoples.

> Relations which hold between the ideas of things are assumed to hold equally between the things themselves. Since distance is of no importance in thinking—since what lies furthest apart both in time and space can without difficulty be comprehended in a single act of consciousness—so, too, the world of magic has a telepathic disregard for spatial distance and treats past situations as though they were in the present. (1950, 85)

Freud explained such magical thinking as a survival in adult culture of the child's prelogical effort to understand his world. Unfortunately, however, Freud went beyond this position to suggest (somewhat ambiguously) that tribal peoples were themselves immature and intellectually stunted at the level of children in our own culture. From a more modern perspective, however, we can conclude that much of human thought in all societies represents what analysts have called a "compromise formation" between the demands of reality on one hand and, on the other, the compelling "overvaluation of thought" characteristic of childhood. In certain areas of culture, reality-oriented thought prevails. Ask a Mehinaku why the fishing is better in one stream than another, and he sounds like an ecologist tracing out food chains and connections between predator fish, their prey, and the fruit-bearing trees along the banks and flood plains of some of the rivers.[1] But if we were to ask the same villager about the origins of men and women, the causes of sexual maturation, or the connections between tongue and penis in the myth, we would find ourselves on an entirely different level of explanation.

The point is that when an explanation or a myth rests on metaphor and the overvaluation of thought, we are surely dealing with emotionally based material. The informant's answer comes, not from a realistic search for a solution, but from his own desires and conflicts. When he and other villagers explain the tale or elaborate upon it, and as we bring in additional cultural and psychological evidence, we gradually move closer to the Mehinaku concepts of masculinity and femininity. But we have a ways to go before arriving at this goal. We must begin with the basics: the patterns of marriage, sex, kinship, and work that form the background of all relationships between Mehinaku men and women.

1. The interdependence of fish and the fruit-bearing tress along the flood plains of the Amazon Basin has only recently been discovered by ecologists (see Goulding 1980) even though it has long been part of the Mehinaku's knowledge of their environment.

TWO

Mehinaku Men and Women: A Sociology of Marriage, Sex, and Affection

> Kikyala! your "little hammock" just went down to the water.
>
> —Kama, referring to his friend's wife

AMONG THE MEHINAKU, THE "BATTLE OF THE SEXES" IS MORE THAN A metaphor. Men and women make insulting sexual jokes in each others' presence and engage in knock-down, drag-out brawls in the course of certain rituals. Much of this book describes the antagonistic character of men's and women's relationships and the price the men pay in fear of women and insecurity about their masculine selves. This focus is of theoretical interest, and it reflects the concerns of Mehinaku masculine culture. It is the oppositional nature of male and female interaction that draws the attention of the villagers. But it is well to remember that Mehinaku men and women are also united in enduring relationships of work, residence, kinship, and affection. Before describing the tensions between the sexes, we must document the institutions that link village men and women and provide a basic background in the sociology of Mehinaku male-female relations.

Work, Marriage, and Affection

MEN, WOMEN, AND THE DIVISION OF LABOR

A division of labor is a separation of tasks, yet a basis for interdependence. Among the Mehinaku, the assignment of separate jobs to men and women is the fundamental economic contract. Even a casual observer of village life will notice that men and women are usually found in different places, following different schedules, and engaged in different tasks.

The six haystack-shaped houses that surround the central plaza are the focus of female activities (see figure 2). A glance into one of these buildings during the late morning hours catches the women of the house at work: making hammocks, processing manioc flour, spinning cotton, or making twine cord. All of these tasks, like women's work in most cultures, are compatible with child care. The job can be quickly put aside to keep a child away from the open hearth or the hot tub of manioc porridge and then resumed with little difficulty. The association of women with the houses and domestic activities is built into the way the villagers conceive of their community. The village is perceived as two concentric rings. In the innermost are the plaza (*wenekutaku,* "frequented place") and the men's house. These are public regions for casual male interaction and organization of community activities. In the outermost ring are the houses and their back yards. This region is feminine in its connotations. A man who hangs around the backyards is derisively called a "trash-yard man," and he is said to be "like" a woman. Boys who spend too much time in these

Fig. 2. Aerial view of village, May 1976. The village is conceived by the Mehinaku as a great circle formed by the perimeter of houses and the brush and scrub forest beyond. Within the circle is the public plaza and the men's house. These are primarily masculine areas of the community, and they are used for public oratory, rituals associated with the men's house, and wrestling. The houses and the "trashyards" immediately behind them are feminine regions where the women process manioc and take care of young children. Bisecting the community are broad paths that the men clear in order to see visitors well in advance of their arrival in the village. Also visible are two houses under construction and several manioc drying racks, which are built during the rainless months of the dry season.

areas are scolded by their parents and ordered away. Only women properly belong in these regions. When they leave, it is for specific tasks, such as getting water, visiting their gardens, and participating in public rituals.

But the women are never quite comfortable beyond the house and yard and move about in circumspect groups of two or three close relatives. On the paths and in the gardens, they are uneasy about the hazards of jaguars, snakes, and "wild" Indians. And on the plaza, the younger women are concerned that the men are staring at them from the men's house and perhaps making sexual comments. The men are more wide ranging in their movements. At a random moment, we find them dispersed about the village. Some are hunting or fishing many miles from home. Others are clearing distant gardens or working on arrows and baskets in the men's house. And a few are to be found aimlessly wandering through the forest in search of whatever adventure may befall them. The men feel at home where the women are out of place.

A Mehinaku feminist who added up the many tasks allotted to the sexes would sense that, as in our own society, the equation does not balance. Steel tools and fish hooks have greatly eased men's work as farmers and fishermen but made no dent in the women's drudgery of producing manioc flour. Following Robert Carneiro's comparable data gathered among the neighboring Kuikuru Indians (1957, 223), I estimate that the Mehinaku men spend only three-and-one-half hours a day in subsistence tasks. Admittedly the work is hard and occasionally dangerous, but it is far less time-consuming than the women's seven to nine hours of processing manioc, fetching firewood, and carrying tubs of water from the stream. When at last these tasks are done, the women are still the main caretakers of small children. Meanwhile, rich in free time, their husbands are off on trading trips to the Indian post, meanders through the forest, and long periods of socializing in the men's house. Only for a few weeks during the dry season when the men clear new fields do they face work that is as demanding of time as that of their wives.

The Mehinaku have made rough but similar calculations, and most will agree that women work longer hours than men. But they do not draw the conclusion that the women are therefore exploited. Rather, they maintain, men and women have different jobs for which they are suited by temperament and biology. Thus Kalu, one of the more assertive women, remarks, "I could not go fishing. The line would cut my hands. I am afraid of big animals. We women have no strength . . . the men are worthy of respect." For Kalu and the other women, the significance of the division of labor between men and women lies in exchange and interdependence. The principal institution that mediates this economic relationship is marriage.

MARRIAGE AS THE BASIC ECONOMIC PARTNERSHIP

On the first morning of his marriage, a young man awakens long before any of the other residents of his house. Slipping out as quietly as possible, he goes to fish in a distant but well-stocked lake. The trip is long, but he would be ashamed if he were to return empty-handed on such an important day. His bride is busy at home, making the sweetest and most delicate manioc bread of the finest flour. On her husband's return, she greets him at the door, takes his catch, and cooks the fish stew. Called the "mistress of the fish stew" (*wakula weketu*), she sends gifts of fish and bread to her relatives and in-laws. Neither manioc or fish alone would make a meal, but when they are distributed together, they are a powerful symbol of the new economic partnership of husband and wife.

Men's and women's craft work is also connected to the symbolism of marriage. Women are known for their ability as hammock makers, and everyone speaks admiringly of the best craftswomen in the village. An essential reason for making a hammock is to fulfill an obligation owed to a man, especially a husband. Properly, a man's hammock is woven from cotton thread, while a woman's hammock is a loosely tied net of palm fiber. As Palui put it as she wove a cotton hammock, "A man's hammock is hard to make, a woman's is easy. A woman's hammock breaks easily. It has so many holes that the mosquitoes eat you when you sleep. This good woven hammock that I am making I will give to my husband." Unlike Palui, some village women weave poorly made hammocks and make them so infrequently that their families are said to sleep "practically on the ground." The contemptuous and derisive descriptions of these women underscore the more than utilitarian significance of the hammock within marriage. The gift of food and well-crafted material goods celebrates the relationship of husband and wife.

THE PLIGHT OF THE BACHELOR

There is no better way to appreciate the value of Mehinaku marriage than to look at the pitiable bachelor. Consider, for example, the case of Tala, a man in his fifties, who has been without a wife for nearly fifteen years. His tattered hammock barely keeps him off the ground, and he has been unable to obtain a manufactured one at the trading post despite his constant importuning. Thinner than many of the other villagers, Tala complains that he never gets enough manioc bread. His sister-in-law usually keeps him supplied, but he cannot ask her to start the fire and bake a new batch as her husband can. Tala is also dependent on other men's women for manioc porridge and water. None of the women, however, get him firewood. On the coldest of nights, he reluctantly hauls his own. When the evening chill has less bite, he wraps himself in a ragged blanket cadged from the post and shivers through the night. But at least he has avoided women's work.

When Tala leaves his house, his frayed arm bands and bead belt show that he has no wife to supply him with cotton thread essential for masculine adornment. Moreover, his unmarried status prevents him from participating in the public ritual and political life of the village as an equal of other men. Only married adults may become "owners" of significant spirits, sponsors of important rituals, and respected chiefs. Bachelors cannot provide the bread and porridge that is the spirit's food and a chief's hospitality. The Mehinaku marital partnership is therefore a unit of participation in vital social events.

Tala is fully aware of the advantages of marriage, and only a shortage of eligible women among the Mehinaku and neighboring tribes has kept him from finding a wife. Once he brought home a woman from the despised Carib-speaking Txicão tribe, but she was never accepted by the village women and soon left. At all times, Tala tries to compensate for his low status by being a particularly energetic fisherman and farmer. Each year when the rains come, he keeps his household well supplied with fish caught in his extensive network of traps along the Tuatuari River. And yet he is never on the same footing as the other men. Lacking basic possessions and living on the margins of the village system of ritual and politics, he is not respected. To his friends, he is an object of pity.

AFFECTION BETWEEN HUSBANDS AND WIVES.

For the Mehinaku, the idea of romantic love is absurd. Nothing is more ridiculous to the young men who understand some Portuguese than the love songs they hear on their transistor radios: "What is this 'I love you, I love you'?" Amairi asked me. "I don't understand it. I don't like it. Why does the white man make himself a fool?"

Although all romantic love is suspect, romance between spouses borders on bad taste. Husband and wife should respect one another and, to a degree, stand apart. Each represents a set of in-laws to whom the other owes work, gifts, and deference. Whatever potential remains for romantic attachment is further diluted by coresidence with many kinsmen and an elaborate network of extramarital affairs. In this setting, only a new couple (*autsapalui*) is permitted anything more than a low-keyed expression of affection. Typically, a newly married husband and wife sleep together in the same large hammock and spend much of the day in each other's company. As their marriage matures, however, this degree of affection seems foolish. Those who persist risk the laughter of their comrades and supernatural dangers. Excessive thoughts about one's spouse, the villagers say, attract snakes, jaguars, and deadly spirits.

Despite the absence of romance, some husbands and wives take an enduring pleasure in one another's company. Ketepe tells me that his wife is "good" and that she is "dear" (*kakaiapai*; literally, precious or expensive) to him. He likes to take her and his children on long fishing trips so that they can be alone together. Far away from inlaws, village gossips, and the tension of sexual intrigues, they spend the days fishing, collecting wild fruits, and paddling together in their canoe to explore distant streams and lakes. On my most recent visit to the Mehinaku, Ketepe asked that I buy him a large tarpaulin as a roof for his family when they pitched their hammocks together under the trees.

Even couples who are less affectionate than Ketepe and his wife spend a fair amount of time together. It is true that their daily work separates them, but each day, a husband and wife go bathing together and speak to the other couples whom they meet on the trail. In the late afternoon, they may pair off to visit their garden. On the way, they talk about the day's events, their children, and the social life of the community. Unlike the communal houses, the gardens are intimate places where husband and wife have sexual relations and speak in privacy. Returning home, couples eat together around a common hearth, share a common water bowl, and rest in hammocks that are slung closely together. Each of these activities is regarded as an expression of the solidarity of the marital relationship. When husband and wife no longer eat together, when they drink from different bowls and separate their hammocks, they are not far from divorce. Hammock position is an especially good barometer of the pressures and pleasures of marriage. When spouses get along well, they hang their hammocks so that the woman is suspended just a few inches below her husband. Whispering to each other after the children are asleep, they discuss the day's events.

More often, husbands and wives prefer to separate their hammocks, suggesting a degree of distance (though not hostility) in their relationship. In this position, the hammocks are tied to separate poles so that the intimacy of the first arrangement is broken. To place even greater distance between themselves and their mates, spouses attach their hammocks to separate house poles and build the family hearth between them. During severe quarrels, a wife may sleep so that no matter how her husband turns, her feet lie alongside his head. Hammock positions are part of the Mehinaku language of marital intimacy and estrangement, just as double beds, twin beds, and separate bedrooms can make the same point in middle-class American homes. But the Mehinaku use the system to convey one message that is beyond the scope of American sleeping arrangements. When enraged at her husband, a wife may take a machete and cut down her husband's hammock. More than ropes are severed, for this symbolic act may initiate divorce.

The most dramatic evidence of the concern that most spouses feel for one another occurs during prolonged absences. The men's two-week fishing expeditions take them through forest that is believed to be the haunt of dangerous spirits and "wild" Indians who prowl the borders of Mehinaku territory. Wives worry about their absent husbands. The men are concerned about the well-being of their women and families. When the men are away, the village is a quiet, empty place, but in each house there is a symbol of connectedness and concern. On his departure, a husband gives his wife a knotted cord and retains an identical one for himself. Each knot stands for "one sleep," and in the evening, husband and wife loosen a tie, so that they can keep track of the days. When at last the string is untied, a wife knows that her husband will return no later than the next evening.

On one occasion, I recall that Kikayala did not return after the final knot had been loosened and night had fallen. Even though his wife, Pialu, had never seemed to display any special affection for her husband, she became increasingly concerned. Anxiously peering down the trail, she wondered if her husband had been carried off by a forest spirit or attacked by a jaguar. She finally borrowed my flashlight and walked with her son to the edge of the woods to wait. When at last Kikyala arrived, she greeted him calmly, but he must have sensed Pialu's concern and her pleasure in his safe return.

The most extreme form of separation is that occasioned by death. Among the Mehinaku, the death of a spouse initiates a period of seclusion and mourning that is more prolonged and intense than for any other class of relative. The villagers say that the purpose of mourning seclusion is to cry for one's lost spouse. The period of isolation, closely supervised by the deceased's kin, can last as long as a year. The mourner (*katumbachu*) must stay behind a palm-wood partition and speak in a hushed voice. Although initially the bereaved cry copiously, the meaning of mourning seclusion varies. For some it is an expression of propriety and an obligation to in-laws rather than an outpouring of grief. It is a mistake to interpret the institution too romantically, as we might be inclined to do from the perspective of our own society, which lacks long periods of formal mourning.

Nonetheless, Mehinaku mourning is a ceremonialization of marriage and an expression of one facet of the idealized relationship of spouses.

Sexual Relationships

Within the roles of marriage and kinship, Mehinaku men and women express mutual affection and respect and advance their economic well-being. The bond of sexual attraction is basic to understanding their complex relationships.

EARLY SEXUAL EXPERIENCES

A Mehinaku child grows up in an erotically charged social environment. Living on close terms with his sexually active older kin and occasionally following them out to the gardens to watch their assignations, a ten-year-old child is already a sophisticate by American standards. His parents openly joke about sex in his presence, and he is likely to be well informed about the village's latest extramarital intrigues. In the open setting of the Mehinaku community, parents cannot wall off sex in a secret adult world. Many of them do just the opposite, openly attributing sexual motivation to their children. As toddlers play and tussle in a promiscuous huddle on the floor, parents make broad jokes about their having sexual relations: "Look! Glipe is having sex with Pairuma's daughter." As a result, there are few mysteries about the facts of life, and some children grow up with a relatively matter-of-fact attitude toward sexuality. "I haven't had sex yet," one eight-year-old remarked to me, "but in a few years I will."

Sex and marriage, like virtually every adult activity, have their counterpart in children's games. In a game called "marrying" (*kanupai*; literally, "taking a wife") little boys and girls sling their hammocks in the trees around the village. The boys bring home "fish" (actually big leaves) to be cooked by their "wives." After the "food" is cooked and consumed, the game has a number of variants. In one, "being jealous" (*ukitsapai*), the children sneak off on extramarital assignations, only to be surprised by furious spouses. In all versions of the game, however, a few of the children may drift off in pairs to experiment in sexual play. Parents do not seem overly concerned about this kind of activity while their children are young and so long as they are discreet. If exposed, mothers and fathers are merciless in their teasing. Children rapidly learn that sexual activity and public exposure do not mix.

By early adolescence, parents are far more concerned about their children's, and especially their sons' sexuality. Maturation, say the villagers, is not an inevitable process. Sexual and physical development must be induced by medicines and sexual abstinence. When a boy is eleven or twelve years of age, his father erects a seclusion barrier of palm-wood staves across one end of the house. The son ties his hammock behind the partition and begins a term of seclusion that, with interruptions, will last for approximately three years. Watching over him during this lengthy period is a spirit, "the master of the medicines," who makes sure that his charge confines himself to quarters, takes medicines to augment his growth, speaks softly, and follows all the dietary rules. Above all, the boy in seclusion must avoid sexual relations. Unlike the little girls he played with when he was young, sexually mature women are dangerous. Their menstrual blood and vaginal secretions can poison the medicines and even induce the medicine spirit to pass a fatal sentence: *makatsiki*, a paralytic disease striking young men in seclusion (see chapter 7).

THE NETWORK OF SEXUAL AFFAIRS

A boy in seclusion is almost invariably celibate, especially while taking medicines. Toward the end of his stay, however, it is common for him to succumb to temptation and sneak out at night for an affair. Upon hearing of such adventures his father rips down the seclusion barrier and expels his son into public village life. Now the boy is nearly a man, ready to cut his own garden, go on long trips away from the village by himself, and get married. At this point, too, he gingerly enters the elaborate village network of sexual relationships. Arranging sexual encounters with most village women can be a risky and humiliating business. Unmarried girls present no problem since they have no jealous husbands. Their fathers are pleased by a potential son-in-law who sends occasional gifts of fish over to the house as an acknowledgment of his indebtedness. So casual is the attitude toward premarital courtship that girls are said to unabashedly return from an assignation smeared with their boyfriends' body paint.

Unfortunately, from a young man's point of view, there are never many unmarried women. Despite the villagers toleration of premarital sex, pregnancy out of wedlock is wrong. The *pukapi ɨnu*, "mother of the illegitimate child," is an object of scorn. The "fatherless" child is himself subject to abuse. As a result, most girls are married as soon as they emerge from the period of adolescent seclusion that follows their first menses. Virtually all sexual affairs, therefore, are extramarital affairs. These are fraught with danger because husbands and wives are sexually jealous. To use the Mehinaku idiom, they "prize each other's genitals" and do not like to see them appropriated by an interloper. Numerous cautionary tales warn the would-be adulterer against the fury of the jealous spouse. In these myths, adulterous couples are beaten, dismembered, put to death, and in one story, glued together in a permanent copulatory embrace. The tale of Patijai and his girlfriend is very much in this genre of cautionary myths (see Gregor 1977, 139, 145–46 for other examples). Our narrator is Ketepe, who has both more girl friends and more cautionary tales than anyone else in the village.

PATIJAI

> Patijai went to the garden to have sex with another man's wife. He did not know it, but the husband was following close behind. Patijai and his girlfriend had sex together, and they they worked a little in the garden, weeding. Just then, they heard the husband coming, whistling as he walked on the path. Quickly, Patijai hid in a pile of sticks and leaves. But his foot was not covered up, and the husband said, "Oh, I think I'll clean the garden a little and burn off these sticks and leaves."
>
> "No, don't do that. My mother hid her knife there," said the wife.
>
> "Well then, look for it."
>
> "No, only mother knows where it is."
>
> "I'll burn it all the same," said the husband, and he did. A huge fire sprang up, and out of the blaze ran Patijai, his hair ablaze.
>
> "There goes your mother's knife, there goes your mother's knife, there goes your mother's knife!" shouted the husband. "You had sex with your lover. I'll club you."
>
> And he struck her, and that was the end of her and the end of her former lover's semen, still in her vagina.
>
> Meanwhile Patijai, his hair burned off completely, went to hide. "What has become of my son," his mother asked the villagers.
>
> "We don't know. Maybe he went off fishing," everyone replied. But one women had seen what had happened, and she said, "It's good that your son caught on fire after having sex with another man's wife. Sex fiends like Patijai are no good."

In real life, extramarital affairs seldom provoke serious confrontations. Only in the early years of marriage are spouses so jealous that they openly quarrel. As they mature, jealousy is tempered by social pressure that enjoins discretion in managing affairs and avoiding confrontations. A Mehinaku like the jealous husband in the myth is called an *itsula*, "kingfisher," a bird noted for its raucous scolding and aimless flapping about. Only a few of the younger villagers seem to deserve the title.

Even though sexual jealousy is muted, entering the network of sexual affairs is still a delicate matter. One low risk strategy is "buying" (*aiyatapai*) the girl's services with the help of one of her established lovers. In exchange for a small gift to both the lover and the girl, she will agree to meet him for sexual relations and perhaps become a regular girlfriend. A second, bolder alternative is to approach the girl when she is alone in a public place. The path to the river and the bushes behind the houses are favored areas. Here the young man takes the girl firmly by the wrist and says, "Come, let us have sexual relations together." On occasion, the suitor may sweeten his offer with a gift, such as a bar of soap, a comb, or a small handful of beads. If the girl accepts, they will have sexual relations immediately in the bushes; or, fearing her husband, she may suggest that her lover come "alligatoring" (*aiyakatapai*) later in the day. "To alligator," in the vernacular of the Mehinaku men, means to summon women to assignations from small areas behind the houses known as "alligator places" (*yaka epuga*). The use of the alligator (actually the cayman, *Caiman crocodilus*) as a sexual metaphor derives from Mehinaku mythology, which describes the alligator as a libidonous animal who in ancient times had repeated assignations with two village women.

Like the real-life alligator who lies submerged for hours until his prey comes into range, the would-be lover remains concealed in his "alligator place" until his girlfriend comes into view. Even though she may not appear for an hour or more, he has to be patient, knowing how risky a direct approach may be. At last she steps outside of her house, perhaps to prepare some manioc flour. Smacking his lips, he signals her to come to him. The sexual behavior that ensues varies according to the participants' preferences. The most common position is "having intercourse while seated" (*putakene aintyawakapai*), in which the couple sit flat on the ground facing each other, the women's legs over and around the man's thighs. In a frequent variation of the position, the man kneels, resting on his legs, knees spread apart. As in the first case, his partner places her legs over his thighs while he clutches her about the back so that they are both supported. The prone position favored in our society is less frequently used by the Mehinaku, since lying on the ground leaves one vulnerable to insects and is considered unattractive. Most commonly, this position is reserved for "having sex on top of a log" (*ata penwitsa aintyawakapai*), with both partners lying down, the man on top.

These positions are employed when couples have sufficient time and privacy. There are a number of other methods, however, adapted to particular situations and considerably less privacy. The most demanding of these is "having intercourse in the hammock" (*amakwaitsa aintyawakapai*), a feat that requires considerable gymnastics on the part of both partners. Although the basic side-to-side position has been described to me, I cannot understand how a couple can arrange themselves in a small swinging hammock so that they can have intercourse. The task is made doubly difficult by the minimal privacy in which such encounters occur. Occasionally, I am told, a woman will have sexual relations with a lover in her hammock even though her husband sleeps only a few inches away. "Danger," say some of the villagers, "is pepper for sex."

"Standing intercourse" (*enwitsa aintyawakapai*) is a fourth position, best adapted to the fleeting moments of chance encounters along the side of a path or in back of a house. Holding his partner about the buttocks and lower back, the man lifts her slightly off the ground while she raises one knee. "In-the-water intercourse" (*unya aintyawakapai*) is the final commonly used position, occurring in the bathing area when a man is briefly alone with his girlfriend. Easiest to perform when the water is about chest level, the physical arrangements resemble those in standing intercourse.

This list of five coital positions does not exhaust the Mehinaku repertory and indicates somewhat more inventiveness than is typical of many societies, including America.[1] Not limiting themselves to one stereotyped act, the Mehinaku vary their techniques to match their mood and situation. Ketepe, for example, prefers the prone position because the penetration is deepest; but, he says "the women usually makes the choice."

REPRESSION AND DESIRE

"All men," Ketepe informs me, "like sex. But women are different." My data supports Ketepe's belief to the extent that sexuality has a somewhat different meaning for the women than it does for the men. Men are more overtly sexual, and hence it is possible for women to use their sexuality to secure food and support in exchange for intercourse. Moreover, women are subject to repressive beliefs and practices that confine and even suffocate their sexual natures. From an early age, a girl knows that she is "just a girl" and in many respects inferior to boys. As she matures, she learns that her vagina is "smelly" and "disgusting." She must take care that others do not see it when she sits or walks. With her first menses, she discovers that she is a danger to others. She can be held responsible for contaminating food, defiling sacred rituals, and making men sick. When she

1. The relatively stereotyped pattern of sexual relations is noted in Kinsey's classic study of American male sexuality: "Universally, at all social levels in our Anglo-American culture, the opinion is held that there is one coital position which is biologically natural, and that all others are man-devised variants which become perversions when regularly engaged in" (Kinsey, Pomeroy, and Martin 1948, 373).

enters the network of sexual affairs, she finds that she must comport herself carefully. A casual boyfriend may seize on any unusual or uninhibited conduct in sexual relations and joke about it among his friends. One of the reasons that a woman expects gifts of her lovers is that a token of commitment is insurance that she will not be denigrated in village gossip. Even discreet sexual relationships are risky, however, since pregnancy is known to be painful and dangerous.

A Mehinaku woman's sexuality is thus linked to a sense of inferiority to men, to feelings of disgust about the genitalia, to concern about menstrual contamination, and to fear of unwanted pregnancy. No wonder that some of the women are *kanatalalu,* literally "rejecting women," and in this context "women who do not like sex." At the moment there is only one Mehinaku woman who is widely stigmatized as a kanatalalu, but the men complain that the others are less than enthusiastic. They are, in the male vernacular, "stingy with their genitals." This lack of interest is disturbing to the men. It puts into question both their own attractiveness and the legitimacy of their sexual demands. Women who consistently reject their suitors are the subject of gossip and are referred to as "worthless women" (*teneju malu*).

The men's complaints about the low level of female sexuality may also be related to their own lack of sophistication in sexual technique. With a few notable exceptions, the men do not engage in foreplay or touch the genitals of their partners. Significantly, there is no word in the Mehinaku language for a woman's sexual climax. From my questioning of male and female informants, I am uncertain if any of the women are orgasmic. Certainly it is not an expectation that they have in participating in sexual relations.[2]

Most women, however, take some pleasure in sexual relations even though their level of interest is lower than that of the men. As Kama puts it, "Women act as if they do not want to have sex. You take them by the wrist and say, 'let's go over there.' And they say, 'Not me. I don't want to have sex.' I don't know why they say that. Perhaps they are afraid of the semen. Perhaps it is revolting to them. But when you sit on the ground and the penis goes in, then they like it. They thrust their hips. It is sensual for them."

Once a couple begin to have sexual relations regularly, they regard themselves as "boyfriend" and "girlfriend," a relationship that is in some respects like marriage. Boyfriends and girlfriends exchange food, spindles of cotton, baskets, and even shell jewelry, just as do

2. The preceding discussion was suggested to me by Emilienne Ireland, whose research among the Waura (neighbors of the Mehinaku) has increased my awareness of the difficulties faced by the Mehinaku women.

spouses. As we shall see, men may even assume a quasi-parental role in relation to the children they have fathered.

As of my last visit to the Mehinaku, the thirty-seven adults were conducting approximately 88 extramarital affairs. This figure is only an estimate because the relationship is noncontractual, and opinions vary within the village as to who is having a genuine affair, and who is engaging in an occasional liaison. To put this number in perspective, it would be possible for the villagers to pair off in 340 extramarital (heterosexual) partnerships if they were unrestrainedly promiscuous. If affairs that are in violation of in-law avoidances, the incest taboo, and the respect owed older persons are eliminated, 150 theoretically possible pairings remain. Given that the actual number of partners is 88, I conclude that the villagers' taste for extramarital liaisons is limited primarily by social barriers, such as the incest taboo, and only secondarily by personal preference. In short, village men and women tend to have relations with each other unless they are specifically prohibited from doing so by the rules of their culture.

The sheer number of affairs is evidence of the villagers' intensely sexual orientation. The network of liaisons, however, is more impressive than the modest frequency of actual sexual encounters. These are limited by long taboos associated with rituals and the life cycle, by the absence of privacy within the community, by competition from jealous husbands and more attractive rivals, and especially by the difficulty of finding a willing female partner. These constraints on sex create shortages in the midst of apparent abundance. Nonetheless, several of the young men have told me that when they make the effort (importuning, gifts, verbal coercion), they are able to have sex on a once-a-day basis. The frequency of sex for the average Mehinaku, however, is far less.

MOTIVES FOR BECOMING LOVERS AND SOME STANDARDS OF ATTRACTIVENESS

Table 1 below shows that the number of affairs per person varies widely from zero to fourteen, with age and physical appearance as the main source of variation. Young, physically attractive men and women have more lovers. A youthful woman with long sleek hair, heavy yet firm calves and thighs, large breasts and nipples, small close-set eyes, little body hair and "attractive genitals" (those that do not show the inner labia) is an avidly sought after sex partner. Appearance in men is also important. A heavily muscled, imposingly built man is likely to accumulate many girlfriends, while a small man, deprecatingly referred to as a *peritsi*, fares badly. The mere fact of height creates a measurable advantage. Men over 5′4″ (N = 7) had an average of six girlfriends at the time of my study, while those under

Table 1. Mehinaku Sexual Affairs (1972)

Number of Affairs per Person	Number of Persons Having the Affairs	
	Men	Women
0	0	3
1	2	0
2	3	0
3	4	3
4	3	1
5	0	4
6	4	1
7	2	1
8	1	1
9	0	1
10	1	0
11	0	1
14	0	1
	20	17

5′4″ (N = 8) had only 3.4 girlfriends. To a degree, these data reflect the advantage height gives men in their political relations with other men rather than simply their sexual attractiveness. As in our own society, men who are socially successful are more attractive to women as sexual partners.

An additional factor that correlates with numbers of affairs is gender. The average man engages in 4.4 affairs, and most of the men are fairly close to that average. In the case of the women, however, the range or variation is greater. The three most sexually active women in the village account for almost forty percent of the total number of liaisons, while the three least active women account for none of the community's extramarital relationships. In contrast, all of the men have at least one sexual partner, and the three most active men engage in only twenty-eight percent of the total number of extramarital affairs.

The data reflect the different meaning of extramarital relationships for men and women. The men's principal motivation for initiating affairs is sexual desire. The women, on the other hand, seem to value the social contact and the gifts they receive in the course of the affair as well as the physical side of the relationship. The result is that women who do not excite sexual interest (the old, the sick, the extremely unattractive) have little opportunity to engage in affairs. All the men, however, no matter what their age or appearance, can have an affair, or at least a sexual encounter, by offering a gift. All village men, therefore, have some sexual contacts, while some women have none.

The case of Tamalu, the most sexually active woman in the village, illustrates the different meaning of affairs for men and women. At the time of my study, Tamalu had fourteen lovers whom she had rapidly accumulated upon her arrival among the Mehinaku. Her initial reception in the village had been less than enthusiastic, since she sought refuge there after abandoning a husband in another Xingu tribe. Though she was welcomed by her cousins and aunts, the men grumbled about her voracious and bothersome children. Each day, her two daughters were mercilessly teased by the village boys and girls. After Tamalu had been in the village for a while, however, these problems largely abated. Gifts of fish from her lovers began to arrive with clockwork regularity, making it apparent she was an economic asset to her household. In addition, some of her paramours took it upon themselves to protect her daughters from the other village children. Tamalu's case suggests that the pressures and incentives for a woman to engage in extramarital affairs sometimes leave her very vulnerable to the men's advances.

EXTRAMARITAL AFFAIRS AND MEHINAKU SOCIETY

Despite husbands' and wives' occasional jealous quarrels, I believe extramarital attachments among the Mehinaku contribute to village cohesion. Within the community, affairs may consolidate relationships between persons in different kindreds. Not only must a man find most of his mistresses among distantly related kinswomen, but he may be obliged to recognize children born of the relationship as his own. The network of blood kinship is thereby greatly expanded. There are few Mehinaku, no matter how marginal they may be to the village kindreds, who are wholly outside the orbit of these extensions of normal paternity (see Gregor 1977, 292–94).

Liaisons also enhance community stability by promoting enduring relationships based on mutual affection. Many lovers are very fond of one another and regard separation as a privation to avoid. In a community whose boundaries and unity are not structured by fear of war or by regular patterns of marriage with other groups, the relationship of lovers is centripetal. The traveler to other villages or the man who takes his family to a distant dry-season garden is never far from home in his thoughts. Eventually, he will return to his community and the pleasures of his extramarital affairs. Finally, even indivious gossip and jealous intrigues are a part of the beat of Mehinaku community life. The culture of sexual liaisons makes the village an exciting and interesting place. As Ketepe often explained to me, "Good fish get dull, but sex is always fun."

Mehinaku men and women enjoy an organic and complex relationship. Attracted to each other by an enthusiastic heterosexuality, benefiting from the affection they owe each other as spouses and kinsmen, and profiting from their exchanges of material goods, they appear to stand united and indivisible. Yet within this pattern of attraction, they are in many respects opposed. Mehinaku society is separated into a male and a female world by fears of sexual pollution, antagonism, and anxiety. The following chapters document the culture and psychology of Mehinaku gender and explain the ambivalence of men's and women's relationships.

THREE

Facts of Life and Symbols of Gender

Kwaumutĩ made women so that men could have sex with them.
—From a Mehinaku creation myth

Nature provides us with few true opposites. The colors of the spectrum appear to be poles apart, but in truth, all colors differ in continuous degrees of variation of wave length (hue), saturation (purity of wave length), and brightness (amplitude of the wave). It is culture that dissects and classifies a seamless nature into opposing categories. In the case of the opposition of male and female, we seem to have an exception, but a look at the biological and social facts of life suggests many permutations on the nature of sex and gender. Biologists discriminate between chromosomal, endocrinal, and genital sex. Normally, all match, but in approximately one in a thousand births they do not, producing one of a variety of hermaphrodites. The reaction of medical personnel to such an event in our own society is instructive, for it illustrates how we can suppress recognition of a natural world that stubbornly refuses to fall in line with our culture's suppositions. The first response to the birth of an intersex infant is to try to determine its "true" sex through medical tests. Regardless of how ambiguous these tests may be, the child is surgically assigned a sexual identity, and the anomaly is apparently eliminated (Garfinkle 1967).

On rare occasions, cultures take recognition of and provide a special position for additional sexes. The Navajo *nadle* seems to have been a true hermaphrodite who occupied a role halfway between male and female in dress and behavior. Somewhat more frequently, other cultures have provided physically normal but behaviorally intersex individuals with respectable careers that take on elements of both male and female identity. The *berdache* of the American Plains Indians is an example, as is the transvestite *xanith*, the male prostitute of Oman (Wikan 1977). Admittedly such recognition of intersex and intergender individuals is rare. Far more commonly, cultures deny such persons a respectable status. The Mehinaku, for one, are even more ruthless than the surgically inclined medical practitioners of our own culture. Even though hermaphrodites are all but unknown (as would be expected in a society of eighty-five persons), the villagers are quite clear about what they would do. They would put a sexually abnormal child to death at the moment of its birth. The Mehinaku recognize only two kinds of sexually differentiated humans: man (*enɨja*) and woman (*teneju*). Later we shall see that there amendments and exceptions to these recognized categories, but none—be they homosexuals or transvestites—are decent human alternatives. Let us now look at the biological and social characteristics the Mehinaku use to mark off male and female as the only classes of respectable humanity.

The Biology of Sexual Differences: Primary Sexual Characteristics

In our society, clothes and modesty screen the body and help conceal the secrets of sexual anatomy. Although the Mehinaku have codes of modesty and are interested in proper dress and adornment, these concerns do little to hide the facts of life. Moreover, as in our own society, the physical contrasts between the sexes is augmented by life style. Men are powerfully built and heavily muscled, reflecting both their masculine heredity and their vigorous and demanding work, such as paddling dugout canoes and clearing gardens. Women are even more hardworking, but many of their activities are sedentary: processing manioc, spinning cotton, weaving hammocks. These jobs do little to visibly augment female musculature. Perhaps even more important in affecting appearance is the woman's role in childbearing. Lacking contraceptives, a Mehinaku woman can expect to have a child every two-and-one-half years. In relatively short order, the burden of bearing, carrying, and nursing infants takes its toll on her figure. By the second or third birth, her breasts are large and pendulous, and the muscles of her abdomen are stretched and slack.

The villagers use the unconcealed anatomical differences between men and women to define masculinity and femininity and justify the differences between the sexes. Evidence of the significance of these sexual characteristics in marking male and female identity comes from a series of drawings by the villagers. The sketches of men reproduced in figures 3 and 4 are examples of some of the two hundred pictures drawn by most of the members of the community in response to my request to "draw a man and a woman." In examining the drawings for clues as to their psychological meaning, it is well to keep in mind that there are no artistic conventions among the Mehinaku for drawing the human form other than to outline the abdomen in a representation of a genderless human, very much as we would sketch a stick figure. The regularities we find in the representations of gender, especially insofar as they stray from realistic portrayals, are my artists' concensus about the importance and connotations of gender-marking characteristics.

The villagers differentiate men from women in the drawings by primary and secondary sexual characteristics, hair styles, and adornment. Of these, primary sexual characteristics are clearly of great significance. In a number of drawings, the artist paid closest attention to the genitals of the person depicted, envincing only passing interest in differences of form and dress (fig. 3). This pattern of using the

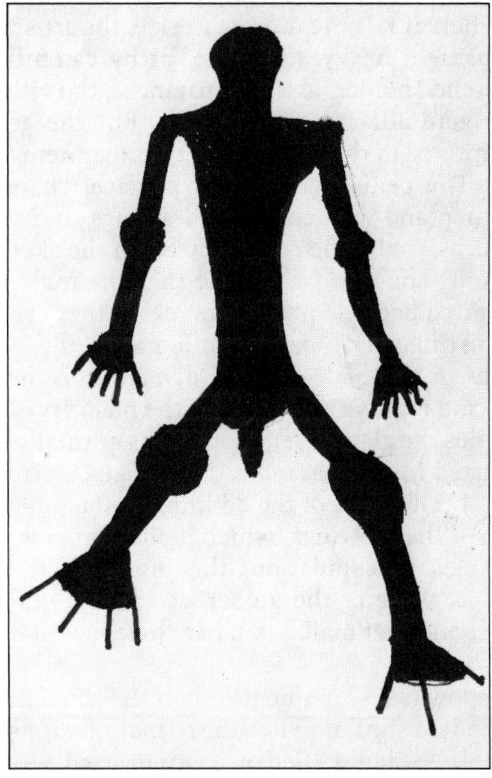

Fig. 3. Male figure. Kuya's sketch of a man is typical of many others in that the genitals are exaggerated. There are, however, a few other clues as to gender in this picture, including the broad shoulders of the figure and the arm and knee ligatures.

genitals as the major cue for signaling masculinity and feminity was particularly characteristic of younger individuals and children, suggesting that for the Mehinaku, primary sexual characteristics are among the earliest recognized markers of sexual identity. The attention to primary sexual characteristics is evident, however, in the drawings of older villagers as well, underscoring the fact that the genitalia are a visible and observed part of an adult's appearance. Certain villagers are even occasionally described in terms of their genitals. An older woman is derisively known as "long labia," and one of the more marginal men is slurringly referred to as "hairy penis."

In reviewing the sketches of male genitalia, I am immediately struck by the distortions of size and shape. In more than eighty percent of the sketches, male genitals are depicted as far larger than they are in real life. In a few sketches (usually those by the women), the penis extends below the knees, and in several it reaches the ankles. Even where it is more modest in size, the artist gives it added emphasis by using a heavy solid line, or by carefully filling in a previously sketched border. In a few instances, the villagers exaggerated the male genitalia for comic effect. But the general pattern should be interpreted in the context of my assignment to draw a man and a woman. The penis is the major physical characteristic that differentiates men and women in the drawings, and its presence or absence was occasionally the only contrast in the sketches of otherwise androgynous couples. I conclude that the male genitals were greatly exaggerated because my artists regard them as the principal element that distinguishes male from female.

The drawings of the male genitals diverge from nature in other ways than size and relative emphasis. In the majority of the sketches, the artist includes the glans, even though it is normally not visible on the uncircumsized Mehinaku male. The artists' intention is to suggest sexual potential as one of the defining characteristics of masculinity. In some of the drawings, which include men with erect phalluses and couples in copulation, the intention is overt. A few pictures, such as those of the archer (see figure 4) also hint at an aggressive component of male sexuality that we will discuss further in chapter 6.

The vagina appears less frequently than the penis in the villagers' drawings. Often it is similar in outline to male genitals drawn by the same artist, but it is seldom filled in or emphasized with a heavy solid line. Almost invariably the drawings are unrealistic in that the vagina appears to be suspended between the woman's legs (see fig. 12). Moreover, the artists often provide us with X-ray views of the organ, depicting it as a large hollow space. As in the depictions of male

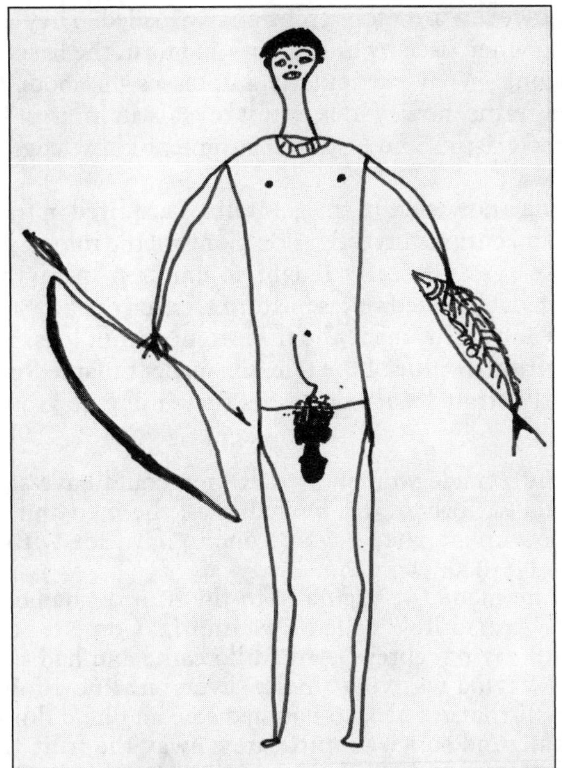

Fig. 4. Male figure. Shumoin's drawing of a fisherman is particularly interesting because it suggests a link between male sexuality and archery, a connection that is also emphasized in several of the villagers other sketches. Additional markers of masculine gender in this sketch include the shell collar and the bowl haircut of the fisherman.

genitals, the villagers thereby call attention to the sexual and procreative uses of the vagina rather than merely its appearance. The drawings tell us that being male and female is a matter of sexual function as well as sexual anatomy.

CARNAL KNOWLEDGE: THE GENITALIA

American sexual culture lacks an ordinary language for the genitals and their parts. We have a rich clinical lexicon and a prolific vocabulary of degrading four-letter words, but no terms with which we feel comfortable in ordinary conversation. The Mehinaku are somewhat freer in that they lable the genitalia and their functions with completely acceptable words. The terms that refer to the less visible parts of the genitals, such as the inner labia, the clitoris, and the glans of the penis, however, are more emotionally loaded. They evoke anxious tittering when used by informants and form the basis for insulting expressions. What particularly impresses us about the entire collection of terms, however, is that it reveals an interest in primary sexual characteristics and a solid anatomical knowledge of the exterior genitals.

Much of the knowledge of the genitalia is acquired in the course of sexual play and curious investigation. Some of the information, however, is more systematically taught to children in myths. One of these, part of an extended series of stories, describes how Kwaumutĩ, culture hero and spirit, made the first women from logs. To appreciate the educational value of the tale, the reader must realize that it is sometimes illustrated with diagrams drawn on the ground with a stick.

> Kwaumutĩ made women so that men could have sexual relations with them. He looked at all the men and said, "Ah, poor men! They have no one to have sex with." And so he made women.
>
> First he made the vagina from the fruit of the buriti palm.[1] "Armadillo!" called Kwaumutĩ, "Come try out sex with my daughter." Armadillo came and had sex, but the vagina was very smelly. Everyone knew from the smell that Armadillo had had sex, and he did not like that. And so Kwaumutĩ threw away the fruit vagina, and made one of the soft tissue of a clam. "Come Armadillo," he said, "Try this one out. Have sex with my daughter."
>
> "Ah, Kwaumutĩ," said Armadillo, "this is good. It does not smell. Your daughter's vagina is fine. Make all the women's vaginas like this, including those of the Brazilian women."
>
> But then Mawari, a really clever person, looked at the women's genitals: "Ooh, these are not good," he said. "Kwaumutĩ, you were not so smart. You did not make a clitoris. For this reason the inner and outer labia are not sensual enough."
>
> And so, Mawari made the clitoris: "Do you see, Kwaumutĩ?" he asked, "I have made the clitoris, and it makes the man's penis delicious for the woman. It is just like a penis and grows erect, looking for its 'food.' The inner and outer labia, they do not grow erect. Only the clitoris, and that is what makes sex sensual."

1. This is soft, foul-smelling, inedible, banana-shaped fruit, occasionally used by the Mehinaku for medicinal purposes.

We will have an opportunity further on to follow up the equations of clitoris and penis, sex and food, but for the moment, we can regard this myth as an eductional device and a fairly sophisticated expression of anatomical knowledge.[2] We should note in addition that it is far from the only such story. Other myths describe the origin of genitalia, including a story of Tsapa, who sculptured each configuration of the penis with an arrow point to produce a shape enjoyable for women.

Secondary Sexual Characteristics and Adornment

In the villagers' drawings and explanation of sexual differences, the genitalia are the clearest markers of male and female identity. Secondary sexual characteristics are also significant. Men are sketched with broader shoulders, greater height, and heavier limbs than women. Women are frequently shown with large breasts, somewhat broader hips, and generally smaller proportions than the men. These characteristics are used by the villagers to justify the social differences between the sexes. Women are said to be weaker than men and consequently frightened of animals, large fish, and lonely trips through the forest. It is natural that they stay close to their homes and gardens and keep out of the political arena. They are simply not endowed with the strength and "anger" needed to make public speeches, participate in men's intrigues, or practice witchcraft against their enemies.

Although secondary sexual characteristics are not as much a focus of cultural attention as the genitalia, they had the same origins in ancient times. Fashioned from arrows and logs, men and women and their anatomical differences are deliberate cultural creations. Even today, each individual continues to shoulder responsibility for his sexual maturation and the development of normal sexual characteristics. This control begins prior to birth, when parents' wishes and dreams can influence the sex of their child. Within the womb, a tiny Mehinaku spirit woman (atsikuma, "Grandmother Spirit") shapes and sculpts the baby from accumulated semen. A strong wish on the part of the parent for a child of a particular sex or a dream of certain male and female symbols (discussed below, chap. 5), influences Grandmother Spirit to make a child of a particular sex. Once born, the child comes under the special care of the parent of the same sex. This parent cares for (*ipyeitsa*: in a narrow sense "feeds," in a broader

2. Notice that the Mehinaku, unconfused by Freudian pronouncements on the subject, have needed no Masters and Johnson to discover that the clitoris is the seat of female sexual pleasure.

context "raises") the child. The child is regarded as recapitulating the life of the parent, he is referred to as the parent's "former self," and he naturally takes on the appearance and temperament of his parent.

Parents protect and make improvements on their "former selves" by honoring an elaborate set of restrictions associated with childbirth, and by ensuring that their children follow food taboos and the other restrictions associated with seclusion at adolescence. Men's heavy musculature, full adult stature, handsome appearance, and sexual maturity depend on the careful observation of the rules of adolescent seclusion. Girls acquire beautiful figures, long hair, heavy calf muscles (a desirable trait), and the control of the flow of menstrual blood through similar means. The Mehinaku belief in the cultural control of natural processes suggests that it is difficult to draw a neat line between biological and cultural markers of sexual identity, a point that becomes especially clear when we examine some of the most visible of male and female differentiators, adornment and body paints.

MALE AND FEMALE ADORNMENT

Patterns of adornment mark gender differences in the villagers' drawings only slightly less frequently than primary and secondary sexual characteristics. Ornaments, belts, ligatures, and paints are, for the Mehinaku, a second skin. A naked man (*mowantalutsi*, literally, "beltless") is asocial, unprepared for interaction with his comrades. Let him dress up, however, and he becomes a walking signboard of messages about his position within the society and about his personal moods. So closely identified is a villager with his wardrobe that bits of armbands or ligatures are good substitutes for bodily effluvia (hair clippings, for example) in a witch's spells.

Like biological differentiators, gender-specific adornment has its origin in mythic times. Once again, we move back to the time of the creation of the first woman:

> Kwaumutĩ made women from wood. He made their hair from palm fibers and cut it long. But it was too white, like a Brazilian woman's, and so he used the down of a bird. Then he added a twine belt (*ɨnɨja*) and painted the legs with *yana* pigment in the proper designs and covered the forehead with *epitsiri* paint. "My daughters!" said Kwaumutĩ, "Don't dress yourselves like me. Your paints are different from mine, and so are your designs. *Epitsiri* pigment is different from men's *yucu*. You paint yourselves with *ulutaki* and with special red pigments." Then Kwaumutĩ's daughter addressed her people: "My friends," she called, "don't

> paint yourselves like men! Do not use ashes or *atwanakiya* pigment—these are men's paints, not ours. Paint yourselves like women!"

The daughter's address was far more than a sermon urging women to follow fashion, for proper dress is an affirmation of proper male-female relationships. And so we learn in myths of role reversal that the restoration of men's and women's normal relationship began with the forcible imposition of the dress code. Here is the conclusion of the myth of Iripyulakumaneju, a female chief, who led all the women away to a distant land where they lived like men. The abandoned husbands, fathers, and brothers followed the women to their new home:

> The men, like wild Indians, attacked Iripyulakumaneju's village at dawn. They chased and caught each of the women and ripped off her belts and leg bands. They forced all of the women down to the water, rubbed them with earth and soapy leaves to wash off all of their masculine paints and designs. "No good, no good," they shouted. "Your leg bands and belts are no good! You have stolen our designs and paints. We paint up in this way, not you. You wear belts of twine and palm bark. You wear different paints from us." Oh, but the women were unhappy!

As the myth suggests, the Mehinaku are opposed to radical experiments in fashion. Inextricably tied up with the diacritical marks and cues of sexual identity, styles of dress have been frozen since the time of creation. Let us now take a close look at two garments that above all others are the hallmarks of male and female identity.

The ɨnɨja belt. As seen in figure 5, the *ɨnɨja* is a twine G-string. The "tail" leads from the body of the garment, which rests on the pubis, through the labia and the buttocks, emerging in the rear, for all the world like an actual tail. For the men, the ɨnɨja is a titillating symbol of female sexuality, irresistibly focusing attention on the vagina. In part, it is so attractive because it is worn during rituals and in the late afternoon, when the women wish to make themselves especially attractive. A man who might be indifferent to an unpainted and beltless woman suddenly finds she is of sexual interest when she paints up, and especially when she wears an ɨnɨja. This attention to appearance, say the men, occurs all too infrequently: "In ancient times," grumps one young man, "the women put on ɨnɨjas every time they went out of the house. Now it seems they just wear them when they go to dance." The provacativensss of the ɨnɨja may have a practical basis since it is said to make sexual relations more gratifying. During intercourse, the tail of the ɨnɨja is removed (the men fear

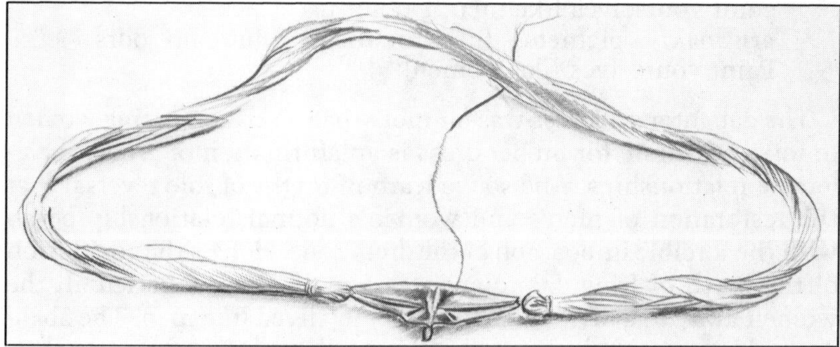

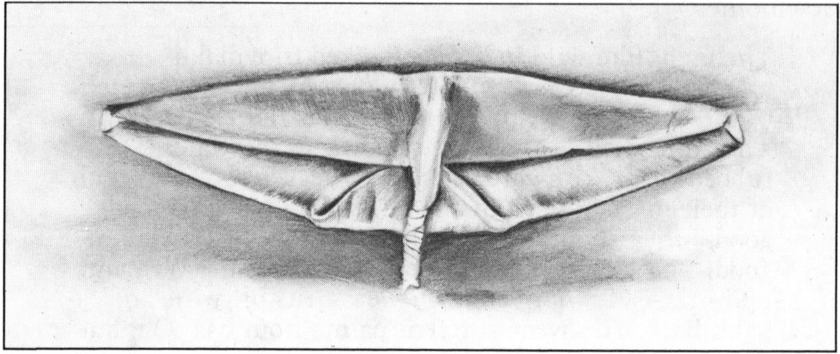

Fig. 5. The ɨnɨja belt. The *inɨja* is the most distinctive garment worn by the Mehinaku and the other Xinguanos. Unique among South American Indians, the use of the inɨja only occurs among the ten culturally similar tribes of the Upper Xingu region. In the detail, we can discern the areas of the inɨja that are said to resemble the human face, including the "nose" and "forehead." The twine "tail" of the garment, which leads from the "nose," is also visible. Drawings by Marshall L. Capps.

that it will injure them) and the rest of the device remains in place, to rub against the clitoris and external genitals.

The symbolism of the inɨja provides additional grounds for its sexual attractiveness. The garment is divided into regions that partly resemble those of the genitals it frames. Like the female genitalia, its parts are those of a human face, including a "nose," a "forehead," and "lips" (see detail, figure 5). The incorporative function of the woman in sexual relations is restated in the language of dress and adornment.

Recalling that in myth women were created to meet men's sexual needs, we can see that from the masculine point of view, the inɨja is a primary visual symbol of female identity. But what is its role from the perspective of the women? To the woman, the inɨja is a symbol of adulthood. It is ceremonially presented at an intertribal ritual (Aka-

Fig. 6. Women's adornment. The village women wearing ɨnɨjas celebrate the ritual of Akajatapa, in which they ceremonially confer the ɨnɨja upon the young girls of the tribe. Although the ɨnɨja is one of the main symbols of femininity, the ritual also incorporates some elements of role reversal: the women wear men's headdresses, shell collars, and carry arrows.

jatapa) in which the girls form life-long formal friendships. The garment thereby has connotations that go well beyond those understood by the men.

Earrings: tuluntɨ. Primary markers of male identity, feather earrings are the most visible ornament worn by the men. These are conferred upon the boys of the tribe in a ceremony that brings the nine tribes of the region together for a festival of singing, dancing, wrestling, and formal speeches. In the course of the ritual, boys are paired off in *jatsa* relationships, formal friendships that form the basis of political cooperation throughout adulthood. A second symbolic association links men's earrings to wrestling, the most dramatic expression of male strength and assertiveness. The feathers utilized for the earrings are those of the parrot and the toucan, among the most powerful wrestlers in the mythical Village of the Birds, where the first ear-piercing ceremony was held. Finally, earrings are among the symbols of maturity that declare a boy's approach to manhood.

The ɨnɨja and tuluntɨ are a principal part of the uniform of masculinity and feminity. Like all symbols, however, they are polysemic, and their messages are often ambiguous. The reader will note that the

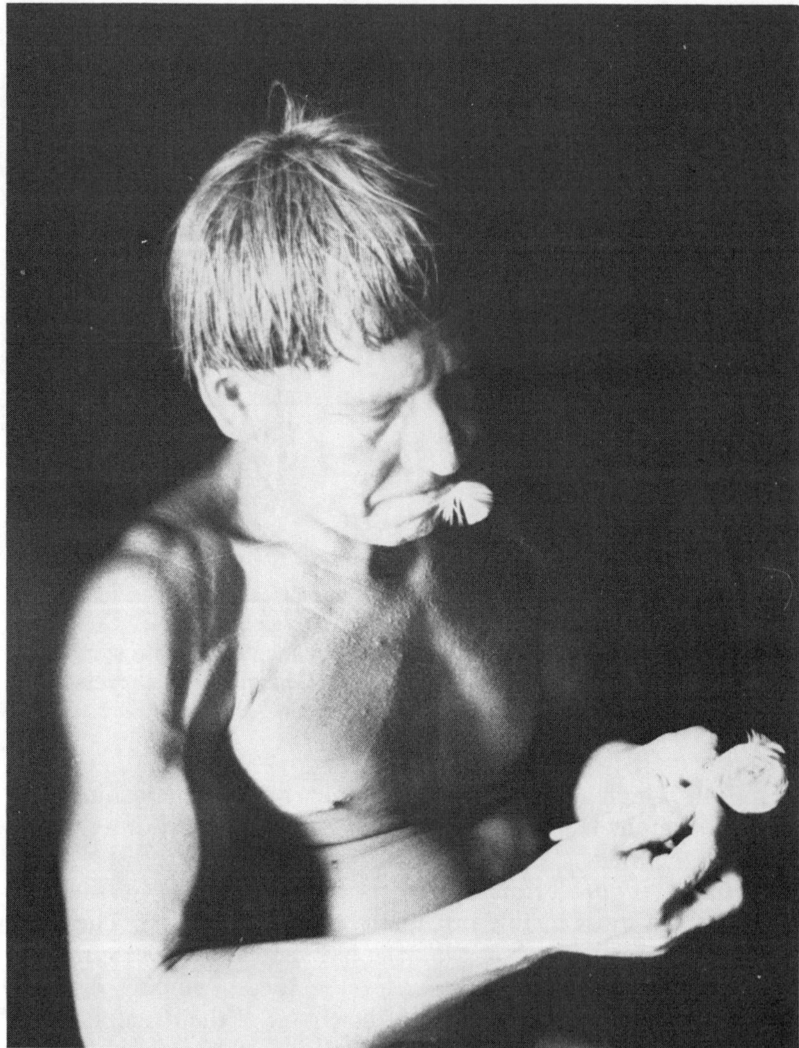

Fig. 7. Making feather earrings. Kuyaparei works in the narrow shaft of light that illuminates the doorway of his house. He ties feathers to a wooden dowel that serves as the rigid element in an earring. The ornament is an emblem of his masculinity and a reminder of the ear-piercing ritual that united him with his *jatsa,* a group of ceremonial friends who go through the life cycle together.

earring and the belt seem to express parallel ideas in that both are awarded at major intertribal ceremonies and symbolize sexual maturity. Surprisingly, as we shall see in chapter 10, the earring is also a feminine symbol. But before we explore this facet of sexual identity further, let us consider how gender is played out in male-female interaction. We begin with the symbolism of sexual relations.

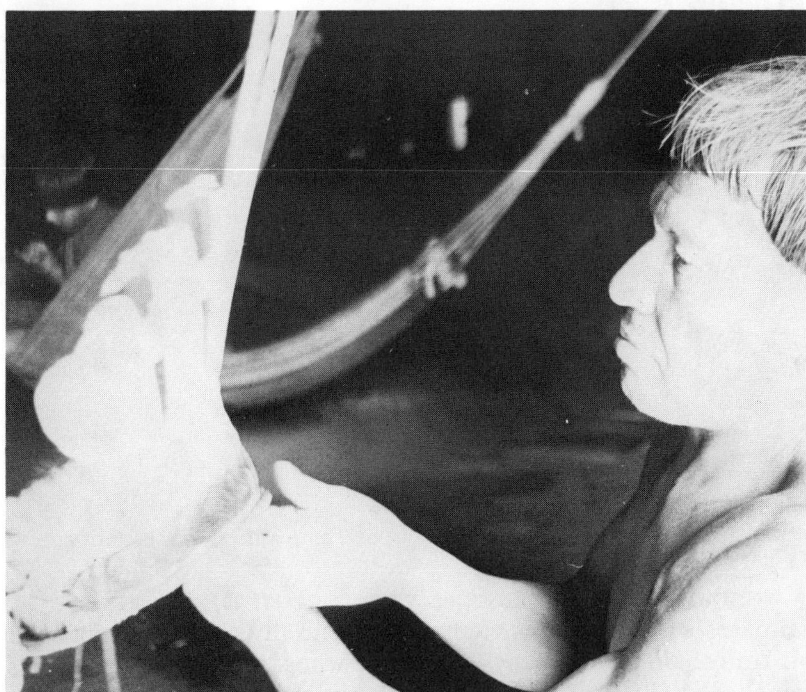

Fig. 8. Making a Headdress. The headdress, which Kuyaparei has nearly completed, requires many hours to make. The band of red down along the lower rim of the headdress is said to be especially "expensive" because of the effort of hunting macaws, parrots, and other species with decorative feathers. A red macaw is so highly valued by the villagers that it can be traded for a rifle, which is among the most expensive of all trade goods.

FOUR

Sexual Relations

Why are you crying over a worm?

—From *Tepu,* a myth of bestiality

A FUNDAMENTAL CONTRAST BETWEEN OURSELVES AND THE LOWER primates is that the human female is potentially sexually receptive at all times. Unlike monkeys and apes, whose estrus cycle confines female sexuality to a brief period each month, humans may use sex as the basis for stable mating relationships. Marriage, the family, and the other institutions of human kinship thereby harness the sexual drive and use it as a system of rewards to ensure individual conformity with their laws. This view of human sexuality is associated with Freud, who regarded the erotic or "life" instincts as the basis of the social order, and is implicitly accepted by most anthropologists. Alongside this theory, however, is a compatible view (also held by Freud) that sees the sexual drive as generating a potential for incest and adultery that threatens the integrity of the family, the rules of kinship and ultimately human culture: "As a powerful impulse, often pressing individuals to behavior disruptive of the cooperative relationships upon which human social life rests, sex cannot safely be left without restraints" (Murdock 1949,4).

In the debate on the unifying and humanizing nature of sexuality versus its disruptive potential, the Mehinaku come down in favor of the former. Above all else, legitimate sexual relations distinguish men from animals and tribes of men from each other. "Humans," say the villagers, "have sex with other humans who are their cross-cousins. Animals don't care who they have sex with." In this chapter, we shall see how the Mehinaku choose objects of sexual interest and thereby define their human identity.

Bestiality

The Mehinaku are careful observers of animals. Fish, birds, and monkeys are a vital part of their diet, and the villagers themselves sometimes fall prey to jaguars, snakes, or herds of aggressive wild pigs. This close link to the natural world means that animals loom large in the Mehinaku psychological environment. Virtually every myth includes animal characters and every ritual assigns them a symbolic role. It is therefore understandable that the villagers give thought to the possibilities of bestiality.[1] Their beliefs about the consequences of sex with animals interest us as a statement about the nature of being human and as a perspective on sexuality.

There is no special expression for bestiality in the Mehinaku language other than the phrase "having sex with animals" (*aintyawakapai apapainyemune etenu*), or the all-purpose term meaning "to misuse" oneself (*atalaitsua*), which is equally applicable to other sexual and nonsexual delicts. According to the villagers, no one would be so "mindless" as to have sex with animals. It is a foolish, unheard of act, and whenever I raised the topic, I was closely questioned as to whether Americans and other tribes of white men degraded themselves this way. And yet the subject exercises a compelling fascination for the villagers, since in the mythical past, sexual relations with animals were a frequent occurrence.

Numerous tales describe bestial encounters, for the most part between women and snakes. There appear to be two general classes of such stories, reflecting sexual anxieties on one hand and hostility toward out-groups on the other. The myth of Tepu, the worm, is an example of a tale from the first group, and it is told by Ketepe, a man in his early thirties:

TEPU

> Long ago, in ancient times, there was a woman named Kataihu. While walking to the forest, she saw Tepu emerging from his hole. "What's this?" she said. "It looks like a penis." Tepu wriggled a little, and Kataihu pulled him out of the hole with a stick. "Let's have sex, Tepu. You are just like a man's penis, with your round head and a mouth like the penis opening. Let's have sex, Tepu—your head-penis is delicious for me."

1. The actual incidence of bestiality among American farm-raised males is four to eight times higher than among city-dwellers (Hunt 1974, 354), suggesting that the proximity of animals is a temptation and a basis for the Mehinaku's concern with the topic.

Kataihu took Tepu home and placed him in a gourd: "I'll be your wife, Tepu," she said. She kept him in the back of the house where it is very dark and fed him manioc porridge through a small hole in the gourd. "Be sure to be quiet, Tepu," she warned him. "If somebody sees you, he will club you."

Later, Kataihu combed her hair and put on body paint to make herself beautiful for her Tepu. She kept him under her bench as she processed manioc. There Tepu waited until she was grinding up manioc tubers. Then he crawled up her leg into her vagina. "Oh, Tepu, Tepu," she moaned, "how delicious your penis, Tepu. Oh, Tepu, Tepu . . . *ateke, ateke,*[2] aaah!" Day after day, Kataihu slipped off to the gardens to have sex with her worm.

Oh, this woman, this woman Kataihu, this fool-of-a-woman from ancient times, she was not very intelligent. Now, none of us, none of us would have sex with a worm.

But finally, one of Kataihu's lovers saw her with her worm in the garden. "What is this?" he said. "It is Kataihu having sex with a worm. Oh, this worm is revolting. His head is covered with semen, he does not bathe, he is disgusting."

And so later, when Kataihu was away, the lover smashed the worm with a stick.

The next day, while grinding manioc, Kataihu called to her lover, "Tepu, Tepu, come have sex with me, Tepu, my delicious one." But there was no response. Looking in the gourd, Kataihu saw her multilated worm-lover and wailed, "Ah, my husband has died, my husband, my lover, my sexy one. Ah, how delicious was his penis!"

One of Kataihu's lovers overheard her and asked angrily, "Why are you crying over a worm?"

"Oh, his penis was so sensual, Tepu's penis, so much better than a man's."

"Kataihu, you are a fool. Real men, those are the ones you have sex with. Not worms. Tepu is smelly and disgusting!"

"Revolting! Disgusting!" said all the villagers, so that the words fell on her.

Tepu was buried, and Kataihu mourned him by reducing her belt one strand. But Tepu's semen was in her; he had put a child in her womb. When the baby

2. *Ateke* is also used to express pain, for example, after a burn.

> came out—that disgusting baby—its head was Tepu's head, its body that of a human, and its penis just like a worm.

On the superficial level, the story of Tepu is a cautionary tale about the hazards of sex with animals. As in other tales, we find a Mehinaku attracted to an animal with genitals that resemble a human's. Snakes, worms, and long-penised lizards copulate with women, while less frequently, men have intercourse with the mouths of stingrays and with herbivores and rodents. In all cases, the results are immediately gratifying but, as in the tale of Tepu, have unpleasant long-term consequences for both the animal and the human.

Looking more closely at these tales, we see that they cut far deeper than simple warnings. Better than human intercourse, animal sex appears in the tale as a threat to normal sexual relationships. Recall in this context Kataihu's lament: "Oh, his penis was so sensual . . . so much better than a man's." Hence, the vaginas, mouths, and penises of stingrays, lizards, and deer become the exclusive sexual outlet for the protagonists of these stories, to the neglect of their legitimate wives and lovers. In typical fashion, the slighted lover discovers what is happening, informs the village, and kills or drives off the seductive animal. When questioned about the characters in these myths, the villagers interpret their behavior from the same perspective: "Kataihu's lover killed Tepu because he was jealous. Because Tepu was so attractive to her."

In the myths, the animal world is dangerously tempting. Let a villager try animal sex once, the stories seem to say, and he may never return to human partners at all. The stories warn of sexual atavism and suggest that the line between animal and human may be all too easily crossed. We should not be misled by our raconteur's assurances, "Now, none of us, none of us would have sex with a worm." In fact, the tales of human and animal coitus are a kind of fantasy about the animal world and its close relationship to human sexuality. The fantasy is distanced, projected well back onto the frozen tableau of mythic times, and made still more comfortable by the humiliation of the protagonist and the death of the animal. But there is some evidence to suggest that the temptation and fear of animal sexuality is current and not just an ancient story. Not only do the villagers take evident pleasure in the tales and their inevitable denouement, but the same themes are found in individual fantasy material.

Dreams of having sex with animals, for example, occur fairly regularly, though the dreamer often employs a variety of devices to distance himself from the action of the dream. These defensive mechanisms include attributing the transgression to another villager while the dream self merely observes the act of intercourse or having the animal change its nature at the last moment, as in this dream report by Kailu, a woman of about forty years: "A snake, a big one, chased me. 'Run, run, run!' everyone shouted. But the snake suddenly turned into a man. He said, 'I want you as my wife.' We had sex. But then I said, 'No, no, you are a snake.' And he kept coming after me."

Dreams such as these are very frightening to the villagers. A measure of their emotional impact is the frequent use of defensive distancing devices, not only during the dream, but also in its subsequent interpretation. The dreamer never attributes the events to his own desires, but rather to a witch who induces the nightmare. Kailu, for example, explained that Yuma, a well-known witch, had caused her snake dream by constructing a small snake image.

The psychological association of animals with human sexuality is so compelling that even ordinary animal dreams are interpreted as having concealed sexual messages. Dreams of worms, turtles, and snakes foretell sexual activity. A man's dream of an anaconda is an omen of assault by a sexually aggressive woman. Animal and human sexuality are thereby closely connected in the villagers' fantasy life.

A second set of myths about animal-human sexuality continues the themes established by the first but adds an element of hostility toward other tribes. The Mehinaku, as we recall, are not alone in the Xingu Basin but are surrounded by friendly tribes who participate with them in a system of barter and intermarriage. These peoples (*putaka*) are distinguished from the tribes outside the Xingu system, the so-called wild Indians (*wajaiyu*), who are hated and despised as violent and uncivilized. For the most part, it is the wajaiyu who are the principal characters impugned by stories of sex with animals. In the following myth, we learn of the origins of the Suya, a Ge-speaking tribe that in the past has raided the Xinguanos, kidnapping women and children. The tale is told with malicious pleasure.

The Origin of the Suya

> Once there was a Suya woman who had an enormous vagina that looked about for its food. Oh, it was revolting, for she never bathed. She is now dead, that Suya woman with the enormous vagina.
>
> Once, while gathering manioc in her garden, she put a snake egg into her basket, but did not notice. The basket was heavy, and the day was hot. She did not notice when the snake egg hatched. Slipping through the weave of the basket, the snake wriggled down her back into her labia, deep into her vagina.
>
> Gradually, this woman got pregnant: "Ah, but why am I pregnant? I haven't had sex. There is no semen inside me," she wondered.

> After many moons, the snake got bigger and bigger, but the woman herself shriveled away. Just her abdomen was fat, but the rest of her wasted away. The snake baby was eating all of her food, eating out the inside of her body. When she went to defecate, the head of the snake would emerge to eat her feces. Oh, its was revolting! Her brothers and her sisters would have nothing to do with her. When they saw her on the path, they said, "Move over to the side! Walk on some other path! You have a snake inside of you. You aren't like any other women. Only you have a snake inside. You are revolting to us!"
>
> The woman went off to live with her one brother who would tolerate her, and together they built a shabby house, way off in the forest." Oh, the snake hurt her: "*Aka, aka*! It hurts inside," she groaned.
>
> As the snake grew bigger, it took to slipping out to wander through the woods, returning to the woman's womb when it wanted to sleep. Finally, when the snake was ready to be born, the woman called her brother, "Cut down a tall palm, the straightest and tallest you can find." The brother cut off the foliage of a tall palm and planted the trunk in the soil. Sitting on the ground in front of the tree, the woman spread her legs. Slowly, the giant snake emerged from inside here and ascended the pole. Way up to the top. Higher and higher it went. Oh, it was long, from its round head to its tail. And as it climbed, the brother hacked it with his machete into many small pieces.
>
> The woman and her brother ran from that place. But the next day, the brother cautiously returned to see what had happened to the snake. And there, where the snake had been, was a house and a village! There, where there had been pieces of the snake were people—the Suya!

"The Origin of the Suya" is not the only myth that ascribes a bestial origin to Xingu tribes, nor are these myths entirely confined to the hated wajaiyu. The Trumai, who are probably the most recently integrated of the Upper Xingu groups, and who are regarded as most marginal to the intertribal system, are also the butt of such tales. In one story, we learn how the grandather of all the Trumai lived alone in a deep forest and lusted for sexual relations. He approached the tapir, who kicked him away with her hooves, and he was similarly rejected by the wild pig and the deer. Finally, the capybara (a semi-aquatic rodent that can weigh as much as one hundred pounds) accepted him as her lover. She delivered seven children, all of whom had sex with each other, and together they founded the Trumai nation.

The intention of these tales is to impugn the human origins of the Suya and the Trumai. Like animals, these tribes are said to be given to repulsive habits in their personal hygiene and diet. Their skin, it is said, is black; they sleep on the ground, defecate in the water from the prows of their canoes, and are crawling with lice and vermin. They are prone to violence, and their speech (which none of the Mehinaku has ever mastered) is likened to the barking of dogs and the slobbering of wild pigs. The Suya, who are especially despised, are said to be subhuman, occupying a class below even the Cebus monkey, which is linguistically classified as a kind of human (*neunei*). When pressed, it is true that a villager will reluctantly admit that in a biological sense, the Suya and other wajaiyu qualify for human status: "Yes, they have tongues and lips and hair as we do; they are human." But socially, so far as most of the Mehinaku are concerned, the Suya and all those who would have sex with animals might as well be animals themselves.

Some of the contempt and revulsion that the villagers feel for bestiality, whether by wajaiyu or kajaiba (white men) is expressed by Kikyala, a man in his early forties: "The wajaiyu and the kajaiba have sex with animals. With lizards, with snakes, with tapirs and birds. All of the wajaiyu and the kajaiba do it. With deers and pigs. I myself saw a kajaiba having sex with a female ox in Batovi. The kajaiba is a fool. He misuses himself to have sex with oxen. This kajaiba had a big penis. The ox was on the ground. I saw this myself, in Batovi. It was disgusting."

The stories of bestiality now take on a new meaning. Sex with animals is a metaphor that expresses who the villagers are and who they are not. Like food habits, speech, and adornment, sexual conduct is a dramatic marker that identifies those who practice it. Indeed, in some ways, sexual behavior is the most powerful of these symbols since it is more likely to be charged with emotional intensity. In the Mehinaku case, this emotion may be composed of a hidden sexual interest in animals and a fear that the temptation may be acted upon. The result is a prohibition that draws its strength from the conflict. The keen pleasure the villagers take in the insulting myths of bestiality may therefore reflect their own suppressed emotions as well as their opinion of the despised wajaiyu.

Sex with Wild Indians and Whites

The animal world is sexually off-limits. Strange humans, be they kajaiba or wajaiyu, are also officially forbidden, but their status as prohibited sexual objects is more ambiguous. From the Mehinaku perspective, the major reason they and the other Xingu tribes have been approached by the wajaiyu and the kajaiba is for sexual relations. In the past, the Suya and other wild tribes have kidnapped Xingu women, and even today the Mehinaku men keep their wives well away from the soldiers at the Jacarei air force base on the fringe of the Xingu reservation. Regrettably, on rare occasions some of the better-credentialed white visitors to the Xingu tribes have also confirmed the Mehinaku view of the sexually predatory kajaiba.

From the Mehinaku perspective, all such interactions are disturbing and improper. Not so improper that the men will shun sexual relations with wajaiyu or kajaiba women when they think they can get away with it, but there is little pride in such conquests. Sex with outsiders "misuses" Mehinaku sexuality. At best, it is "worthless sex" that creates neither legitimate offspring nor enduring relationships. At worst, it is "revolting sex" with a partner who is said to have a bad smell and a disgusting vagina. Revolting sex is known to lead to sores on the genitals and other venereal diseases, which are a part of the "white man's witchcraft." Although the villagers did not quite spell it out, their descriptions and feelings about sex with wild Indians and whites were like muted reactions to sex with animals. Proper human sex is with Mehinaku and other Xingu tribes. But even here, there are important limitations, such as the prohibition against homosexuality.

Homosexuality

The very idea of homosexual relations is considered ridiculous by the villagers. It is the kind of behavior characteristic of whites and wild Indians, but not the Mehinaku and their neighbors. "Why," Ketepe asked me, "would anyone want to have sex like that?"

We gain a sense of the villagers' attitudes toward homosexuality by considering a series of events that took place in the Xingu reservation many years ago. To place what occurred in context, we must realize that the Xingu peoples and their exotic tribal culture slip easily into the fantasy life of emotionally disturbed individuals from our own and Brazilian society. From time to time, these persons obtain access to the Xingu reservation, and incorporate the villages into their fantasies with comic or even tragic results. Such was the case many years ago when a regular visitor began to recruit Indian men for homosexual relations. As word of his activities spread and as young men began to sport such high-status gifts as radios and bicycles (useful on the hard flood-plain during the dry season), the visitor had no shortage of consorts.

The Mehinaku regarded the episode as characteristic of the kajaiba. White men are known to have relations with animals, so why not with other men? In support of this reasoning, the villagers pointed to numerous other examples of bizarre conduct on the part of the individual in question, including extreme sadomasochistic sexual practices filmed with a self-timing camera. In dealing with the white man, the Mahinaku have discovered, anything is possible. The villagers' explanation of the motives of the Xinguanos who consorted with the visitor is simple. They wanted his gifts. They had no sexual interest in him whatsoever. Admittedly they were foolish to have participated, but no man really desires homosexual relations.

The minimization of homosexual interest is reflected in the Mehinaku language, which has no term for the role of homosexual. Homosexual acts are referred to simply as "having sex with a man" (*aintywakapai enɨja etenu*) or as "misusing" (*atalaitsuapai*) oneself with another individual. The culture of homosexuality is also minimal, though it is suggestive of what homosexuality means to the villagers. Kikyala tells the only myth I have recorded in which homosexuality figures prominently:

> A man went fishing with his comrade. His name was Kiyayala. I do not know the name of his friend. But this is a real myth, from ancient times. Kiyayala had sex with his friend through the rectum. His friend got pregnant. His abdomen grew big. Then the child, a boy, was born. "*Aka, aka,* it hurts," cried Kiyayala's friend. He was all torn inside. He picked up the little boy and held him to him. The boy grew up. A woman gave him her breast. He grew to be big and handsome.
>
> The myth is over. It wasn't a long one. What Kiyayala did we would not do today. There is no word for what he was. If a man were to be like Kiyayala or his friend, he would be very ashamed. Everyone would tease him.

The story of Kiyayala is of special interest because it suggests that the passive male homosexual develops the reproductive capacity of a woman. This follows logically from the villagers' male-centered theory of conception (see chapter 5) but also implies the absurdity of homosexual sex and the men who might practice it. The tale is thus a warning, but with its thin characterizations, lack of detail, and implausible plot, it may also be read as a denial of homosexuality. So impoverished is the tale that the narrator feels obliged to apologize for its low entertainment value and to alert the listener when it has reached its conclusion: "The myth is over. It wasn't a long one."

In mythology, homosexuality hardly exists. The case of the visitor who hired Xingu men is seen as reflecting more on the strange kajaiba than on the Indians. Only in one historical instance must the villagers explain the behavior of a Mehinaku who, though uninfluenced by perverted outsiders, stepped beyond the boundaries of the masculine role. Tenejumɨne, "Slightly a Woman," as this person is referred to today, died more than forty-five years ago and is remembered by only two persons in the community. Even for them, however, the details of his life and behavior are somewhat sketchy and contradictory.

Born to a father who "wished for a girl while he was having sexual relations," Slightly a Woman grew up to assume the dress and role of a woman. He wore an ɨnɨje belt, painted his body with feminine pigments, and used women's patterns and hair styles. He performed women's work and was said to have been a prodigious weaver of hammocks, processor of manioc flour, and spinner of cotton. The women liked Slightly a Woman since he carried great quantities of water back from the stream and brought home stacks of firewood from the forest. Some of the villagers claim that Slightly a Woman had small but feminine breasts and a high voice. Others insist that he was like a man in voice and physical appearance. All are agreed, however, that he formed special relationships with a few of the men that resembled those of lovers. The men, it is said, would get into the same hammock as Slightly a Woman and "pretend" to engage in sex play. But they did so "only because they wanted presents," and they did not have sexual relations with him.

What strikes me as an ethnographer is how little I was able to learn of Slightly a Woman. Details were hazy, and different villagers told contradictory stories. Other Mehinaku historical figures, such as chiefs or witches, are remembered with far greater clarity. In a generation or two, if Slightly a Woman is remembered at all, I suspect it will be as a mythological character from ancient times. His physical transition to a female (with "small breasts and a high voice") in some of the villagers' renditions has already begun the metamorphosis from history to mythology.

The amnesia that surrounds Slightly a Woman is akin to the near absence of homosexuality in mythology and the oblique way in which it is expressed in the language of sexuality. All serve to mute the villagers' awareness of homosexuality. This pattern may well be a denial of homosexual impulses since, as we shall see in chapter 10, there is evidence of unconscious feminine identification among the men. What clearly emerges from the data thus far, however, is the unacceptability of homosexuality.

Incest

The main current of Mehinaku libido flows toward persons of the opposite sex. Among the channels that guide its course, the most clearly defined are those marked by the prohibitions against incest. According to the villagers, sex and most forms of kinship do not mix. Only relatives who stand in a cross-cousin relationship, that is, the children of opposite-sex siblings, may have sexual relations. Many of the Mehinaku say that even these cousins are "too close" and that sex and marriage is only proper for the grandchildren of opposite-sex siblings. These villagers emphasize the concept of closeness between blood kin in their discussions of sex with relatives by pointing to their navels and declaring "we are kinsmen here and therefore cannot have sex." There is thus a common biological connection between near kin that makes them too close for sex.

Other villagers explain their avoidance of incest with a particular kinsman by tracing the genealogical links that connect them. Eventually, they reach a point where their ancestors were, for example, brothers. They then explain their avoidance of incest by saying, "Our grandfathers were one group." The key term *teupa*, "group," refers to a cluster of things that have a common origin, such as arrow cane from the same grove or fish caught in the same trap. Kin who are of such common origins are called "true kin" (*epene waja*) in contrast to more distant and merely putative relationships. True kin should not have sex or marry unless they are cross-cousins (children of a brother and sister).

Frequently, however, it is not clear which relatives are in the forbidden category. Approximately sixty-five percent of marriages are to other Mehinaku; thus kin relationships are complex and overlapping. In the absence of written records, these links are easily forgotten after several generations. As I have argued elsewhere (Gregor 1977, 263–64), the Mehinaku practice a kind of "genealogical amnesia" that actively discourages the retention of kinship lore. Let the anthropologist question a young man about his ancestors, for example, and he is likely to respond: "What? You want the name of my grandfather's brothers? I never saw them. Go ask an old man. I'm not from mythic times!" The net effect of this system is that the boundary between the incestuous and the acceptable is sometimes ambiguous. And so the villagers play with the system, selectively maximizing the possibilities for interesting sexual relationships and supporting their choices with after-the-fact genealogical alibis.

Given the flexibility of the system, the villagers are not preoccupied with the possibilities of incest, especially with distant kin. We find there is no way to refer to incest other than to state the specific nature of the forbidden act (*aintywakapai pitsukakalu ɨtenu* "having sex with your sister") or to use the more general term for "misusing" the relationship. Moreover, as is common among many peoples, including ourselves, the Mehinaku are able to provide no precise explanation of why incest is wrong. When pressed, an informant will provide the sort of explanation prized by structurally oriented anthropologists: "No, you do not have sex with your sister. Your sister marries men who will become your brother-in-law and with whom you go fishing." The villagers thereby recognize that a violation of the incest taboo obliterates the distinction of in-laws and blood kinship. But the objection to incest cuts deeper. We press the informant further, and he says that kin are too close (*aitsa mawaka*, literally, "not far") for sex and that sex with them in any case would be wrong (*aitsa awushapai*), stupid (*aitsa katamapapai*), and animal-like. We persist: Why is it so foolish? In despair over his interrogator's obtuseness, the informant plays his final card: "Do you have sex with your sister? Do Americans think incest is good?" And so, we have reached bottom. Incest is wrong, ultimately, because it is wrong.

But not all incest is equally bad. Distant kin of the wrong degree regularly engage in quasi-incestuous relationships and even get married. Once the relationship is well-established, the attendant gossip rapidly dissipates. Affairs between close kin are far more serious, but here too, we find a range of variation. Father-daughter incest, for example, occurs on very rare occasions, but of the possible nuclear family transgressions, it is the least serious. Brother-sister incest occurs in myth, but probably almost never in reality. As for mother-son incest, the villagers simply do not believe it could occur. Not even in mythic times, when seemingly anything was possible, did sons couple with their mothers! Perhaps the best way to gain an appreciation of the villagers' reactions to incest is to look first at a myth of incest between father and daughter and then at a recent historical case involving such a relationship.

Tuluma, the Woodpecker

Tuluma was sick in his hammock, very, very sick. Or so he pretended.

He saw his daughter, the line of her labia, her black pubic hair. He wanted to have sex with her.

Tuluma called his daughter to him: "Come here, my daughter. In the future, I will send your cross-cousin to you. He calls me "mother's brother," he is your real cross-cousin, your father's sister's son. He looks just like me. He has my nose, my eyes, my body, my feet. Just like me. You'll see in the future, my nephew will come to you. When he does come, I want you to marry him; I want you to have sex with him."

Ah, then the daughter began to cry, out of sorrow for her dying father: "*Papai yu, papai yu*. Oh, my father," she wailed.

"Come to me, my daughter, I will soon die. When I am dead, I want you to have me buried under a ceramic cauldron, in the ground. But don't bury me too deep—just a shallow grave, not too deep."

"Yes, I will do it," said the daughter.

Then Tuluma completely relaxed his body and played dead. They decorated his body and put him in his hammock, painting his head with a red design, like that of a real woodpecker. They carried him out in his hammock, and he was buried under the ceramic cauldron, in a shallow grave.

Later that night, when it was very dark, Tuluma began to peck at the cauldron: "*Tak, tak, tak* . . ." It broke. The cauldron broke! Tuluma came up from the grave, in the middle of the night. All that night, Tuluma hid in the forest. The next day, he went to his daughter and said, "My uncle, Tuluma, has he died?"

"Yes he has."

Tuluma pretended to cry for his "uncle": "*Ua ku, ua ku, ua ku, ua ku*. Oh, my uncle . . ." Then he said, "Let me tell you what my uncle told me: 'When I die in the future, my nephew, I want you to marry your cousin, my daughter.'"

"Yes, so my father told me."

Tuluma tied his hammock above his daughter's, and he had sex with her.

But then, a few days later, Tuluma called to his daughter: "Come over here to groom me for head lice." She sat down beside him and began to look through his hair for lice: "Ah, here is one. And here is one . . . here is one—What's this!?" All over Tuluma's scalp she found earth, earth from the grave.

"Mama! This one—my husband—he is my father!"

They struck him with clubs. Up, up, up, he flew away over the village to the forest and landed on a tree limb.

"*Tsiik, tsiik, tsiik hururu* . . . I had sex with you . . . I had sex with you . . . I had sex with you," he said to his daughter.

What strikes us about this story is that, unlike other Mehinaku myths of incest, *Tuluma* is a light-hearted tale. At worst, Woodpecker is an outrageous sexual trickster who wins his daughter so implausibly that we are almost won over to his side. Even today, Tuluma seems to have the last word as his onomatopoeic call taunts the villagers from the safety of a high perch: "You have sex with your daughter . . . you have sex with your daughter (*paintyawaka pitsupalu*)." Our amused reaction to the myth is affirmed by the Mehinaku themselves, who told me the story as I sat with a group of men in front of the men's house. A few minutes after the tale was told, while the men were still offering humorous additions and comments, a woodpecker flew over the village, occasioning a tremendous whoop and shout from the assembled men: "There he goes, there he goes, Tuluma, Tuluma, Tuluma!"

But we should not be misled by the whimsy of the tale and the men's apparent lack of concern. Incest is wrong, and there is a price to be paid by those who find the temptation too strong. A case in point is that of the infamous Eweje and his daughter Kwalu. The story is still fresh in the villagers' minds, even though it is now many years since Eweje and his daughter died. Kikyala, who also recounted the myth of Tuluma, is again our narrator.

> Eweje left the Mehinaku. He took refuge in another tribe because he feared he would be killed. He was a big witch, and everyone knew it. His daughter, Kwalu, was a little girl when he left, but she entered adolescent seclusion and grew into a beautiful woman.
>
> When Eweje returned to the Mehinaku, his wife had died and his daughter was living with kin. He took his daughter off to the woods and said, "Let's have sex."
>
> "Oh no," she cried, "you are my father."
>
> But Eweje threw her on the ground and raped her. When he returned to the village, he hung his hammock over his daughter's. Everyone was very much afraid of him. None of Kwalu's lovers continued to see her because they were afraid of Eweje's anger. Only one man dared criticize Eweje openly, and that was an old man, one of Eweje's close kin who did not fear his sorcery. All the others taunted him in falsetto voices from behind the houses at night so that he could never be sure who it was: "Woodpecker, woodpecker, you have sex with your daughter," they shouted. But none of that stopped Eweje. He lived with Kwalu as her husband until he himself died from witchcraft.

This case of Eweje and his daughter is an extraordinary one. The fact that it occurred in the open over a period of many years suggests unusual freedom in sexual choice and a relatively relaxed attitude toward father-daughter incest. We shall see in chapter 9 that brother-sister incest is far more emotionally painful. Yet it is well to note that Eweje and Kwalu's relationship was costly to them. In the context of a small tribal community, a man who has lost his good name has lost everything. Eweje, "the Woodpecker," lived at the fringe of Mehinaku society, which although sexually permissive, is not a sexual free-for-all.

"Having Sex with the Hand"

Interest in sex and avoidance of bestiality, homosexuality, and incest do not ensure a social relationship. When expressed in masturbation, for example, the erotic drive is individualizing rather than social. In our own society, Kinsey, Pomeroy, and Martin declare that ninety-two percent of the male population engage in autoeroticism (1948, 499). Hite's more recent data puts the figure at ninety-nine percent (1981, 486).

Confronted with this data, I am reluctant to say that the Mehinaku never masturbate, but I am convinced that it represents a relatively small portion of their total sexual outlet. I find, for example, that there is no single-word term for masturbation or way of referring to it other than such descriptive phrases as "having sexual relations with one's hand" (*aintyawakapai pawejuku ɨtenu*). Further, the villagers have a relatively relaxed attitude toward masturbation, suggesting that we are not dealing with an emotionally loaded topic such as bestiality. Masturbation is foolish, and anyone who masturbates is surely misusing his own sexuality. But certainly the practice is not subject to anything like the same kind of censorship or repression that was until recently characteristic of Western society.

In further support of the low incidence of autosexuality, we have the testimony of the villagers themselves. According to the Mehinaku, the only ones who would masturbate are lonely old men whose wives and lovers have died and who have no other regular sexual outlet. Late at night, while everyone is asleep, these solitary and marginal men relieve their sexual tensions, alone in their hammocks. For everyone else, especially young men, there are far more pleasurable opportunities. As Ketepe responded to my query, "Having sex with the hand? Why would anyone bother? There are plenty of women around."

The low salience of autosexuality is reflected in the paucity of myths and dreams about the subject. The relatively few stories of masturbation, however, are sufficient to demonstrate that the physical environment, like the world of men and animals, has sexual potential. All manner of unlikely crevices and protrusions may be pressed into service for autosexual gratification, as is the case in the tale of the wax phallus.

The Wax Phallus

Once there was a woman who was quite old. No one wanted to have sex with her. But one of the men in her house had a rod of wax, which he used to haft his arrows. It was shaped just like a penis. Late at night, when everyone was asleep, the woman painted herself

> with epitsiri dye and combed her hair to make herself beautiful for her wax lover. Then she had sex with it. Oh, how sensual was her rod-of-wax lover! She would spit on it to imitate semen and make it even more delicious for her. But she kept the wax rod well hidden. Until one day, a man looking for wax happened upon the rod: "Ooh . . . what is this?" he said. "This wax smells like a vagina!"
>
> Later that night, he awoke and watched the woman masturbating, but he said nothing. The next day, while she was out, he rubbed the wax rod with the hottest pepper. Then, going from house to house, he dumped out all the water in the village. After it got dark, and all the villagers were sleeping, she began once again to make love to her wax rod. Pain! Pain! Pain! Soon she began to burn in pain. She looked about for water, but there was none. She raced to the neighboring house: "Do you have water?"
>
> "No, there is none here."
>
> And so she went to every house in the village. Finally, she had to race all the way down to the bathing area to wash herself out.

I have been able to find only two other stories of masturbation, and in both, men are the principal actors. In one tale, we learn of a man who discovered a remarkably gratifying hole in a tree, which he began to use to the exclusion of his wife and girlfriends. In the second story, a man made an artificial vagina of leaves to which he became similarly attached. In both myths, the culprits were seen by other villagers who hacked away the hole with an ax and tore the leaf vagina to shreds. In both stories, the masturbators behaved as if their leafy companions had been real women. They wailed for the deceased plants, cut their hair short, and took off their belts as a symbol of mourning.

In these tales, we find some of the same themes we noted in the case of bestiality. Let a villager be fool enough to be seduced by animals or plants, and he is punished. Only human beings are proper sexual objects, and the person who wastes his sexuality in the pursuit of animals or in the solitary practice of masturbation is bound to be found out and come to a bad end.

Each Mehinaku is at the center of a sexually charged universe. All around are potentially enticing but inappropriate objects that must be discharged of their sexual electricity. The grounding wires are the villagers' contempt, the warnings of the myths, and the images of inhumanity reserved for those who succomb to the lure. At the extreme end of this sexual universe are physical objects, plants, and animals, all of which are strongly forbidden. Distant human sexual objects, such as wild Indians and whites, are closer but also prohibited. Moving excessively close to the individual, we find that near relatives, persons of the same sex, and autoeroticism are forbidden. Across the entire spectrum of conceivable sexual objects, there is only one sanctioned choice: a Xingu Indian of the opposite sex who stands as a cross-cousin.

In actual behavior, the Mehinaku are able to find ways around these rules. Intercourse between kin of the wrong degree is common, and sex with wild Indians and whites occasionally occurs even though it is supposedly distasteful. There may even be some casual experimentation with masturbation and homosexuality. But the intention of the culture of sexuality is clear. Sex defines human and tribal identity. It brings members of different kin groups together in relationships that lead to economic exchange, parental responsibilities, the division of labor between men and women, and the obligations of in-laws. For the Mehinaku, sex is a supremely social drive in which the libido is harnessed in service to society.

FIVE

Food for Thought: The Symbolism of Sexual Relations and Eating

Eating is the form of sex. Copulation is oral copulation.
—Norman O. Brown, *Love's Body*

Your children are big because your food is sweet.
—Kikyala

SEX IS A NATURAL SYMBOL WHOSE CONNOTATIONS AND MEANINGS GO WELL beyond the act of procreation. In some cultures, such as the "Sambia" of New Guinea, male sexuality is linked to the dissipation of life force and energy, which the Sambia replace by drinking tree sap. In our own society, the colloquial language of sexuality regards intercourse as the conquest of a passive female by an aggressive male. Among the Mehinaku, we have seen that sexual relations define who a person is with respect to his kinsmen, his tribe, and the natural world around him. But the imagery and connotations of Mehinaku sexuality are richer still. For the Mehinaku, sex intertwines with biological processes and with the social relationship of men and women. At the base of their system of ideas about human sexuality is the postulate that supports the entire edifice: sex is a kind of eating.

Eating and Sexual Relations

In the Mehinaku language, the word for having sexual intercourse is *aintyawakapai*; eating is *aintyapai*. Analyzing the words, we find that the affix *pai* is a durative (roughly equivalent to the "ing" form in English), while *aintya* is the root of the verb "to eat." The medial *waka* is an augmentative that enlarges the scope or action of the verb. Hence "walking" is *etunapai*, "trekking" or "wandering" is *etunawakatapai*. A literal rendering of the verb to have sex might thus be "to eat to the fullest extent."[1] The Mehinaku are fully conscious of the metaphor: "Sex," they claim, "is a kind of eating." It therefore comes as no surprise to hear the villagers using the verb "to eat" to mean "I eat" or "I have sex." The "eating" that occurs in the course of sexual relations is reciprocal. Unlike the most commonly used Anglo-Saxon terms for sexual relations, both men and women "eat" each other. Thus *aintya ja ha* ambiguously means "she has sex with him" or "he has sex with her." The assumed activity of men and passivity of women in the sexual act is not built into the verb as in English. Linguistically (if not behaviorally), the sexes have an equal role in intercourse among the Mehinaku.

But precisely what is it that is "consumed" in sexual relations, and what is doing the "eating?" The colloquial language of sexuality provides the answer. Let a villager inquire about his girlfriend, for example, and he may be told, *Pitsi inula iye unɨ taku*, "Your penis's food is going to get water." Or a young man may point to an attractive girl and say, "Her vagina is my penis's food." Although this expression is often used jokingly, the idiom is also heard in the everyday speech of both men and women. The essential idea is that the genitals of one sex are the "food" of the other's. We are now in a better position to understand the anatomical labels the villagers employ in discussing the genitalia and the ɨnɨja belt. The female genitals and the belt are divided into a number of parts, some of which resemble the human face. In this picturesque taxonomy, they are equipped with "foreheads," "lips," "mouths," and "noses." The act of sexual relations from this perspective is the joining together of body parts that actually engage in eating.

The equation of the female genitals with facial parts requires further elaboration. We recall that the clitoris (*itsi kiri*) is the "vagina's nose." In the manner of the hunter of monkeys who sniffs the air in pursuit of his quarry, the clitoris is said to move about, "searching for its food." The entire vagina is symbolically identified as a mouth, an idea that appears at many levels of cultural imagery. In dreams, for example, fish traps are interpreted as seductive feminine symbols in which the "mouth" (*kanatɨ*) of the trap is equated with the vagina and the entrance of the fish into the trap becomes a symbolic sexual act. The doorways of houses (*paintyanatɨ*, the "mouth" of the house) are also feminine since, framed with thatch, they are vulvalike in appear-

1. I acknowledge the assistance of Emilienne Ireland in analyzing the term *aintyawakapai*.

ance. In the course of highly sexual harvest rituals, the doorways are penetrated by an "anteater" who is then beaten off by the women (see Gender Wars picture essay, page 122). The sexual meaning of this ritual is no secret to at least one of the men: "The anteater's nose is a penis; the doorway of the house is a vagina."

The equivalence of mouth and vagina finds additional support in mythology. In a story we will examine in more detail later, we find the large-mouthed bass playing the female role in the invention of sexual relations because its "big mouth is like a vagina." Here we offer another illustration from one of the many in Mehinaku mythology.

THE TOOTHED VAGINA

> In ancient times, there was an angry man who constantly berated others. One evening, a woman took many tiny shells—they looked just like teeth—and put them in her inner labia. Later, when it got dark, the man wanted to have sex. "Oh, she is beautiful," he thought. The woman was pretending to sleep. "Let's have sex," he said. Oh, but his penis was big. In it went. He ate her, he ate her, it went all the way in. . . . *Tsyuu*! The vagina cut his penis right off, and he died right there, in the hammock.
>
> "Ahhhhh. . . . my lover has died, my lover has died," she cried. "Come here, come here, come and see!" Everyone came to see. "What has happened here?" they asked. But the woman did not tell. She was ashamed to tell. She pretended to cry for her lover.

With the myth of the toothed vagina, we are introduced to the dark side of male-female relationships among the Mehinaku, an area shaded with anxieties about castration. We shall have more to say about this facet of Mehinaku sexuality in chapter 7, but it is well to add at this point that the eating-sex equation includes the notion of destruction and harm. Among the major classes of spirits in the Mehinaku pantheon, for example, are the "spirits that eat" (*apapainyei aintya*). A villager luckless enough to meet one of these monsters is consumed on the spot and never heard from again. Myths frequently tell of encounters between Mehinaku and animals or monsters that threaten to eat them. Finally, the verb "to eat" suggests harmful or painful experiences. Thus a wrestler, bleeding from scrapes and wounds after being thrown on the ground, may explain, "The earth ate me."

We can understand, then, that the term *aintya* for sexuality may convey a threatening message. When, as the villagers say, a man's penis is "hungry" for its "food," it grows erect and "angry" (*japu-*

japai). At these times, male sexuality may have an aggressive component to which the women fall victim. But we now hold in abeyance a discussion of the anxieties and tensions in Mehinaku sexuality and more happily turn to the pleasures of sexual relationships.

SEXUAL FEELINGS

In the syntax and grammatical construction of the Mehinaku language, physical sensations tend to be separated from the individual and ascribed to an organ or bodily system. Mehinaku do not say, "I am thirsty" or "I have a headache" but ascribe the sensation to the part of the body experiencing the discomfort. "I am thirsty" is rendered "my tongue is hurting" (*kowpai nupiri nein*), and "I have a headache" becomes "my head hurts" (*kowpai nutu*). Through these expressions runs the idea that the affected part has a life of its own, a detachability from the possessor. In the case of sexual sensations, we find the same pattern combined with the use of oral imagery.

The prototype of all sexual sensation is hunger. One's genitals are said to be "hungry" (*iyumenakapai*) for their food, the genitals of the opposite sex. Several adjectives are used to describe the flavor of this food, most of which have an explicitly oral component. A "taste" (*eteme*), may be "delicious" or "succulent" (*awirintyapai*), one of the most common descriptors of both good food and good sex. Dull sex, on the other hand, like dull food, may be *mana*, "tasteless," a term that refers to a category of unspiced food such as cold manioc porridge and water. Sad to say, sex with spouses is said to be mana, in contrast to sex with lovers, which is nearly always awirintyapai. Only one major descriptor of sexual sensation, *weiyupei*, has no oral references. Not easily translated into English, this term is used for a variety of intense feelings, such as itching or tickling, as well as sex. In direct quotes, I gloss this term as "sensual" or "voluptuous," to differentiate it from orally derived terms.

In using the vocabulary of sexual sensation, the villagers tend to ascribe the feelings to the genitals themselves, as in *awirintyapai pitisi*, "your genitals are delicious," or *pitsi upai weiyuki*, "your genitals have sensuality," though it is also possible to describe the experience more personally (as in *awirintyapai nupiri*, "it's delicious for me"). Let us now cite a myth that brings together the themes of sex, food, and the self-distancing we have identified in the linguistics of physical sensation.

The Wandering Vagina

> In ancient times, all the women's vaginas used to wander about. Today women's vaginas stay in one place. One woman of ancient times, Tukwi, had a vagina that was especially foolish. While Tukwi slept, her vagina

would crawl about the floor of the house, thirsty and hungry, looking for manioc porridge and fish stew. Creeping about snail-like on the ground, it found the porridge pot and slid the top off. One of the men awoke and listened: "Aah, nothing but a mouse," he said, and he went back to sleep. But as the vagina slurped up the porridge, another man awoke and took a brand from the fire to see what was happening. "What is this?" he said. To him it look like a great frog, with a nose and an immense mouth. Moving closer, he scorched the vagina with his torch. Oh, it scurried back to its owner, slipping right inside her. She cried and cried, for she had been burned. Then Tukwi called all the women and lectured them: "All you women, don't let your genitals wander about. If they do, they may get burned as mine were!"

And so, today, women's genitals no longer go wandering about.

RESTRICTIONS AND LIMITATIONS

Culture, anthropologists argue, is built of rules. Sensible rules, arbitrary rules, painful rules—they are the framework for social life. More often than not, the rules that are most burdensome are those that limit life's pleasures, notably food and sex. The Mehinaku are no exception to this pattern, in that rules and taboos hedge and control both diet and sexual relations. Moreover, as among many peoples, the prohibitions are backed by magical sanctions. What makes the Mehinaku unusual is that one conceptual language frames both sets of restrictions.

The simplest of the prohibitions is the concept of *kanupa*, "not consumed." Kanupa foods are those that are taboo to a particular person. A man avoiding certain species of fish because of a dream of a fish spirit honors the avoidance because it is kanupa to him. By extension, a woman may be kanupa to a particular man because the relationship would be incestuous.

A taboo having broader scope and greater intensity is suggested by the term *keinke*, "forbidden" or "under prohibition." Here the focus is on the individual rather than the forbidden object, and the term usually refers to the major taboos surrounding individuals at significant points in the life cycle. A young girl menstruating for the first time, for example, is *keinkepei*, "fasting; under a prohibition," and eats and drinks nothing at all for twenty-four hours. The concept also applies to sexual relations, the unity of language being nicely expressed in such phrases as "she is keinkepei; therefore he does not eat (have sex with) her genitals" (*keinkepei ipiri ja ha; yukaka aitsa ainytapai itsi*). Interestingly, one may be under prohibition for the benefit of another individual. Hence a new father honoring the couvade is said to be *keinkepei patain ipiri*, "under restrictions for his son." Let the father violate the prohibiton by eating forbidden foods or engaging in sexual relations, and the child becomes ill.

No guesswork is required to assess the father's culpability, for the village shamans stand all too ready to diagnose an infringement of the prohibitions as the cause of an infant's sickness. Gathering around a child suffering from a stomachache, they suck out the disease-causing *kauki*, which have magically intruded themselves in the child, thanks to the father's irresponsibility. By sleight of hand, one shaman may remove a fishbone if the father has negligently eaten fish; a second holds up a small amount of saliva, said to be the father's semen, thereby demonstrating that he recently had sexual relations. The prohibitions are taken seriously. The villager who harms his child risks the scorn of the community.

The final rule we examine is the concept of "frustrating and endangering" (*waritya*). "Frustrating and endangering" are actually rough glosses of a term that is difficult to translate. Waritya is based on a belief that when one leaves another in "hunger," that individual is in an emotional state conducive to becoming sick or losing his soul to a spirit. Unlike the kanupa and keinke prohibitions, however, the waritya concept is a prescription that enjoins generosity with food and acquiescence in sexual relations. The sanction that backs up this prescription is different from the others in that an infraction harms only the individual whose hunger has been frustrated. The following semihistorical account of a victim of such frustration provides a sense of how the concept is applied.

A Frustrated Lover

> A man went to solicit sex from a really pretty girl. He called her from behind her house again and again, but she did not like him. He was not attractive to her to have sex. "*Aitsa neutɨ aintya pitsi*, my genitals will never 'eat' yours," she said. Oh, but the man was hungry. And therefore he fell victim to convulsions (*mapwanapwa*, possibly epilepsy).

The villagers explain that the man became ill because he wanted to have sex very badly—his "hunger" was great—and was refused. And so he was put in a state of waritya and therefore became sick.

The strength of the waritya concept as a sanction that enforces generosity is not easy for members of an urban society to understand. If all that robbers had to fear was the discomfort of their victims, no bank in town would be safe. In a small-scale society, however, each man shoulders some of the responsibility for the well-being of his fellows. In this setting, the price paid in reputation for harming others is far higher than the cost of generosity with food and sexual services. A reasonable request for food or sex is seldom turned down without good cause.

THE ASSOCIATION OF FOODS AND SEX

The interpenetration of ideas about food and sex that we find in taboos is further developed in associations that the villagers have about edible plants and animals. Fish, for example, accounts for nearly all of the animal protein consumed by the Xinguanos. The sexual associations of fish are multiple and complex. At times, they are seen as feminine in nature. More commonly they are phallic and sexually active. A fisherman may take advantage of the sexual nature of his quarry by using charms and spells to lure the fish into the feminine trap (see figure 9). In Mehinaku dream interpretation, a fish trap is a symbol of a woman. The entry to the trap is her genitalia. When he sets a trap, a fisherman may say, "Trap, when you see a fish, tell it, 'Come here for a moment. I want to talk to you; I want to have sex!'"

Once caught, fish play a special role in marking masculine and feminine behavior. Let us watch a fisherman returning home with his catch. As he enters the village he is proclaimed by a tremendous whoop from all the men. Basking in the attention of the entire community, he hands his catch to his wife, who has been stoking the fire and preparing manioc bread in anticipation of his return. After she prepares the fish, as "mistress of the fish stew" (*wakula weketu*), she sends heaps of stew on slabs of flat bread to her in-laws and relatives in other houses. Catching and cooking fish are symbols of the marital relationship as well as men's and women's roles. But there is another more secret side to this exchange of food.

Let us again follow the husband as he returns from his traps. Well outside the village, not yet seen by the men on the plaza, he detaches a large and oily fish with few bones—the pick of his catch. He calls to one of the boys playing by the path and whispers: "Take this to Kiyalu, but make sure her husband is not in the house." Kiyalu's fish is *yamala*, a gift exchanged by lovers. Women receive other presents from their boyfriends, such as wooden spindles, baskets, and more recently, soap or beads. But fish, as a token of men's productive efforts and as a symbol of male sexuality is, above all other gifts, quintessentially yamala. A sexually active woman is therefore a recognized economic asset in her family, bringing in a modest but regular supply of fish from grateful lovers.[2]

2. Even after the fish is caught, cooked, and consumed, its sexual influence is not entirely over. Along with flesh, fins, and scales, the eater also ingests the male fish's milt. Living in the body, it is believed to eventually surface on the skin in the fluid that accumulates in pimples and small sores.

Fig. 9. The fish trap. During the rainy season, the villagers dam the slow-moving streams near the village and set large woven traps. A fisherman with several trap sites can expect to bring home a good catch at a time when arrows and hook and line are less successful. In Mehinaku dream symbolism, a trap represents the body of a woman. A dream of a large *mutu* trap with many fish swimming inside it portends marriage to a fecund women. A dream of a narrow *atapinya* trap like the one shown here, is less fortunate. Just as the atapinya usually kills the fish that enter it, the dreamer is likely to have a stillborn child.

Janet Siskind, who has worked with the Sharauana Indians of Peru, believes that the exchange of animal protein for sex has a very wide distribution among hunting peoples and that it tends to act as an incentive for increased productivity (Siskind 1973). Among the Mehinaku, it would be difficult to measure the impact of sex on the size of the catch, but the cultural and symbolic effects are clear. Fish is the currency that rewards sexuality and thereby takes on more than ordinary significance. Sex and economics so interpenetrate that even a staple food is charged with sexual connotations. We are therefore not surprised to discover that in mythic times it was the fish who invented sex. Appropriately, the male fish is the phallic-shaped needle fish (Hejupi) and the female is the large-mouthed bass (Kirityuma).

THE FISH TEACH MEN HOW TO HAVE SEX

Kaipura went fishing with his friend Tala. Hearing a strange noise, they came upon Kirityuma having sex with Hejupi.

"What's going on here?" asked Tala.

"Shhh," said Kaipura, "they are having sex."

"Sex?" replied his friend. "What's that?"

"Quiet . . . let's get closer."

Oh, the fish were having sex: "*Ateke*! *Ateke*! *Ateke*!" Kiritỵuma thrust vigorously as she called out in pleasure. Hejupi and Kirityuma were nearly like people, wearing necklaces, belts, and designs. Hejupi's penis was big, like the log bench in front of the men's house. But then Hejupi had an orgasm, and the two lovers turned back into fish and jumped into the water.

"It looks as if they had sex," said Kaipura. "Would you do that, too?"

"Not me!" said Tala.

The two friends returned to the village and told everyone what they had seen. Everyone laughed, but the next day, Kaipura and Tala went to solicit sexual relations from their girlfriends. "Come on," said Tala, smacking his lips at his girlfriend Tunti. "I'll teach you what the fish taught me." But Tunti was ashamed.

"No, Tunti, don't be ashamed. We will do it very far off." And so they walked into the woods.

"*Ateke, ateke*, Tunti; how sensual, Tunti!"

"Shhh, quiet, someone might hear."

"But I'm doing it like the fish, just like Hejupi."

"Well . . . O.K."

"Does my penis feel good to you, Tunti?"

"More, more, more, more! *Ateke, ateke*!"

But hidden in the woods, a man saw what they were doing. "Tala," he called, "what are you doing to yourself?"

"We are just imitating the fish," said Tala. "I told you about it yesterday. We are having sex."

"Ah, well, it is good that you are having sex. Go ahead, have some more. I am going back to the village to speak about you on the plaza." And he did, telling everyone in the village. Tala and Tunti were ashamed to return, coming back only after dark. Everyone laughed at them.

We never do learn how the remainder of the tribe learned "the lesson of the fish," but in taking leave of the subject, it is well to note a theme we have discussed earlier and will have occasion to recall further on. To the Mehinaku, the physical and mental development of a human being is controlled by culture and experience rather than by innate characteristics. Not only does individual growth and sexual maturation require a set regimen, but even human sexuality cannot be taken for granted. The myth of the fish tells us that, far from being "naturally" human, sex is learned behavior.

PLANT SEXUALITY: PEQUI

By their habits, appearance, and connotations, fish are the most sexual of the natural species. However, other plants and animals have sexual associations, including wild fruits and domesticated crops. Among the more important of these, both in the Mehinaku diet and in cultural significance, is *pequi* (*Caryocar butyrosum*). Originally planted in manioc gardens around the village, pequi trees continue to bear fruit many years after the gardens have been returned to fallow. As a result, even long-abandoned Xingu villages are surrounded by orchards of pequi trees and are identifiable from the air by the distinctive nature of their leafy cover (Da Silva 1978).

Ripening in the fall of each year, pequi is harvested in enormous quantities until early December, when the last of the season's fruit falls to the ground. In size, appearance, and firmness, pequi resembles a large green baseball. Cutting through the bitter and inedible husk, one comes to a pit surrounded by rich, oily meat, tasting like an amalgam of avocado and sweet potato. Baked in the embers of a dying fire, mashed into a porridge with manioc flour, or fermented for many months in underwater silos, pequi is a major supplement to the villagers' diet, providing a rich source of oil, protein, and vitamin B.

Like all seeds, fruits, and nuts, pequi are categorized as *euti*, "genitals." Unlike other plants, however, its sexual associations are built into myth, ritual, and belief. Let us look at a myth that unmistakably establishes the sexual nature of pequi fruit.

The Origins of Pequi

> Long ago, Iripyulakuma and her younger sister went down to the river to bathe. There, to their horror, they were greeted by Yakajakuma, "Great Alligator Spirit." Enormous in length, extending all the way around the bend in the river, Yakajakuma terrified the women. But before they could run away, his skin zipped open just like a duffle bag, and out stepped a handsome man, beautifully adorned in arm bands, knee ligatures, shell belts, necklaces, paints, and feathers. He called to the women, who returned to him. They had sex together, and the women promised to come back the next day.
>
> The following afternoon, the women returned, beautifully dressed and painted, carrying a pail of manioc porridge and a sheaf of freshly baked manioc bread. Together they called to their lover, "Yakajakuma! Great Alligator Spirit! Come, let us have sex." As the day before, Yakajakuma surfaced from the depths of the river, his skin slid open, and the handsome spirit-lover appeared. But this time, one of the villagers was hidden in the forested riverbank, and saw what occurred.

> Later that evening he told all the men what he had seen, and they agreed to help him. The next day, armed with bows and arrows, the men pretended to go on a fishing expedition. Circling around on a back path, they crept up to the banks of the river and watched as the sisters called their lover, "Great Alligator Spirit! Come let us have sex."
>
> As Yakajakuma rose up from the water, the men shot him with many arrows and then clubbed the spirit to death. The cuckolded husbands beat their wives for their infidelity and rashness at having sex with a spirit and left them with the body of Yakajakuma. Grieving for their spirit-lover, the women buried him a shallow grave, cut their hair short, and removed all but one strand of their belts as tokens of mourning.
>
> The sisters returned to the grave some days later. There they found a pequi tree, which had grown from Yakajakuma's genitals. The tree rapidly reached immense height, with a thick trunk and huge spreading branches. When the fruit was ripe, the sisters found the outside bitter, but the inside, the penis of the Great Alligator Spirit, was sweet and good.

The sexual origins of pequi fruit are a part of a system of thinking in which food, eating, and sexuality are regarded as similar. The myth of the Great Alligator Spirit, however, takes us beyond this mundane equation to suggest that the cycle of food, sexuality, and fertility transcends death. At the end of the story, the protagonists are reunited with their reborn lover through the eating of Yakajakuma's metamorphosed genitalia. Behind Mehinaku ideas about sex and food lies an implicit folk philosophy about the human condition as well as about masculinity and femininity. The villagers' theories of procreation, to which we now turn, provide us with the framework of that philosophy.

Food, Sex, and Procreation

The Mehinaku concept of procreation consists of closely integrated ideas about sexuality, human anatomy, and the division of labor. We break into this system of thought at the level of the production of food and the division of labor between men and women.

MEN'S WORK, WOMEN'S WORK

Just as fish are a primary symbol of male sexuality, so is fishing men's work. Women may occasionally assist by harvesting nearby fish traps or by accompanying their husbands on short trips. They almost never participate in fishing on a day-to-day basis, however, and are forbidden to accompany their husbands on long trips, especially where *ituna*, "fish poison" (*Paullinia pinnata*), is employed. The men offer a variety of reasons for keeping the women at a distance. Women are weak and afraid of big fish. They are not strong enough to paddle a canoe. They are scared that fish lines will hurt their hands. In any case, there is plenty of work for them at home.

But male objections go farther and deeper. Pressed for additional explanations, men say that the presence of women, or even contact with women, reduces the size of the catch. On the eve of major trips, chiefs and sponsors of fishing expeditions urge the men not to have sexual relations, going so far as to list the names of sexually active single women the fishermen should avoid. On fish-poisoning trips, men disperse the poison-laden vine through the water, but turn the shooting of the fish over to young boys who have not yet had sexual relations. The men explain that fish are fastidious. Revolted by women's genitals, they know the smell of a fisherman who has had sex.

Although women's work is not jeopardized by male participation, the men are not tempted to join in the tedious labor. The staple crop is bitter manioc (*Manihot esculenta*), a root containing deadly quantities of prussic acid. To the women falls the unending drudgery of harvesting the tubers, carrying them back to the village, and extracting the toxin. This process is accomplished by scraping the brown husk from the tubers with a shell, grinding the white pulp to a mash on a thorn board set over a large ceramic tub, repeatedly washing and rinsing the mash, and finally shaping the mushy flour into loaves to dry in the sun. The highly volatile cyanide compounds remaining in the flour are driven off when it is baked into bread.

Seen from the perspective of our own culture, it would be hard to imagine such contrasting patterns of work as those followed by Mehinaku men and women. Table 2 provides a quick summary of fishing and manioc processing in the form of an American job description. This list of tasks and their characteristics, though useful, obscures the Mehinaku point of view. Although the villagers would accept our summary of the differences between the two kinds of work, they see a deeper, more profound similarity. This similarity is expressed in Mehinaku dream symbolism. In the villagers' interpretation, a man's dream of digging up manioc tubers portends success in fishing. The tubers are pictures (*patalapiri*, "representations, symbols") of fish, and a man fortunate enough to see many in his dream will have a good catch the next day. But why are tubers like fish? The women point out the resemblances. The abdomen of many fish, like the skin of the tuber, is dark, while the flesh of both is white.

Table 2. The Division of Labor

	Men's Work (fishing)	Women's Work (manioc processing)
Location	Forests and Rivers (wide ranging)	Gardens and residences (restricted)
Schedule	Intermittent flexible hours	Many regular hours, especially during dry season
Variability	Much variation	Monotonous, repetitive
Skill level	Many skills needed, including canoe building and navigating and aptitude with bow and arrow. High level of skills required.	Few skills required for food processing and production. Relatively menial, unskilled work.

In addition, sweet manioc (*Manihot dulcus*) is yellow-orange on the inside, just like the flesh of some fish. The resemblance goes past appearances. Our informant explains: "Men get fish from deep in the water; women get manioc from deep in the ground. Harvesting manioc is a kind of fishing."

The analogy goes further still, finding correlates and associations in language and conduct. The tubers dug from the earth and piled in baskets, for example, are a woman's "catch" (*meipiya*), just like a man's string of fish. Returning with her "catch" of manioc to the village, a woman assembles with friends and relatives in small work teams to process the manioc into a nontoxic flour. After reducing the tuber to a watery mash, it is folded between woven mats so that it can be repeatedly washed with water from a large ceramic tub. Here, the villagers recall the resemblance of manioc to specific fish, labeling the flattened mash by several fish species according to the shape it assumes when the mat is unfolded. Even when molded into loaves to dry or cut into trapezoidal slices, the manioc retains its identity as a fish, being called at this stage a *pyuluma*, "piranha."

MANIOC AND SEXUALITY

Manioc tubers are symbols of fish, and fish, we recall, are equated with male sexuality. The Mehinaku bring these equations full circle, by linking manioc tubers to phalluses. The metaphoric thinking that makes these connections possible requires that we partly retrace our steps in the processing of manioc flour. Dug up from the ground, manioc tubers vary in size and shape, but despite irregular twists and bulbous protrusions, they are unmistakably phallic in appearance. In jokes and obscene remarks, the villagers recognize the resemblance, saying that "manioc tubers are patalapiri of penises." We can thus look at the production of flour not only as a facet of the division of labor, but also as a symbolic act of sexuality. Returning from the gardens, the women scrape the coarse brown skin from the tuber with a freshwater clam shell. We recall from the myth of Kwaumutĩ's creation of women that after a period of experimentation, he made the first vagina from a clam. According to the villagers, the clam is a symbol of the vagina because of its shape, texture, and color. Scraping the skin from the manioc tuber with a clam shell (*amalakapai*) is thereby infused with sexual meaning that does not escape the villagers.

After scraping, the manioc tubers are washed and prepared for grinding. Holding a tuber firmly in both hands, a woman squats on a low bench, knees apart, in front of a large ceramic tub. Across the tub and directly in front of her is a large grater made from a board set with thorns or, quite frequently nowadays, from flattened tin cans whose surface has been roughened with nail punctures. The thorn board (*imya*) is called by the same term as a woman's pubic area. Grasping the tuber firmly in both hands, she thrusts it back and forth across the thorns, grinding it into a soft pulp. The work is hard, and to make it easier, nearly all the women follow a breathing technique that they claim gives them more endurance. Through nearly closed teeth and lips, they breathe loudly and rythmically so that their efforts are audible a considerable distance away. Above all other ordinary activities, grinding manioc replicates the sounds, movements, and standard seated position for sexual relations. I must stress that this judgment is not imposed by me, but is that of the Mehinaku themselves, who openly regard this phase of processing as sexual, describing it as a "picture of intercourse." As one of the men puts the matter: "When a woman grinds manioc, she is having sex with the manioc tubers. The tuber is a symbol for the penis, and the thorn board is a symbol for the vagina. She is scraping the penis against her vagina."

Cultural evidence conveys the same message. We recall the myth of Tepu, the worm who had sexual relations with one of the village women. Installing Tepu under her bench, she was able to have intercourse while grinding manioc without immediately alerting her workmates as to what she was doing. From the Mehinaku perspective, this phase of manioc processing is so similar to sex that the ruse was at least plausible.

Language reinforces our interpretation. The term for grinding manioc is *ulutapai*, a word that provides us with an unexpected insight. The root of the word, *ulu*, means "clam." The medial *ta* indicates causality, and the final *pai* is a durative. Literally translated, the term might be rendered "causing with the clam," or more freely, "working

Fig. 10. Processing manioc. Women spend hours in processing manioc tubers. During the dry season, the men construct drying platforms for the flour loaves, which provide shade for their wives who must work long hours out-of-doors. The labor is arduous, time consuming, and monotonous. And yet in this drudgery, the villagers see a symbol of sexual relations.

Here Pitsaulu grinds manioc tubers that have already been scraped of their brown husk. She works together with her kinswomen, and occasionally her friends from other houses. The work is hard, but the company is good and the women take pride in the quality of the flour and the manioc bread they will make from it.

with the clam." The use of this term is at first glance surprising, since the clam shell is used only in the first stage of manioc processing, when the skin is scraped from the tuber. We can only understand the use of *ulutapai* for the grinding of manioc tubers if we conclude that the term recalls the equation of clam and vagina and the sexual meaning of this act. A free translation of *ulutapai* is thus not only the contextually accurate "grinding manioc tubers," but the strongly connoted "working with the vagina."

The Mehinaku provide us with further evidence in their other idiomatic usage of the term *ulutapai*. We have already seen that from the perspective of the village men, not all women are equally desirable. Women's sexual attractiveness varies from the "flavorless" (*mana*) to the "delicious" (*awarintya*). In the indelicate vernacular of the younger men, those who are most appealing and most sexually proficient are the women who ulutapai their lovers. The intention of this picturesque metaphor is to bring to mind the actions of a woman grinding manioc as an unmistakable symbol of sexual proficiency. Sexuality suggests food processing, and food processing connotes sexuality. The chain of symbols thus comes full circle, forming a closed system of associations and meanings.

PROCREATION: THE ULTIMATE MEHINAKU METAPHOR OF CONNECTEDNESS

Our discussion of the metaphors linking food and sex has primarily examined the carnal nature of sexuality. There is, however, another side to the equation that also requires our attention since sex, to the villagers, is procreation as well as pleasure. The multiple links that connect men and women in the creation of new life are complex. Our discussion will move from the villagers' ideas about food, human anatomy, and kinship on to cosmology and symbolism. We begin with the concrete and the practical: the nature of food and its transformation by the human body.

The connection between food and procreative sex begins with the production of manioc flour. The technical steps and their numerous variations in this laborious procedure (nicely summarized in an article by Gertrude Dole [1978]) ultimately produce a number of staple foods, including manioc flour for making bread and thickening fish stews, manioc-based drinks, such as *nukaiya* (a warm, sweet drink made from glucose-rich tapioca flour), and *itsichui* (manioc bread soaked and mixed with water until it assumes the consistency of a loose porridge). Manioc bread, manioc drinks, and other products made from this staple crop are symbolic of women and their role in the division of labor. It is a woman's job to produce these foods, and her good name and reputation as a wife and mother depend on their quality and quantity.

When consumed by the men, feminine manioc is transformed into something quite different. But to understand the critical role of manioc in procreation and in the symbolism of gender, we must first examine some basic Mehinaku ideas about anatomy and physiology. Our instructors are the villagers themselves, who provided me with a series of ethnoanatomical drawings depicting the inside of the human body and basic physiological processes. Two of the drawings are reproduced in figures 11 and 12 below. Since these X-ray pictures are a critical line of evidence in the Mehinaku concept of procreation, we must hold our discussion of the relationship of food and sex momentarily in abeyance to examine the Mehinaku knowledge of human biology.

WHAT GOES ON UNDER THE SKIN: X-RAY DRAWINGS.

The Mehinaku knowledge of human anatomy is primitive by our standards. Respecting their own dead and lacking any motivation for autopsies, none of the villagers has seen the inside of a human body. What observational knowledge they have was obtained some forty years ago at the traditional village of Suyapuhɨ. Like many historical Mehinaku villages, Suyapuhɨ was named after a memorable historical event, in this case, the killing of a Suya Indian who was caught in the vicinity of the community.

We recall from the myth of the origins of the Suya that their status as human beings is held up to question. The corpse of the Suya therefore presented the village's amateur anatomists with a once-in-a-lifetime opportunity to carve up a body unprotected by the taboos and codes of respect surrounding a Xinguano cadaver. For most, disgust and fear outweighed curiosity, and the job was left to a small group of men led by a visiting Waura Indian. Together they hacked and sliced away, motivated by nothing other than the pure curiosity of wanting to "see what was inside." None of these men is alive today, but their descriptions were handed down, passed along, and combined with information acquired from butchering monkeys. Since the villagers have only this oral tradition to guide them and lack first-hand anatomical knowledge, the inside of the human body is a kind of Rorschach upon which they project their ideas about sexuality and human nature. The X-ray drawings that were made at my request to "draw the inside of a person" are therefore of special value to us, and the reader is urged to refer to them in the course of the following discussion.

According to the villagers, certain kinds of food are transformed within the body into semen, while others are eliminated as feces. A rapid inspection of table 3 shows that foods associated with women are usually transformed into semen while those produced by men are

Table 3. The Transformation of Food

	Food Produced by Women		Food Produced by Men
Transformed into semen	Manioc beverages Tepukaiya Nukaiya Itsichui Manioc bread Fish stew Water	Transformed into feces	Bird meat Monkey meat Grilled fish of all kinds

transformed into feces. Men's production of medicines (*ataiya*) that are fed to pubescent boys for the purpose of producing semen is the only true exception. This practice appears to be part of a larger pattern of masculine efforts to duplicate feminine physiological processes, a topic to be examined in detail in chapter 10. Another apparent exception to this pattern, fish stew (*wakula*), is produced through the cooperative effort of both men and women. Some of the villagers explain, however, that the chunks of fish in the stew are converted into feces, while the stew itself becomes semen.

The Mehinaku do not provide us with a clear idea as to how foods are transformed into semen other than to point out that in the mouth it changes into and mixes with saliva. A man may refer to his semen (*yaki*) as "my former food" (*nulekein wein*) or "my former saliva" (*neihenyu wein*). Our anatomists discern two possible paths for the food-saliva. According to some of the villagers, it moves through the stomach and then is shunted past the bladder to an organ called the *yaki nain* (literally, "semen holder"). In all probability, this receptacle is accurately identified by the villagers as the prostate gland, since it is said to be the source of semen and is occasionally enlarged and uncomfortable. According to a second and somewhat more widely received theory, the food-saliva is swallowed into a special tube at the back of the throat, the so-called semen's path (*yaki apui*). Winding back to the spine, this channel descends along the backbone until it eventually pours its contents into the "semen holder" (see figure 11). In support of this spinal theory, some villagers claim that in the course of intense orgasm, they actually feel semen issuing from the region of the small of the back.

As we move from theories describing the origin of semen to ideas about sexual excitement and the completion of the procreative act, we find that the villagers' explanatory models become less mechanical and more metaphorical. Sexual excitement takes place because

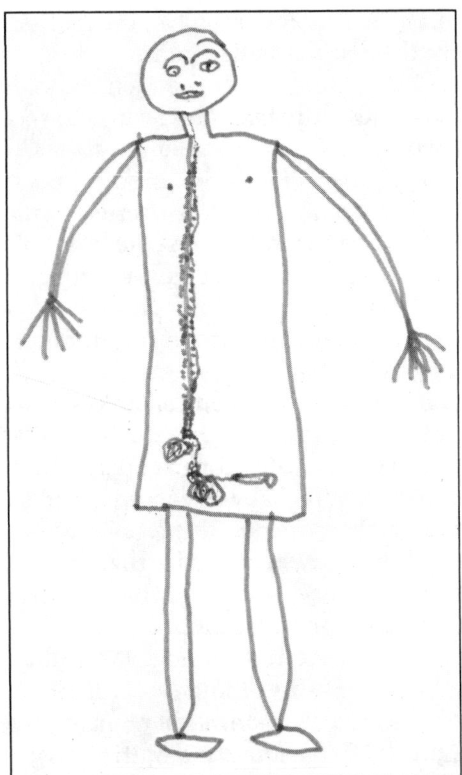

Fig. 11. X-ray drawing of a man. A tube leads from the throat, through the spine (shown as dotted lines) down to an organ that is probably the prostate gland. This so-called semen holder completes the transformation of feminine foods such as manioc porridge into semen. Drawing by Shumoin.

the penis is attracted (*atwata,* literally, "brought") by the vagina. More directly, erection (*inyantɨ*) occurs, according to some of the villagers, because the testicles (*kunyunte*) "make the penis strong" just as the muscle "makes" the arm strong. Pressed further on the role of the testicles in procreation, one informant offered the analogy of a flashlight, suggesting that the testicles are the batteries powering the libido. Hence a man with no testicles could not have an erection, and a person with an undescended testicle (a problem the villagers are aware of) is "revolting" to women. In general, however, the testicles are a mysterious organ in Mehinaku ethnophysiology, and few can tell what is inside or why it is there.

Intense excitement and the flash of sexual pleasure at the moment of orgasm is caused by semen. "Semen," according to the villagers, "makes the vagina delicious" (*yaki awarintyatapuh itsi*). With ejaculation of semen, the metaphor of food and sexuality is brought to a logical conclusion: the penis is said to vomit (*echeke*) the semen into the vagina, also called in this context the "semen holder." Following orgasm, the penis is said to die (*akama*), returning to a flaccid state.

The return of women's food in sexual relations, reprocessed as semen, initiates the creation of new life. In so-called worthless intercourse (*aintyawaka malu*), however, the uterus (*yamakunain*, "baby holder") remains shut, so that the semen comes out of the vagina. To open the uterus, women eat roots that have the rough shape of men's or women's genitals and are therefore symbols of boys and girls. Taking the appropriate medicine opens the uterus and causes the conception of a boy or a girl.

In "true" sexual relations, conception takes place without intervention. The uterus "snatches" or "steals" the semen and the creation of the baby begins. Two theories explain the development of the embryo. The first sees the baby as accumulated semen resulting from numerous acts of intercourse. The fetus shapes itself, the head first, then the rest of the body in the order that the child appears in a normal birth. A second theory, which may have a Carib origin since it parallels a set of beliefs current among the Kuikuru Indians (see Carneiro 1979), is also current in the village. According to champions of the second theory, a tiny Indian woman (variously called Yumeweketu or Atsikuma, "Grandmother Spirit") lives just outside the womb (see figure 12). Grandmother Spirit "makes" the baby by molding and shaping the semen. An ally of the mother, Grandmother Spirit lectures the developing fetus: "Do not hurt your mother; do not make her pregnancy painful." In a dream, Grandmother Spirit shows the mother objects, such as garments that are symbolic of male or female, and thereby communicates the sex of the child.

Both theories assert that one sexual act is insufficient to conceive a child. Rather, the infant is formed through repeated acts of intercourse that accumulate enough semen to form the baby. Since all but three of the village women are involved in extramarital affairs, the semen of the mother's husband may form only a portion of an infant. With comic intent, the men refer to joint paternity as a *wanaki*, an "all-male collective labor project," placing it on the level of a fishing expedition or the clearing of a field. Joint paternity is further recognized at birth when the putative fathers of the baby honor attenuated versions of the couvade and accept some of the obligations of in-laws when the child grows up and gets married. For the most part, however, the relationships generated by extramarital affairs are hidden from cuckolded spouses so that an underground kinship system flourishes alongside the public network of relatedness (Gregor 1977,292–97). The system of multiple paternity has additional

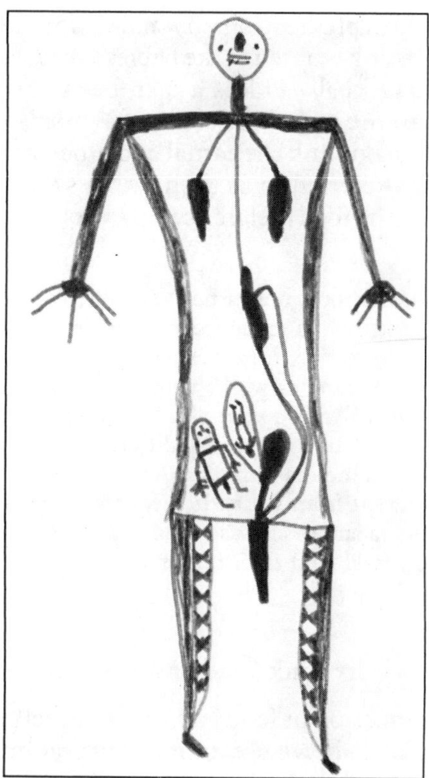

Fig. 12. X-ray drawing: A theory of gestation. Grandmother Spirit molds and shapes the baby in the womb. The substance of the child is semen, supplied by repeated acts of sexual intercourse. When the mother drinks manioc porridge it is shunted through two special tubes that carry it to the breasts, where it is converted into milk. Mother's milk and semen thus have common origins in the foods that women produce. Some water and all foods produced by men are routed through the stomach, which separates liquid from solid and eliminates them through the tubes shown in Kuyaparei's sketch.

limits. Just as too little sexual activity is insufficient for conception, too much is also undesirable. A promiscuous woman risks having a child that is "too large" or twins, which, like all anamalous births, are immediately buried alive. At the least, promiscuity scrapes the hair off the head of the infant, leaving it bald as it comes into the world.

Both of the Mehinaku theories of conception are androcentric: the baby is almost entirely a male product. Only the belief in Grandmother Spirit (far from universally accepted) leaves any role for the mother in the creation of offspring, aside from providing the shelter of her body. No matter how persuasively the case may be put for a fuller feminine role in procreation, my male informants always had a ready reply: "You think women make babies? Well, then, think about this: no woman has a baby unless a man has sex with her."

Birth brings us to the end of the chain of symbols and associations by which the Mehinaku link the carnal and procreative aspects of sex to food and eating. Referred to as their father's "former food," newborn infants reflect the food preferences of every human race. Kikyala explains:

> We are our former food, our father's semen. You whites are different. Your semen is made from coffee, milk, soup, and hot chocolate; from rice, from beans, and from the flesh of animals, from Guarana as well.[3] Your semen, like these foods, is therefore sweet. And so your children are big, because your food is sweet. But our food is very different. Our food is tasteless, and so our semen is different. And so our children are small and different from yours. It is for this reason that the children of the Japanese and the wild Indians are different from us. Their food, and their father's semen, is different from ours.

Food for Thought: Why Link Food and Sex?

The symbolic connection of food and sex may well be a near universal. In American English, we use a variety of oral images for sex that run the gamut from the relatively tame "peach" for an attractive woman to the biblical apple as a symbol of temptation to the tabooed term "eating" for oral sex. Among tribal peoples, the symbolism may be far more evolved. In at least one instance, that of the Hua of New Guinea, food and orality are not ony a metaphor for sex, but swallow up virtually all other areas of thought. Thus the Hua phrase for "everything" translates literally as "that which can be eaten and that which cannot" (Meigs 1984,x).

The psychological basis of the equation of food and sex is that oral sensation is the antecedant of sexual feeling. The infant's quasi-erotic experience of nursing is transformed in adulthood into mature genital sexuality: "The various channels along which the libido passes are related to each other from the very first, like intercommunicating pipes" (Freud 1957,151). We may therefore speculate that a relatively prolonged and indulgent period of nursing (which is the case among the Mehinaku; see chapter 9) leaves the individual in touch with the oral basis of sex. It is then a relatively simple step to construct a system of metaphors that equate the oral cavity with

3. Guarana is a popular Brazilian soft drink much appreciated by the few Mehinaku who have tried it.

sexual anatomy and the act of sex with the act of eating (c.f. Jaffe 1968,525–26).

But the Mehinaku beliefs about food, eating, and sex go well beyond expressing primitive sexual psychology. Taking leave of the villagers' concrete ideas about human biology, we see a philosophy that intertwines natural processes and social relationships. Just as men and women are dependent upon one another for the production of food, so they also cooperate in the exchange of sexual services and the production of new life. Although this idea may be as universal as the division of labor within society, it is given special emphasis among the Mehinaku by a system of beliefs that so nearly equates eating and sexuality. The transformation of female-produced food to semen, and the return of this food in the act of procreation, fuses the multiple exchanges that unite male and female in one closed system. Spiraling away from this metaphor of interdependence, we find specific ideas about sexuality and eating appearing at virtually every level of Mehinaku culture. Religion, mythology, dream symbolism, taboo, kinship, folk science, economics, and tribal identity are incorporated in a complex body of beliefs whose heart is the relationship between male and female.

SIX

Men's House

I don't want to see the sacred flutes. The men would rape me. I would die.

—Itsanakwalu, a young woman in her early twenties.

Without an understanding of the seamy side of sexuality there is no understanding of politics.

—Norman O. Brown, *Love's Body*

In ancient times, the Sun laid down the ground plan of every Mehinaku community, and to this day the villagers are faithful to the original design. They build their houses in a great circle around the plaza or "frequented place" (*wenekutaku*). Two great roads owned by the village chiefs divide the plaza, one leading from the main port, and the other, the "Road of the Sun," leading from the Culiseu River in the east to the bathing area along the Tuatuari River in the west. The Sun decreed that the Mehinaku build the men's house, "the place of the spirits," so that it would bisect the port road and face due east.

Today the men's house is the social and religious center of the Mehinaku community. Within its walls, the men socialize, joke, and work on crafts. From its rafters hang the masks, costumes, and religious paraphernalia of the year's ritual calendar. But beyond these social and ceremonial functions, the men's house is the most visible symbol of the unity of the men and their opposition to the women. Any woman who enters the men's house, or who so much as glances at the sacred flutes stored inside, will be gang raped by all the Mehinaku men other than her closest kin. Even after many years of research and reflection on Mehinaku culture, I am brought up short by this

Draconian sanction. How can it exist within the network of kin obligation and together with the evident affection of Mehinaku men for their wives, parents, and children? The puzzle has a solution when it is considered within the larger context of Mehinaku sexuality. Our starting point is the ethos of masculine solidarity.

A Man's Place

A man's place, when he is not out hunting or fishing, is in the men's house or on the log bench just outside it. A villager who spends too much time in the family dwellings or work areas surrounding them is antisocial and unmanly. He is belittled as a "trashyard man," as a "star" because he is said to come out only at night, or as a "seclusion boy." The barb that cuts deepest, however, is "woman." A man who does not socialize with his fellows in the men's house loses part of his claim to masculinity.

The atmosphere of the men's house is relaxed and friendly. In the daily relationships outside of its clubby confines, men are separated by the codes of respect and deference that are owed to in-laws and men of older generations. But in the secure warmth of the men's retreat, all of that is put aside. "In the men's house," say the villagers, "there is no shame." Correspondingly, there is little respect, since the prevailing ethos demands a smiling, open countenance and a willingness to participate in ribald banter. A man must joke a little (*metalawatain*) and good-naturedly accept the teasing dished out by his comrades.

The men greet Kama, a young man who has just entered the men's house:

> "Here you are, Kama. But where have you been? Out 'alligatoring' the girls?"
>
> "No. Just planting manioc in my garden."
>
> "Planting? Just planting?[1] Come now, you 'sex fiend,' tell us all about it."
>
> "No, no, just planting manioc."
>
> "Planting your penis, you were!"

Everyone is following the conversation, and after the last line, all give a tremendous whoop, audible to the women across the plaza. After the laughter has died down, the men turn to other light topics and resume their work on baskets, arrows, and other crafts. The ethos of the men's house forbids discussions of serious topics such as village witchcraft and quarrels, which cast a pall over the jokes and offend the occasion. The man who walks into the men's house, his "stom-

1. The term "planting" (*panalapai*) is also used for having sexual relations.

ach hot with anger," soon outstays his welcome. No one confronts him (a confrontation is ruder than the act that provokes it); they leave instead. The angry man finds himself in an empty men's house, which is a dismal place, and he too leaves. Gradually the others reassemble, and the high jinks begin anew.

CLOSENESS: TOUCHING AND WRESTLING

The Mehinaku are a "touching" culture, unafraid of the physical contact between men so suspect in our own society. It is common to see friends casually strolling about the plaza in the evening arm-in-arm or holding hands. In the men's house, the pattern is even more

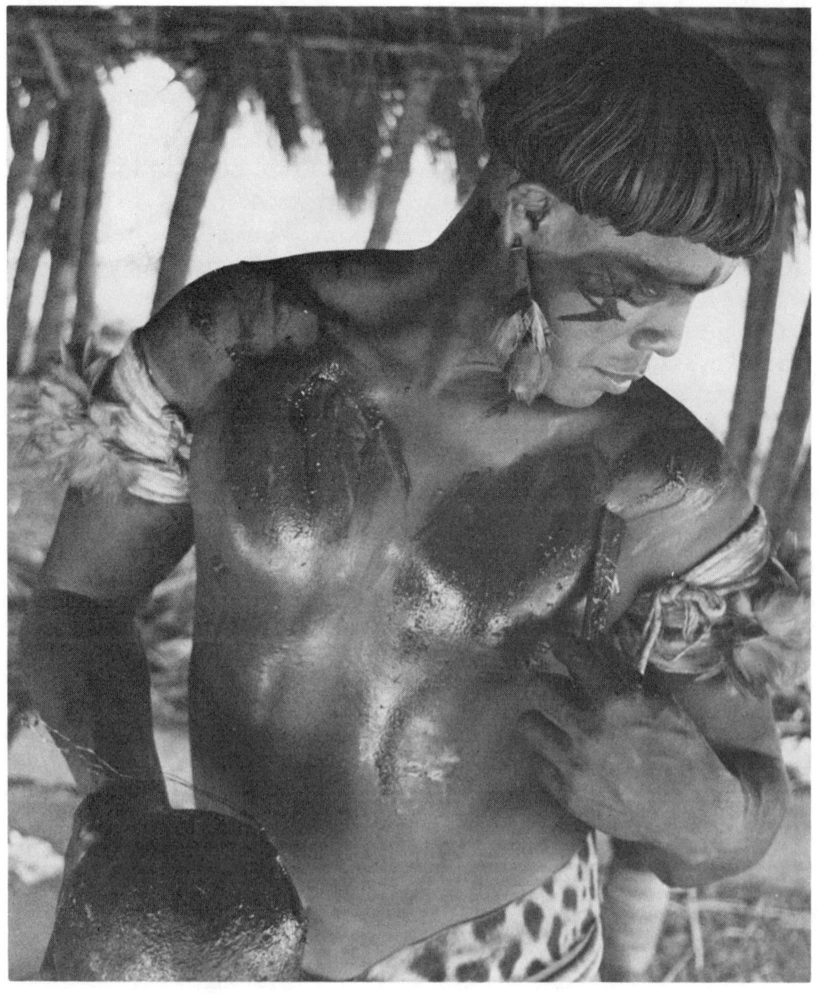

evident amid the prevailing amiability and genial rowdiness. The villagers throw their arms about each other's shoulders, tousle one another's hair, and playfully grab at each other's genitals. More deliberately, the men spend many hours painting their comrades' bodies, applying oils and pigments to backs, chests, legs, and thighs. The villagers do not speak of it, but there is a sensual component to this physical intimacy that enhances participation.

The most physically close and visually dramatic activity of the men's house is wrestling (*kapin*). Every Mehinaku wants to be a champion, able to measure up to the best during matches with neighboring tribes: "When we go to the Kuikuru or the Waura, we

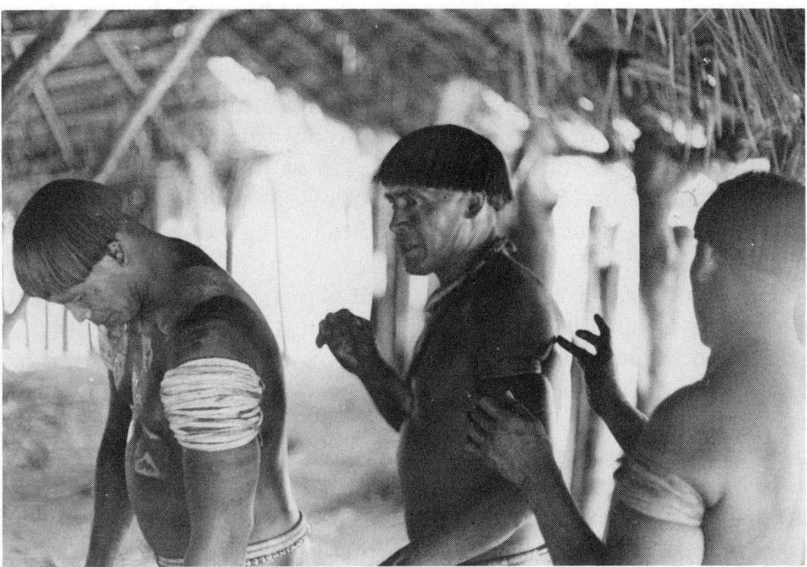

Figs. 13 and 14. Adornment in the men's house. The men's house is simultaneously a social club, a temple, and a rehersal stage for rituals. Normally little light filters in, but in 1971 a thunderstorm blew over a portion of the structure. The sacred flutes were wrapped up in a blanket and stored in the sponsor's house, while the men carried on as before in the well-lit lean-to that remained. Here we see four of the villagers adorning themselves for an afternoon ritual. In figure 13, Shumoin is decorating himself alone, but the men usually cluster together in groups of twos and threes to apply the intricate body patterns and hair designs. Notice the shell belts, which are traded from neighboring Carib-speaking tribes. The arm bands worn by all the men both set off and, it is believed, increase the size of a man's biceps. Less traditional decorative elements include the belt of metal bells worn by the first man in figure 14 and the airplane on Shumoin's cheek, now a part of the villagers' repertory of facial designs.

trade and we wrestle. It has always been that way since the Sun taught us in ancient times." But even in the doldrums of the rainy season when visits to other tribes are few and far between, the tempo of the local matches hardly slackens. Let the rain stop and the clouds part, however briefly, and the wrestlers are back to their holds and throws. A new storm is on the horizon, the roof steams with dampness, but a man senses his wife's admiration even as she complains about the leaks. Above all other skills, wrestling ability is the measure of a man.

A powerful wrestler, say the villagers, is frightening (*kowkapapai*). Likened to the anaconda in the quickness of his holds and the way he "ties up" his opponents, he commands fear and respect. To the women, he is "beautiful" (*awitsiri*), in demand as a paramour and husband. Triumphant in politics as well as in love, the champion wrestler embodies the highest qualities of manliness. Not so fortunate the vanquished! A chronic loser, no matter what his virtues, is regarded as a fool. As he wrestles, the men shout mock advice from the bench in front of the men's house, urging him to keep his face out of the dirt and his back off the ground. The women are less audible as they watch the matches from their doorways, but they too have their sarcastic jokes. None of them is proud of having a loser as a husband or a lover.

The abuse heaped on the weak man is justified by the belief that each person controls his own biological destiny. A man becomes a champion because he has disciplined himself. Unlike the loser, he honored the rules of adolescent seclusion. While the weak man went sneaking out from behind the isolation barriers, he stayed indoors, focusing all his thoughts on imagined matches. Periodically, his father came to scarify his body and rub in medicines to build his biceps and thighs. The scraping was painful, but the pain "killed" weakness, and the medicines from the exceptionally hardy cotton plant ensured lasting strength. As for the loser, one hardly knew he was in seclusion at all. He wandered about in the woods, became a "master of little boys games," (*mapampam wekehe*), and daydreamed about growth-stunting sexual relations. Defeat and victory are more than tickets in a lottery. They are the measure of a man's worth.

It is three o'clock in the afternoon, or "wrestling time." For the past hour, the men have been gathering in front of the men's house, tying protective wrappings around their knees and shins and rubbing pequi oil into each other's bodies to make the skin supple and the bones resilient. One of the villagers finally gets up from the bench and beckons to a comrade. Together they move about in a tight circle, gradually lowering themselves to their knees. "*Hu-hu-hu-hu,*" they call out in imitation of the jaguar's grunt as their bodies come closer

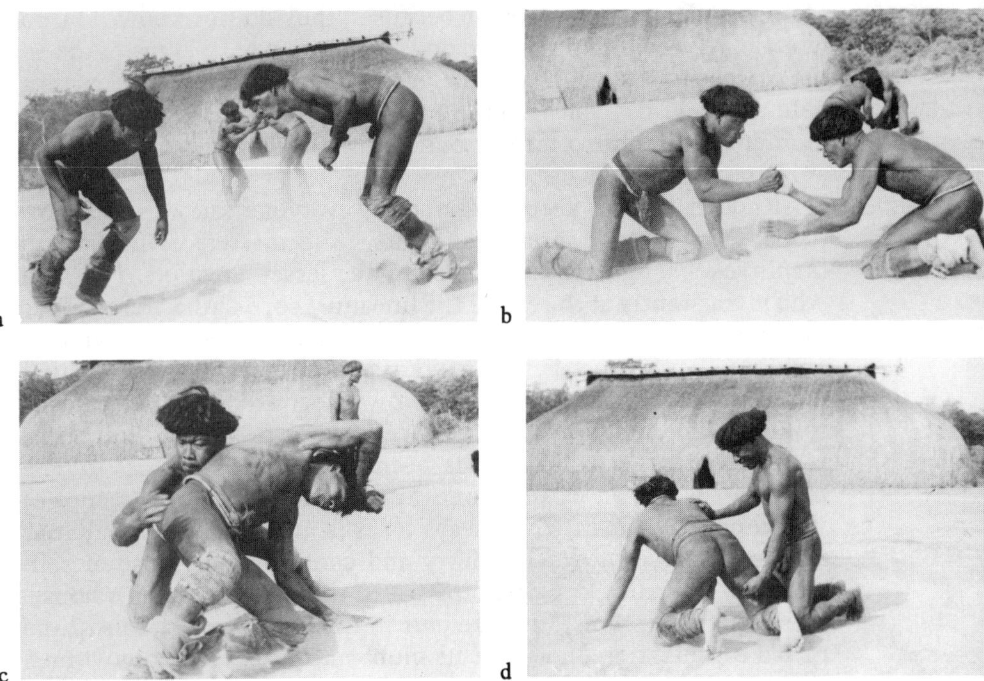

Fig. 15. Wrestling. Wrestling, above all other activities, dramatizes key masculine values. A bout begins when a villager beckons to a partner, and both move about in a tight circle (a). They first make contact on their knees, their right hands coming together with a loud slap (b). The match moves vigorously forward as the opponents strive for advantage (c). In an intertribal bout, the victor may throw his opponent heavily to the ground. Here in the village the match stops as soon as one of the wrestlers grasps his opponent's arm and leg (d).

together. They clasp hands and the match begins. From the bench, the men call out advice and urge friends and kinsmen to use the best holds: forcing the opponent's head down, dragging him down from a standing position, seizing his hand, taking his arm and forcing his body around, and lifting him off the ground. Finally, the moment comes to "throw" (*awaintya*) the opponent. But this match, like all home bouts, is a friendly one, a training exercise for the really strenuous contests fought by tribal champions. Being thrown on the ground risks injury. "The earth," the Mehinaku say, "eats skin and breaks bones." Only the "angry man" throws a fellow villager, and he does so at the cost of hard stares and indignant words of older men who sit as informal referees on the men's bench. Moreover, wrestling in and of itself eliminates anger. A man with "anger in his stomach" wrestles and finds himself at peace. The wild Indians beyond the

Mehinaku borders are violent because "they do not know how to wrestle. All they know how to do is kill people with clubs." And so the match stops short of a throw. A wrestler wins when he secures a hold that would enable him to throw his opponent if he wished. The moment he lifts him off the ground or catches him by the thigh and arm, the match is over.

Although no one keeps close score, everyone knows the champions. At the great intertribal bouts, "the masters of wrestling" (*kapinyekehe*) fight first, followed by the lesser wrestlers. The man who is constantly at the end of the line must cope with a tremendous loss of self-esteem, which is reflected in the terminology of victory and loss. The winner is said to *ukutene* his opponent, a word that literally means "shoot with an arrow" but more generally means to kill or maim seriously. A passive form of this verb, *ukutakɨna*, is applied to the loser; he has been "killed" by the victor. The metaphor is not an extreme one. Such is the social significance of wrestling that a man who always loses is just a little bit dead. But most men have moderate ability and confirm their sense of self-worth by wrestling and participating in the life of the men's house. Even the poorer wrestlers take part in the banter and rituals of the men's organization and share its clubby atmosphere. Only women are excluded, and it is the barriers that keep them at a distance that give the men's house its special role in defining the relationship of the sexes.

The Culture of Exclusion and Intimidation

SECRECY AND SACRED FLUTES

If the Mehinaku women planted a spy in the men's house, they would be disappointed by his reports. The men's secrets are neither "dark," hiding damaging information, nor "strategic," concealing valuable facts. They include little more than the nature and appearance of the sacred flutes and other cult objects and the identity of the participants in the men's rituals. Thus the men's house is similar to many other secret men's associations. Noel Gist (1940) has noted that candidates for admission to American secret fraternal orders are disappointed to discover that the only real secrets are the details of the initiation rituals.[2] The function of "contentless" secrets is to

2. This same pattern holds for most tribal men's cults as well. Charles Valentine's description of the Lukalai of New Britain in the Pacific could apply to many men's secret societies throughout Melanesia and South America: "All the supplementary mystification which surrounds the masks and the performances not only contributes to masculine pride, but heightens the atmosphere of secrecy and the sense of the uncanny as well. . . . Yet virtually the only real secrets beneath all this elaborate

differentiate those who are in the know from those who are excluded. So long as those who are joined by either knowledge or ignorance regard the concealed information as important, there will always be a sense of distance and tension. As Georg Simmel has put it: "Whether there is secrecy between two individuals or groups . . . is a question that characterizes every relation between them" (1950,330).

Among the Mehinaku, the most hidden secret of all is the appearance of *kauka*, the flute representation of the spirit of the same name.[3] Kauka, chief of the spirits, can make people ill by taking away their souls. Appeasing Kauka, and thereby ensuring the well-being of the community, requires that the flutes be played regularly. To organize a concert, the "songmaster" (*apaiyekehe*) whispers his intentions to his accompanists, "those who play on the side." Pretending to leave home on a casual errand, the musicians assemble in the men's house and prepare their flutes. Everyone speaks in whispers. The spirit is in the men's house, and the occasion is solemn. At last the songs begin. All of them are titled and played in a definite order. Iyepe, one of the most proficient of the songmasters, plays "Worthless Fishtrap," "Angry Woman Spirit," "Lizard," and "Sadness." The flutes have a resonant bassoonlike quality, and many of the songs are hauntingly beautiful.

As the songs proceed, one of the men calls out a warning, and the women scurry into the houses, closing the doors behind them: Kauka is about to emerge from the men's house. When the women are safely away, the trio of musicians marches onto the plaza, stamping out the beat of their song with pequi-seed rattles tied to their ankles. Circling the plaza, they come to the house of the sponsor of the flutes. His wife, who is responsible for preparing food for the spirit, calls out through the thatch wall of the house: "Do not come here. We have no food. My husband did not go fishing today. We have nothing for you here." Disappointed, the spirit returns to the men's house. After the four-hour song series is completed, however, the sponsor of the flutes "ashamed for all the hard work done by the musicians," brings large tubs of manioc porridge to the men's house to "pay" the musicians and feed the spirit (fig. 16). The men drink deeply and pass the drink to the others who are present. Fish are also distributed and eaten (figs. 17–18). Kauka has been fed and is pleased.

---

cultural camouflage are the details of the internal structures of the masks and the procedures surrounding their construction. (1961, 481)"

3. The Mehinaku have permitted me to take many photographs of the sacred flutes, but only on the promise that they would never be shown to village women. Inevitably, this book will find its way back to the Mehinaku community, and hence no illustration of Kauka's flutes appear on its pages (though see sketch, Fig. 19). The reader may thereby savor some of the mystery of Mehinaku religion.

Fig. 16. The cauldron of cold manioc porridge was made from tubers harvested from Kauka's garden, a plot of land cleared and planted collectively by the men of the tribe. The kinswomen of the flute sponsor have spent many hours making the porridge, which will be distributed in small buckets to the men.

GANG RAPE

The Mehinaku are hard pressed to explain why the women cannot enter the men's house or see the sacred flutes. Some the of the older men claim that the spirit forbids it: "The women can't come in here! The spirit Kauka would kill us if a woman came in here. A woman's eyes are revolting to the spirits." Still other villagers say that the women are in danger: "If a woman were to see Kauka, she would die in a month." But for the most part, the men throw up their hands and appeal to tradition: "It has always been that way." The women, on the other hand, have a far more down-to-earth reason for avoiding the men's house. As Kialu explained to me, "No, we never the enter the mens' house or see the sacred flutes. We pass our lives without ever having seen the inside of the men's house. If we were to enter the men's house, the men would rape us!"

Only a few of the oldest Mehinaku men have actually seen a woman raped for seeing Kauka's flutes. The last occurence was around 1940. It began like other episodes of gang rape. Returning to the village, a woman inadvertently saw the flutes while the musicians were playing on the plaza. A group of men other than her closest kin got together and decided that she had to be raped. In the evening, one of her lovers lured her into the forest for an assignation. When they arrived, the men rose out of ambush, and the flutes began to play: she had to be raped by Kauka. "She screamed and cried," recounts Teme, "but they held her firmly. The men raped her. I decided not to do it because her legs were fouled with semen." Later, the woman was taken back to the village where she was bathed by a

Fig. 17. Smoked fish are divided among the men, who will eat some in the men's house and take some home with porridge to their wives and daughters.

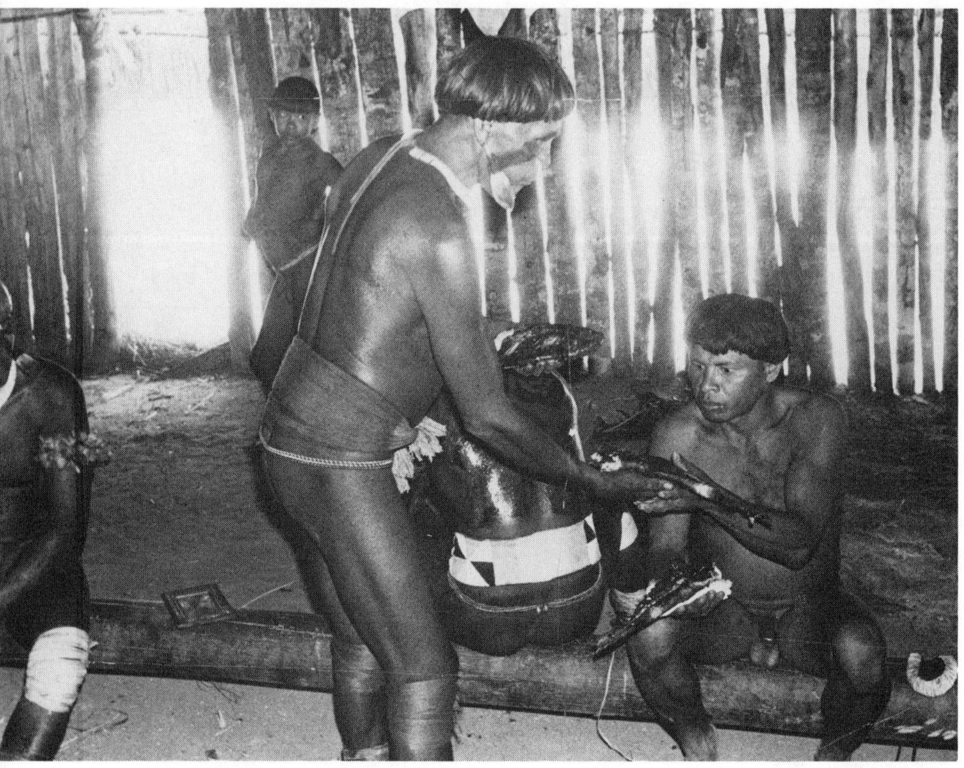

Fig. 18. Food for Kauka. The fish and porridge are said to be the spirit's food even though they will be consumed by the Mehinaku. Kauka is the chief of the spirits and the justification of the men's cult; yet he, like all spirits, is only content when he is fed both men's and women's food.

kinswoman. She subsequently delivered an "oversized" baby that was put to death because "it had too many fathers."

As in our culture, the women express considerable fear about the possibility of rape: "It is an ugly thing. I am afraid of the men. I do not want to see the flutes." The "ugliness" of rape for the Mehinaku women cannot be overstated. To understand rape from the woman's perspective, we must realize that it goes beyond the obvious violence and coercion inherent in the act to include symbolic defilement of the woman's personal and social integrity. This begins with the public exposure of the victim's genitals. Even though Mehinaku women are normally unclothed, they take care to comport themselves in a way that conceals the inner labia and the vagina. Insofar as is possible, this modesty also occurs within sexual relationships. During gang rape, however, the woman's legs are deliberately spread apart and she is humiliatingly exposed to the view of all the participants. Rape is also brutal from a woman's point of view because she is dirtied by the men's semen. Ejaculate, for both men and women, is an unattractive and even "disgusting" fluid that can cause pain and injury. All of my accounts of gang rape mention the abundance and "foulness" of the men's semen with which the woman is said to be covered in the course of the act. Finally, a rape is "ugly" because the victim must continue to live with the men who have raped her. Many of them will be classificatory kin who have taken part in the incestuous act. In the distorted logic of rape, however, the shame is the woman's, and somehow she must live with it.

All Mehinaku women live with the threat of rape. The fear follows them into their dream life where thay are haunted by nightmares of male violence. In twelve of a sample of 109 dreams (see Gregor 1981b), the women were the victims of men's physical aggression. In half of these dreams, the assault was sexual in nature. These frightening dreams were among the most anxiety-charged in the entire sample. The threat of gang rape and masculine violence is real, and the women's fears permeate their unconscious life.

Despite the women's anxiety, they accept the system and even enforce it. They are the main conduits for malicious speculation that some of their sisters have spied on the sacred flutes. It is beneath male dignity to take such "woman-mouthed" gossip seriously, but the men know they can count on their wives and daughters' support when it is time to rape someone else's wife or daughter. Itsanakwalu put the matter like this:

> It has always been like that since our grandfathers' day. I don't want to see the sacred flutes. The men would rape me. I would die. Do you know what happened to the Waura woman who saw it? All the men raped her. She died later. Kauka had sex with her. I don't like it. But I would not get angry with the men if they did it to another woman.

For the men, gang rape is linked to dominance and control, an orientation that is built into the language of forced sex. Thus the word for rape, *antapai,* is used in other contexts to mean "dragging off." As the term suggests, a woman who is raped is overcome by a physically stronger individual. No woman can *antapai* a man. The semantic link of "dragging off" to rape also suggests the aggressive pattern by which a predatory man may approach a woman alone on a path. Taking her firmly by the wrist, he leads her a short way into the forest to have sex. At times, the line between consensual and forced sex is a thin one, and the woman is "dragged" (raped) rather than "led." A second term for rape (*aintyawakakinapai*) is used for gang sex and is derived from the term for sexual relations (*aintyawakapai*). The medial *kina* refers to others who are engaged in the action and in this context denotes the raping of one woman by several or more men.[4]

In mythology, rape is a method of asserting men's control over women. In ancient times, the villagers believe, the women dominated the men. The men established patriarchal rule by stripping the women of their masculine garments, pushing them into the houses, and raping them:

> Later that night when it was dark, the men came to the women and had sex with them. The men forced their wives to have sex, they forced them, they forced them. Then the women could not go into the men's house. Oh, no.

The political rather than the sexual or aggressive dimensions of rape emerges in interviews with the men. In discussions of what would happen if a woman were to see the sacred flutes, they almost invariably place distance between themselves and the act by ascribing the rape to the spirit:

> Look, the men's house now has two sets of Kauka's flutes. The women will not go inside. They are afraid of Kauka. If a woman does go in, someone will say, 'Ah, that one went in and saw Kauka!' Then at night she will be taken, and Kauka will rape her.

It is rare to hear the men use the first-person pronoun or verb form in describing a rape, however hypothetical. Moreover, the men are anxious to emphasize that the matter is dictated by custom rather than personal anger or desire. "Then when all the raping is done, the woman can go to the stream and bathe. It is finished, over. It is always done that way." And also in typical fashion, an informant points out that if it were done any differently, the men would suffer a worse fate than the woman. "If Kauka did not rape the woman, then all the men would die. It must happen."

In contradiction to this last belief, however, the men are reluctant to report a woman who sees the flutes. They not only hold themselves aloof from the talebearers and malicious gossips, but admit (with only one exception) that they would not tell on their closest female kin. Several men spontaneously remarked that they would not report any woman who saw the flutes unless other men also saw her. Rape is not primarily an expression of personal sexual or aggressive needs, but a group response to an open challenge to the patriarchal system.

4. I gratefully acknowledge the assistance of Emilienne Ireland in analyzing the etymology of the term for rape and in outlining the Mehinaku women's perspective on forced sex.

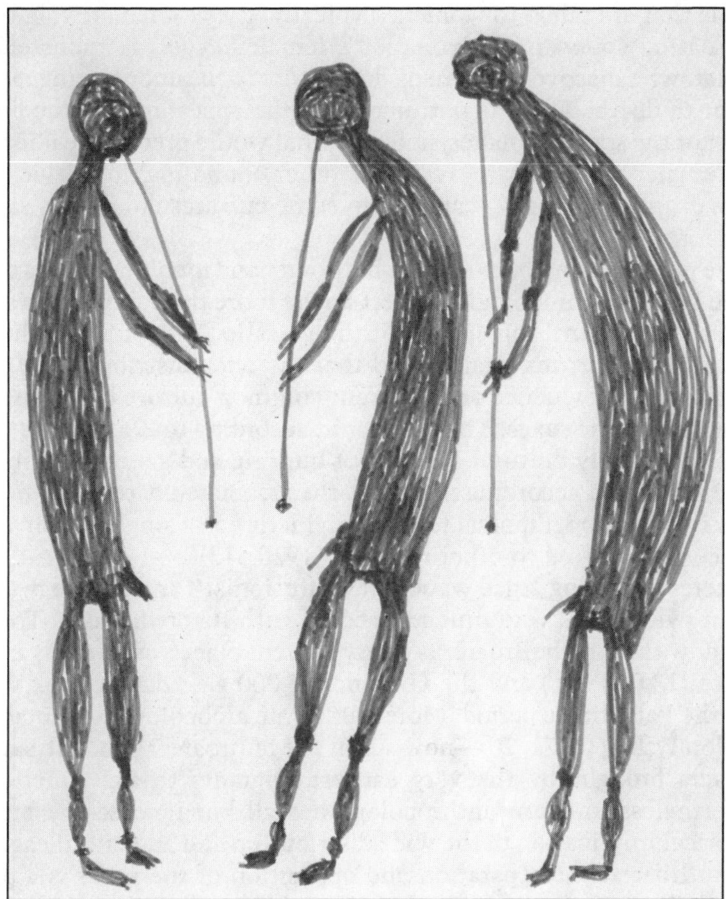

Fig. 19. Three flute players. In Imi's pen-and-ink sketch, three musicians play the sacred flutes. The aggressive phallic symbolism of the flutes is suggested by the artist's attention to the genitalia, which other than the men's knee ligatures, are the only markers of their masculinity.

THE BULLROARER

Among the most fascinating of the paraphernalia of exclusion in the Mehinaku men's house is the bullroarer. A bullroarer is a slat of wood swung on a cord. As the device moves through the air, it begins to spin on its own axis. The two motions of spinning and swinging produce vibrations at different pitches that are heard as a throbbing roar similar to a motorcycle engine. In the Western world, the bullroarer is known only as a child's toy sometimes called a "whizzer." Among a number of scattered but widely distributed traditional societies on every continent, however, the bullroarer is used in rituals that are taboo to women. Typically, the women are told that the roaring sound is the voice of a female-devouring monster. A woman who discovers the men's imposture is commonly gang raped or put to death. There is nothing about the appearance of the bullroarer or the sound it makes, however, that would predispose it for its role in men's secret rituals. Many other sound-making devices—bells, drums, trumpets—can (and in some cultures do) fill the same function.

The puzzling link between the bullroarer and men's cults was first noted by the anthropologist Robert Lowie more than sixty years ago. He, as well as anthropologists of the so-called diffusionist school, such as Otto Zerries, maintained that the wide distribution of the bullroarer was evidence of an ancient common culture based on the separation of the sexes. The bullroarer, according to Zerries, has "its roots in an early cultural stratum of hunting and gathering tribes" (1942,304). And according to Lowie, the associated pattern of men's cults is "an ethnographical feature originating in a single center, and thence transmitted to other regions" (1920,313).

Interest has long since waned in "diffusionist" anthropology, but recent evidence is very much in accord with its predictions. Today we know that the bullroarer is a very ancient object, specimens from France (13,000 B.C.) and the Ukraine (17,000 B.C.) dating back well into the Paleolithic period. Moreover, some archeologists—notably, Gordon Willey (1971, 20)—now admit the bullroarer to the kit-bag of artifacts brought by the very earliest migrants to the Americas. Nevertheless, modern anthropology has all but ignored the broad historical implication of the wide distribution and ancient lineage of the bullroarer: the separation and opposition of the sexes is a profoundly basic human social relationship.[5] A local variant of a men's cult takes on a significance that goes well beyond the frontiers of any one tribe. In the mirror of the Mehinaku culture, we may find images of ourselves and reflections of a nearly universal human sexual nature.

The Mehinaku word for bullroarer and the spirit it represents is *matapu*. Unlike the spirit of the sacred flutes, Matapu is found in the men's house only during the pequi fruit season in the late fall of each year. At this time, the owners of pequi orchards who are the "sponsors" (*wekehe*) of the Matapu ritual choose "makers" (*petewekehe*), who go outside the village to carve and paint bullroarers. The goal of

5. An article by Alan Dundes (1976) is the only recent systematic study of the bullroarer in the literature. The article is tangential to the historical point that presently concerns us, but it is of special interest because of its effort to explore the psychological implications of the bullroarer.

the ritual is to bring the spirit into the village, feed it in the name of the villagers, and thereby ensure the health of the children (who are particularly vulnerable to Matapu) and the fertility of the pequi orchards. From our perspective, however, the matapu, like the sacred flutes, is an object of intimidation.

After the bullroarers are carved and painted, they are attached to twenty-foot cords hafted to ten-foot poles. The women are warned to get inside their houses, and Matapu enters the village. The sound of fifteen or more large bullroarers whirling simultaneously on the village plaza can only be compared to that of an airplane revving its engines in one's living room. Next to a clap of thunder, it is the loudest sound the villagers will every hear. The women are told that they are listening to the voice of the spirit. Most of them, however are only modestly impressed. Matapu is a lesser spirit, not nearly as dangerous as Kauka. A woman who sees Matapu suffers only an uncertain supernatural penalty: all her hair may fall out. But few women take this threat seriously. While the bullroarers whiz overhead, the women peer through the thatch walls of their houses and, incidentally, through the men and their pretensions. Far from being frightened, the women regard the performance with the attitude of appreciative spectators: "Oh, there goes a really big one," was Tuapi's comment to my wife as she watched the bullroarers through her peephole. Ironically, the men are fully aware that the women are party to the secret of the bullroader. In recent years, they have become increasingly casual about the rules, even allowing the women to see the bullroarers that were made for me as gifts. The matapu used in rituals, "real" matapu, remain hidden and are not shown to women.

Although the bullroarer as an object of intimidation does not reach the status of Kauka's flutes, it would be an error to underestimate its

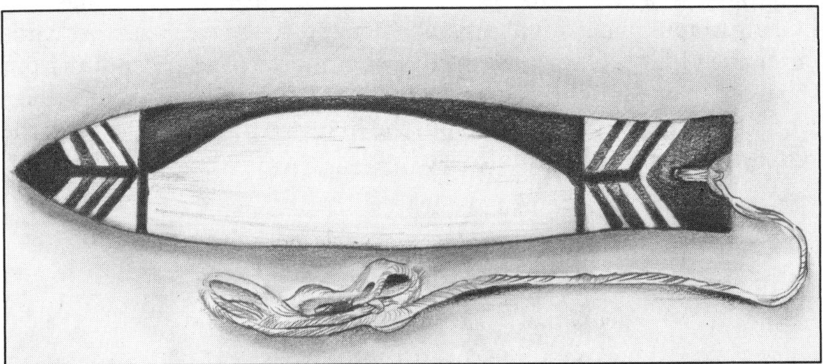

Fig. 20. A Mehinaku bullroarer (actual size 28"). Drawing by Marshall Capps.

symbolic significance. The women watch the show, but they do so from the poorest seats in the house. It is the men who bully them off the plaza-stage and shout abuse when they are not quick enough about it. No woman would dare leave her house and join in the ritual despite her knowledge of the men's secrets. Matapu is a reminder that among the Mehinaku, it is the men who act the principal parts, direct the action, and run the show.

SONGS, JEERS, AND JOKES: INFORMAL INTIMIDATION

The sacred flutes and the bullroarer are representative of a number of rituals that are forbidden to the women. Interspersed with these rituals, as well as those in which both sexes participate, are derisive songs aimed at the women. The most gentle of these are teasers, sung by a chorus of men from the men's bench each evening during the ritual of the bullroarer. Starting with the women who live in the ritual sponsor's house, the men sing about each of the young women in the village. Each song begins with the same two lines, modified only by the insertion of an appropriate name:

> Don't cry Maiyalu
> Kama, your lover, is not far off.

And then it continues with a jab at the woman's taste in boyfriends:

> You like him a lot, don't you?
> His face like a fish, his belly all bloated.

The men who are named in the songs are invariably members of other tribes and often the most outrageously inappropriate choice for a liaison. As the men sing, the women lie in their hammocks somewhat embarrassed by the teasing but on the whole enjoying themselves.

Quite different is the women's response to the men's songs during Mapulawaja, a ritual that is also associated with the pequi harvest. During Mapulawaja, men impersonating spirits of the pequi orchards enter the village. One of the spirits, to a chorus of angry shouts from the women and laughter from the men, addresses a song to the village women. As in the case of Matapu, the first two lines are standard, the remaining material is improvised:

> Look, look, look!
> Do you see your miserable genitals?
> Do you see the blood there?
> Do you see the feces there?
> Your feces are in your rectum,
> Your urine covers your genitals.

Songs and shouted jokes such as these continue through the Malpulawaja ritual and spill over into daily relationships during the entire six-week pequi season. A woman who passes near the men's house becomes the target of verbal assault. As soon as she is in range, a hand holding a wax vagina jabs through the thatch, accompanied by a barrage of derisive taunts about female genitalia. The men's shouts and laughter echo after her as she moves out of earshot.

The women, however, are not simply the recipients of abuse. On occasion, they strike back and briefly get the upper hand. The pequi rituals of Alukaka, Kiriri, and Mapulawaja are examples (see Gender Wars illustrations following page 117), but there are also songs in which the women tease the men about their sexual anatomy. On rare occasions, the women's antagonism reaches a more serious level. A man from a different tribe who enters the Mehinaku village during the Yamurikuma role-reversal ritual will be set upon and beaten by the women. In ancient times, the villagers claim, he would have been gang raped. Nevertheless, except for teasing, the men have little to fear at the hands of their women. A woman who refuses to accept the slurs and jokes and who shouts back at the men forfeits her femininity. Several Mehinaku women have edged in this direction, and the men's response is instructive.

Kalu is a woman in her mid twenties, outspoken and articulate. Married to one of the most marginal and powerless men in the community, she is clearly the dominant partner in her household. Unlike her more timid sisters, Kalu occasionally teases the men as enthusiastically as they taunt the women. During the high jinks of Mapulawaja, she was the one who made a grotesque clay phallus "to get the men back" for their sexual taunts. While in training for intertribal female wrestling matches, only Kalu dared to perform exaggerated imitations of the wrestling styles affected by Mehinaku male champions.

For a while, the men good-naturedly accepted Kalu's teasing, but some of her taunts clearly hit home. During the week prior to the women's wrestling matches the men stepped up the level of their abuse to a point Kalu could never hope to surpass. "Come out and wrestle, you long-labiaed one," they bellowed from in front of the men's house. "Let's see your vagina with your legs spread apart." After some delay, Kalu appeared on the plaza wearing a pair of shorts that someone had cadged from a worker at the Indian post. "Take them off, take them off," shouted the men. "We want to see your vagina's nose" (the clitoris). Ignoring the men, Kalu began to wrestle with one of the other women. Immediately, the men called out mock advice: "Head down! Grab her by the genitals! Roll over and spread your legs." "Not like that," shouted one man racing up to her and throwing her heavily on the ground, "like this!"

Despite her ability to score a few quick points, Kalu is now in danger of losing the entire game. As of my last visit to the tribe, she had lost the support of the other young women who in the past could be counted on to provide some back-up in her teasing matches with men. More ominously, rumors were circulating that Kalu had clandestinely seen the sacred flutes.[6] The message is clear: a woman who challenges the men on their home turf is bound to lose. Much as in our own society, where feminists briefly experimented in sexually taunting construction workers, victories are short-lived and dearly bought.

WHOOPS AND JEERS

Ritual is not the only occasion for intimidating women. On fine evenings, young men like to stroll about the village plaza, arm-in-arm, enjoying the cool night air. Often there is a *metalawaitsi* (a joker or a wise guy) among them who takes advantage of the cover of darkness to hurl insulting falsetto whoops and jeers into the night. An old work horse is *pwitya kamalu*, a phrase that is translated literally as "grab clay," but is understood to mean "go have sexual relations." Clay is a denigrating simile for female genitalia since it is moist, spongy, and foul in odor when newly dug from a riverbank. Other current jeers include *eluhɨ yalai, "your genitals are smelley,"* and *kakaiyaiki*, literally, "stingy ones," but in this context, "you are stingy with your sexual favors." For the jokers, these one-liners are uproariously funny. Even the shamans sitting in the circle of smokers are amused, though too dignified to show it. Only the women are discomfited, perhaps because they understand the political meaning of the jeers: in the battle of the sexes, women are the losers.

Women's House: Myths of Matriarchy

The public life of Mehinaku society is men's life. Acted on the plaza, the men's space, it is composed of men's oratory, men's songs, men's rituals, men's wrestling matches. Women have a culture that paral-

6. Women who conduct themselves like Kalu are very much at risk in male-dominated societies. Robert Murphy describes Borai, a Mundurucu woman, who was very much like Kalu in her bold demeanor: "She eyed all the men with an alert, sparkling gaze, and she expressed amusement by throwing her head back and laughing deeply" (1974, 204). Borai's unfeminine manner and her open sexual interest in men amounted to "an infringement of the public order." Murphy believes that had it not been for his own presence in the village, she would have been gang raped, even though she had never seen the Mundurucu sacred flutes.

Fig. 21. Directing a women's ritual. Women have a culture that in some ways reflects that of the men. They have their own rituals and bartering sessions, and there is even a female chieftainship. These institutions, however, are not as dramatic, as frequently performed, or as politically and socially significant as the men's. Even during the intertribal ritual of Akajatapa, when the women wear some items of men's dress and wrestle women from neighboring tribes, it is the men who direct the show. Here two chiefs, Monai and his father Aiyuruwa, call out instructions to the women dancers.

lels that of the men, but its public displays are pale reflections of a masculine image. Female chiefs speak but rarely to the village women, and then their quiet voices are heard only within the houses. Women's songs are largely confined to after-dinner serenades on the plaza or lullabies at home. On the few occasions that women conduct intertribal rituals, the action is largely directed by the men who superintend their women's movements from village to village. Women's wrestling is an entertainment for the men, a burlesque in which the women are the bullied and often reluctant participants. This picture of patriarchal culture is largely shared by the women themselves, who accept the fact of masculine dominance. Even Kalu, the only woman who dares challenge the men, confesses:

> I am frightened by the men. They are fearful. I could not speak on the plaza. I could not go fishing. The line would cut my hands. I am afraid of big animals. We women have no strength, we have no anger. The men are worthy of respect.

It was not always so, at least not in myth. We are told that the women of ancient times (*ekwimyatipalu*) were matriarchs, the founders of what is now the men's house and creators of Mehinaku culture. Ketepe is our narrator for this legend of Xingu "Amazons."[7]

> THE WOMEN DISCOVER THE SONGS OF THE FLUTE
>
> In ancient times, a long time ago, the men lived by themselves, a long way off. The women had left the men. The men had no women at all. Alas for the men, they had sex with their hands. The men were not happy at all in their village; they had no bows, no arrows, no cotton arm bands. They walked about without even belts.[8] They had no hammocks, so they slept on the ground, like animals. They hunted fish by diving in the water and catching them with their teeth, like otters. To cook the fish, they heated them under their arms. They had nothing—no possessions at all.
>
> The women's village was very different; it was a real village. The women had built the village for their chief, Iripyulakumaneju. They made houses; they wore belts and arm bands, knee ligatures and feather headdresses, just like the men. They made kauka, the first kauka: "*Tak . . . tak . . . tak*," they cut it from wood. They built the house for Kauka, the first place for the spirit. Oh, they were smart, those round-headed women of ancient times.
>
> The men saw what the women were doing. They saw them playing kauka in the spirit house. "Ah," said the men, "this is not good. The women have stolen our lives!" The next day, the chief addressed the men: "The women are not good. Let's go to them." From far off, the men heard the women, singing and dancing with Kauka. The men made bullroarers outside the women's village. Oh, they would have sex with their wives very soon.

7. The myth's title, *Teneju Auta Kauka Iyeyaka*, translates literally, "The Women Find Kauka's Speech." The term "Amazon" that is applied to female warriors comes to us from the ancient Greeks, who believed that tribes of such women lived near the Black Sea. The Amazon River was so named because of the reputed presence of Amazons according to the myths of the tribes of the region.

8. To be "beltless" (*mowantalutsi*) in the Mehinaku dress code is to be naked.

The men came close to the village, "Wait, wait," they whispered. And then: "Now!" They leaped up at the women like wild Indians: "Hu waaaaaa!" they whooped. They swung the bullroarers until they sounded like a plane. They raced into the village and chased the women until they had caught every one, until there was not one left. The women were furious: "Stop, stop," they cried. But the men said, "No good, no good. Your leg bands are no good. Your belts and headdresses are no good. You have stolen our designs and paints." The men ripped off the belts and clothes and rubbed the women's bodies with earth and soapy leaves to wash off the designs.

The men lectured the women: "You don't wear the shell yamaquimpi belt. Here, you wear a twine belt. We paint up, not you. We stand up and make speeches, not you. You don't play the sacred flutes. We do that. We are men."

The women ran to hide in their houses. All of them were hidden. The men shut the doors: This door, that door, this door, that door. "You are just women," they shouted. "You make cotton. You weave hammocks. You weave them in the morning, as soon as the cock crows. Play Kauka's flutes? Not you!"

Later that night, when it was dark, the men came to the women and raped them. The next morning, the men went to get fish. The women could not go into the men's house. In that men's house, in ancient times. The first one.

This Mehinaku myth of Amazons is similar to those told by many other tribal societies with men's cults (see Bamberger 1974). In these stories, the women are the first owners of men's sacred objects, such as flutes, bullroarers, or trumpets. Often, however, the women are unable to care for the objects or feed the spirits they represent. The men band together and trick or force the women to give up their control of the men's cult and accept a subordinate role in society.

What are we to make of the striking parallels in these myths? Anthropologists are in agreement that the myths are not history. The peoples who tell them were likely to have been as patriarchal in the past as they are today. Rather than windows to the past, the tales are living stories that reflect ideas and concerns that are central to a people's concept of sexual identity. The Mehinaku legend opens in ancient times with the men in a precultural state, living "like animals." In conflict with many other myths and the received Mehinaku opinion about female intellect, the women were the culture creators, the inventors of architecture, clothes, and religion:[9] "They were smart, those round-headed women of ancient times."

The men's ascendance is achieved through brute force. Attacking "like wild Indians," they terrorize the women with the bullroarer, strip them of their masculine adornment, herd them into the houses, rape them, and lecture them on the rudiments of appropriate sex-role behavior. On the surface, this assertion of dominance reflects the men's present confidence in their ability to put women in their place. As in ancient times, men are stronger than women and are still capable of locking them back in their houses. But in fact, force of arms is the last resort of the confident oppressor. A far more effective patriarchal strategy is to base the subordination of women on values and teachings that both men and women endorse. In our own society, sex-role differences are grounded in a murky but generally shared folk biology of purported differences in aggression, intelligence, and moral worth. Among the highly patriarchal agricultural cultures of the Near East and Mediterranean regions, this reading of nature is augmented by a rigid double standard that confines women to domestic roles. So powerful are the moral images that buttress patriarchy that women largely support it. In their roles as socializers of the young and as guardians of family honor, they become the enforcers of female subordination, in effect conspiring in their own oppression.[10]

Among the Mehinaku, the skeleton of patriarchy is not well fleshed out with moral arguments and beliefs about sexual morality and innate biological differences. To be sure, the villagers deal out the facts of sexual dimorphism in justifying gender roles, but relative to other cultures, these cards are not at the top of the cognitive deck. There is, moreover, a strong sense that human biology is human creation rather than a natural or God-given product. Hence a myth of Amazons and male rebellion is an explanation of patriarchy for the Mehinaku. Men rule today, not because that is the natural order of things, but because they remain strong. They can, if necessary, once again rape the women and lock them in their houses.

What neither the myth nor the Mehinaku can directly tell us, however, is the dimension of fear that lurks behind the apparent strength. If patriarchy rests upon a successful male insurrection, could not the women stage a counterrevolution? If they were better

9. Within the myth, there is some ambivalence on this point. Even though the women are the creators, the men sense that the creation is rightfully theirs. Thus, the women "have stolen" their lives.

10. Hayes (1975) provides a vivid example in her discussion of female enforcement of clitoridectomey and infibulation in the Egyptian Sudan. Dwyer's (1978) study of women in Morocco also documents how women become party to a highly repressive system.

armed and even smarter than those Amazons of ancient times, what would prevent them from reestablishing the matriarchy? I posed these questions to a number of my male informants, and all, including Ketepe, were confident that patriarchy had a long future:

> Oh, no. The women don't want to go into the men's house and hear the flutes. In *ancient times,* in *ancient times,* the women wanted to play the flutes, to be like men. Now they don't want to go into the men's house. They are not strong. Their speech is not quick, like a man's. They are just "house-stayers" now. But they are sad when they hear Kauka's song. "Alas for us!," they say; they miss ancient times.

As for the women, there seems to be no serious counterrevolutionary spirit among them, even if a few would risk an occasional guerrilla skirmish. Yet Ketepe is perceptive in identifying a certain glow of nostalgia: "Ah, those women of ancient times," said Kalu. "They were really strong and clever. But not us. It was just in ancient times that those things happened."

A restitution of the matriarchy is thus not imminent. Despite the villagers' denials, however, "The Women Discover the Songs of the Flute" reflects genuine male anxieties. There is no other way to interpret the myth if we read it within the larger context of secrecy and intimidation, taunting songs, hostile jokes and jeers, bullroarers and flutes, and the threat of gang rape. The men with their dramatic masculine displays would have us believe that the barriers separating the sexes are walls of granite. The legend of matriarchy, however, almost reveals a dangerous truth: the men's house as a symbol of male identity is a citadel of papier-mâché. The secrecy, the intimidation, and the use of force are the shims and gimcracks that shore it up. Even though male identity and men's house culture are not immediately in danger of collapse, the cost of maintaining the façade runs high. The price the men pay is in anxiety: fear of their own sexual impulses and fear of women.

GENDER WARS

An Interlude and Picture Essay
Watercolors and Sketches by Akanai

We have rituals to feed the pequi spirits. If they don't have their food they are sad. They eat fish and pequi nuts. That's spirit food. If we didn't feed the spirits, there would not be any pequi. We bring the spirits into the village to feed them. First we bring the spirit Matapu. Then we bring the spirits of Anteater, Cricket, Bee, Scorpion, and the spirit Alukaka. Last we celebrate Mapulawaja. That is a happy ceremony. A really beautiful ceremony."

Ketepe

Gender Wars: The Rituals of the Pequi Harvest

> Always, always in the past, our grandfathers, the Ones Who Are Now Dead, spoke together from the center of the plaza: "Let us bring the masters of the pequi to the village!"
>
> —The Mehinaku chief, in a ceremonial speech, beginning the pequi rituals

In the late fall, the pequi fruit in the orchards around the village ripens and falls. Roughly the size and the texture of an avocado, the pequi is roasted in the fire or mashed into a gruel. The flesh of the fruit is rich in oils and B vitamins and is an important part of the villagers' diet when the abundant fishing of the dry season begins to fall off. But pequi is more than nutrition. It is symbolic food with rich sexual associations, as we recall from the myth of Great Alligator Spirit, in which the slain spirit's genitals became the first pequi.

In addition to the symbolic connection between pequi and sex, the harvest of the fruit occurs at a sexual time in the village. The great intertribal rituals of the early autumn are over, the rains of the wet season have begun, and the rhythm of village life slows. During this slack time, the community is more insular, more inwardly focused, and more eager for stimulation. Sexual relations with spouses and lovers help to relieve the tedium. In the stories turned out by the ever-churning gossip mill, intertribal politics takes second place to sexual adventures, intrigues, and jealousies. But it is not just the carnal aspects of sex that preoccupy the villagers. The rains that follow the five months of drought have at last awakened the land and forests. New shoots of manioc turn the gardens green, and the pequi fruit swell, ripen, and fall. The season is a time of growth, quickening, and fertility.

The villagers attribute the abundance of pequi to spirits who are the true owners of the orchards. Collectively the spirits are referred to as the *akain wekehe*, the owners, or masters, of the pequi. The rituals that occur at the time of the harvest feed and entertain the spirits, who in exchange for food and pleasures of the occasion provide an abundant crop. The harvest rituals themselves are simply called "feeding all the pequi spirits" (*kulekeinpei akainwekehe não*). Some of these rituals are organized and over in less than an hour. Others are planned well in advance and engage the community in several days of song, dance, and feasts. But in all the rituals, there is a component of opposition between men and women that ranges from the playful to the assaultive. It is this aggressive dimension of the rituals that leads us to speak of "gender wars."

Matapu: The Bullroarer

The cycle of rituals begins with Matapu, the ceremony of the bullroarer. The owner of the pequi orchards appoints two "makers" of the ritual who act the part of the spirit Matapu. They will carve bullroarers, bring them into the community, and whirl them in front of the house of the orchard owner to make the droning noise that is the spirit's voice. The women, sequestered in the houses, are supposedly mystified, though all have looked in secret upon the devices and seen through the men's impersonations.

In Akanai's watercolor, the men and boys, adorned and painted for the occasion, spin bullroarers from the ends of long poles. Each of the men is paired with a comrade who is spoken of as his "wife." In part, this marital relationship is merely a division of ritual labor based on that of a real marriage. The "wife" follows her "husband" into the village as they bring the spirit of Matapu in from the orchards. The "husband" spoons ceremonial food into individual portions, and the "wife" distributes it. The "husband's" bullroarer is painted distinctively, is large in size, makes a deep-throated roar, is whirled first, and will be stored to the right of the "wife's" in the men's house. But the marital metaphor is more than a sex-appropriate separation of tasks. The men are fully aware of its implications and make broad jokes at the ritual wife's expense: The "wife," remarked Ataiya, referring to the ceremonial male partner, "is our penis' food."

Matapu is the most dangerous of the pequi spirits. He attacks village children by taking their souls (*iyeweku*, literally, "shadow") and thereby making them ill. The parents of children who have recovered from illness are the main sponsors of the rituals. At the end of the ritual, they beg the spirit to return to its home in the forests and orchards: "It is good you have come. It is good you have come, Matapu. Do not be angry. Do not take the souls of our children. It is good that you go back to your home in the orchards."

The ceremony of Matapu, however, does not dwell on the theme of illness. Rather, the central theme is the opposition of the sexes. From the men's point of view, the women should be a mystified and intimidated audience. At night, when the bullroarers are tucked away in the men's house, the women are treated to obscene jeers and insulting songs. On the final day of the ritual, the only time the women are full ritual participants, they are bested by the men in a race that ushers the spirit out of the village. Although the men dominate the first pequi ritual, the cycle of events has just begun. The women, the men know, are looking forward with pleasure to the next ceremony, that of Yupei, the anteater.

Yupei: The Anteater

Unlike Matapu, most of the pequi spirits are relatively benign masters of the orchards. The organization of the harvest rituals associated with these unthreatening spirits depends on generous and prominent men who own the large orchards. They will provide the pequi mash for the villagers who make the spirits' costumes (*nain*, literally, "enclosing garment or skin"), bring the spirits into the village from the orchards, feed the spirits or those who impersonate them, and finally send the spirits away from the village. Among the more interesting of the benign spirit owners of the pequi is the anteater (*Myrmocephaga*). Like the other animals inhabiting the orchards, he is said to include pequi in his diet. Keeping him fed and contented not only guarantees the next year's harvest but at the same time, the villagers recognize, creates a joyful community ritual.

The ritual of Yupei begins along the main trail to the orchards. There the men and boys assemble the anteater from vines and leaves. The men are the body of the animal, and a long pole protrudes in the front as a drooping, phallic nose. With a whoop, the men march into the village, imitating the shambling gait of the anteater. The women are out of sight, waiting in the houses. After circling the village, the anteater approaches one of the houses and penetrates the doorway repeatedly with his nose. The women are waiting in ambush, armed with sticks and clubs. They vigorously beat the nose of the beast until it retreats from the house with grunts and snarls. Not completely defeated, the anteater forces its attentions upon each of the other houses in turn, where it is once again clubbed away. At last, the anteater circles the plaza as all the women gang up to annihilate it. They attack, pounding the nose of the beast into bits and pieces of vegetation. The men do their best to imitate a dying anteater, though their performance is marred by their bursts of laughter.

The sexual symbolism of the anteater ritual is not lost on the villagers. Houses are intensely feminine areas associated with such activities as nursing and caring for children, recovering from illness, and eating and sleeping. Moreover, to the villagers, the doorways of the houses, framed as they are in a narrow fringe of thatch, look like female genitalia. A few of the villagers explained the ritual by saying that the anteater was having sex with the houses, an idea that they found uproariously funny. One of the men's interpretations, however, attributed a psychologically darker motive to the phallic anteater: "Yupei goes into the houses," he insisted, "to get his nose beaten."

Kiriri: The Cricket

The masters of the pequi are animals and spirits that are usually associated with the orchards. The cricket would hardly seem to fit in, but a trip to the orchards proves otherwise. During most of the day, there is a constant background noise of crickets. The voice of each is lost against the shrill of thousands of others, so the sound cannot be pinned down. But beyond doubt, the cricket, a master of the pequi, is there even when he cannot be seen.

To feed the cricket and ensure a good harvest, the men and boys enter the village from the direction of the orchards. Holding onto a circular cord, they sing the song of the cricket in cricket-like wisps of falsetto voices.

> I hear the hammock cords and poles creaking:
> *Pilaw, kulei, pilaw, pilaw, pilaw.*

The last lines are onomatopoeic words for the sounds of sexual intercourse. The men explain that the cricket hears his mother as she has sex in her hammock.

Once again, the women respond to the insult. They emerge from their houses, carrying aluminum pots and cauldrons of water. The previous night, the chief had warned them: "In ancient times the women were practical jokers. They filled pots with dirt and water to dump on the men during the ritual of Kiriri. But you women in the houses who hear my speech: You will use clean water, fresh from the river." No such luck. As the men sing, the women disgorge a mixture of water, household trash, earth, and fermenting manioc on the men's heads.

After the cricket has visited each of the houses, keeping up his shrill song no matter how heavy the innundation, the men whoop and race off to the bathing area to clean up. The ritual is a high-spirited affairs, and the men do not take offense, especially since they are looking forward to a counterattack in the ritual of the bee to be held the next day.

Akanai's picture nicely captures the events of the ritual. Notice especially how one of the women looms like a giant over the men as she covers them with watery garbage.

Yu-yu-tu: The Bee

Early in the morning, the men assemble well outside the village on the path to the pequi orchards. The owner of the orchard has brought a bottle of pequi oil and several large pieces of charred wood. The men rub each others' bodies with charcoal and oil until their skins glisten with a slick black finish. Then, led by the chief, they form a single line and began to run to the village, chanting and humming like bees: "*yu-yu-yu-yu*!" Swarming through the back doors of the houses, the line of men drives the women onto the plaza. Two or three men grab each woman. Little boys capture little girls. They rub their naked oily bodies over the women, smearing them with black grease to represent the attack of the bee. Some of the women are lifted bodily off the ground, clutched in a oily embrace, and only released after they are thoroughly blackened. A few of the men who catch voluptuous village women are sexually aroused by the intimate contact, much to the amusement of their comrades. "Yu-yu-tu," as one of the men explained to me, "is a 'sexy' bee" (*weiyuteri*).

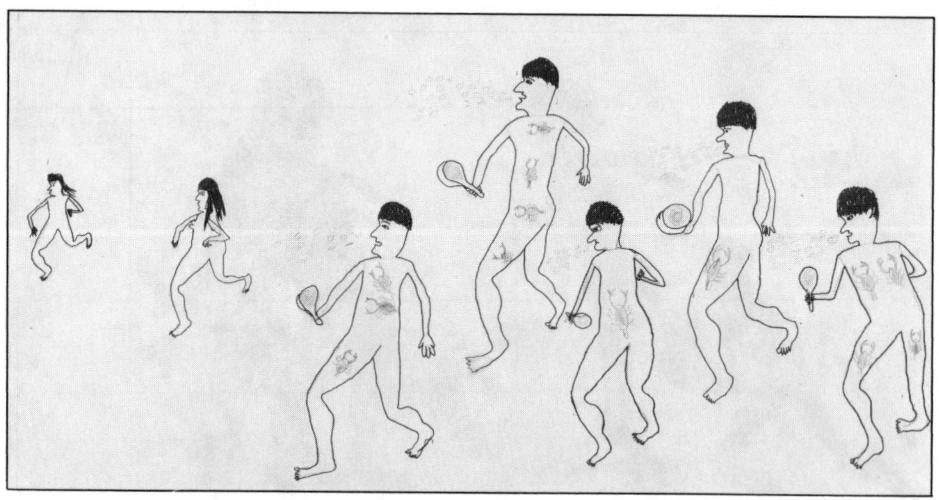

Hopa: The Scorpion

Hopa is the one master of pequi that the villagers would prefer not to meet. Measuring up to six inches in length and carrying his venemous stinger high above his back, he is flushed out of burrows and crevices by the first heavy rains of the wet season. According to the villagers, he can spray his venom a distance of six to ten feet. A spattering on the skin leaves a burning sensation, but a direct hit in the eye leads to blindness and death—or so my informants claimed.

In Akanai's drawing of the ritual, Hopa has arrived in the village to attack the women. Like Yu-yu-tu, the bee, Hopa comes in aggressive swarms of human impersonators decorated with charcoal drawings of the insect on their backs, shoulders, chests, and thighs. Each "scorpion" carries a gourd dipper filled with water, and chants "Hopa, Hopa, Hopa!" while rhythmically moving his arms in imitation of the scorpion's front mandibles. When the women are in range, the men eject a blast of water from their mouths, spraying their prey with Hopa's "venom." After the drenching, the men and women bathe in exuberant same-sex groups. The women have a special reason to take all the teasing good-heartedly: they will get back at the men with interest in the rituals of Alukaka and Mapulawaja.

Alukaka

Some say that Alukaka is a snake spirit. The normally better-informed villagers insist that it is a bird, albeit a spirit-bird that has no living counterpart. One would prefer to believe that it is a snake, for in the ritual, a long snake-like line of men is systematically torn apart by the women of the village.

Whether the spirit represents snake or bird, Alukaka begins outside the village with the men and boys covering their bodies with pequi oil to make their skin slippery, their limbs supple, and their bones springy and resilient. "We will need it," explained one of the men with only a trace of humor. The spirit enters the village in two long lines of men and boys, each linked to his comrades by a loop of rope. The chief, at the head of the men's line, leans heavily on a pole planted deep in the soil. Using the chief as a human fulcrum, each line snaps the whip back and forth across the plaza while the men and boys chant the name of the spirit in falsetto voices: "Alukaka! Alukaka! Alukaka!" Gradually the women of the village, dressed only in leg bands and twine belts, assemble behind the line. Rubbing their hands in dirt to get a good grip, they attack Kikyala, the last man on one line. Kikyala is strong, powerfully built, heavily oiled, and fast moving—not easy to hold down. But at last one of the women catches him about the knees while six others grab him by the arms, legs, and hair. His grip on the rope broken, his comrades cannot snap him free from the avalanche of women who bury him under their bodies. Overcome by their weight and strength, Kikyala is at their mercy as they tickle and poke him. Maiyalau, one of the saucier and less inhibited of the women, seizes the opportunity to fondle his genitals. "Enough!

Enough!" cries Kikyala, but it is not enough for his tormenters. Only after he is reduced to tears of laughter, pain, and embarrassment do the women allow him to get up from the ground.

As the women tear Alukaka up, segment by segment, it is apparent that Kikyala has gotten off lightly. Some of the men, their faces rubbed with dirt, are lifted off the ground, dropped several feet, and dragged across the plaza by their feet. These men are covered with scrapes and lacerations and are genuinely angry with the women. For them, the battle of the sexes is a reality and they are more than a little surprised to discover that they are on the losing side.

Mapulawaja

Mapulawaja is the most elaborate of the pequi rituals and the most important. Three days in length, it engages the entire village in feasting, the manufacture of ritual objects, and all-night dancing and singing. The form of the ritual is roughly similar to others in that the villagers bring spirits into the community where they are fed a mash made from pequi. At the end of the ritual, the spirits are guided back to the gardens that they must protect and make fertile.

For the most part, the spirit masters of the pequi in Mapulawaja are birds that can be found in the orchards. Chief among these are various species of hummingbirds, whose images are carved in soft wood and placed in the village plaza. The spirits of the birds are further impersonated by the villagers who arrive in pairs ("husband" and "wife") from the direction of the orchards. At the end of the ritual, the "husband" and "wife" feed the spirits by placing a small amount of pequi mash in their beaks: "Take this, take this pequi, Hummingbird Spirit; it is good that you have come to us. Do not be angry with us; it is good now that you go back to your home in the orchard."

But there is one pequi spirit who strikes a note very different from the solemn deportment of all the others. She is Aripi, "Old Woman." Like other spirits, Aripi is represented by a pair of dancers who enter the village from the direction of the orchards. Unlike the others, Aripi is a grotesque caricature of a woman, an ancient crone who limps and stumbles her way into the village while singing in a thin, croaking voice. Low, between her legs, Aripi carries large flesh-colored gourds decorated with oversized female genitalia. As she enters the plaza, she points to the gourds and sings to the women:

> I see, I see, I see;
> I see your worthless vaginas
> I see the vaginas with which you are so stingy;
> I see!

The women shout and wave their arms in anger. The chief, as a master of ceremonies, vainly tries to recall the ritual seriousness of the occasion: "Aripi is coming. She is coming to eat pequi. Look at her, but don't laugh! Aripi, it is good that you have come to eat and drink. You are happy to be here. But do not trifle with us, Spirit. Do not tease us, Aripi."

In fact, Aripi is a trickster. In the dances that follow, she will dog the heels of the women, shouting abuse, calling out obscenities and improvising songs about bloody vaginas and foul rectums. The culmination of Aripi's pranks occurs on the last evening of Mapulawaja when there are all-night dances in each of the village houses. Prior to the dances, the men who represent Aripi make wax imitations of women's genitals. Knowing that a few will be stolen and destroyed by the women, they keep a supply in reserve. Some of the genitalia are of menstruating women, others are adorned with imitation feces. Each waxen image represents a woman at a different stage of life so that sexual teasing that is to come can be directed at different targets.

The dance begins in the houses. The women face the center while the men dance in a line in front of them. Most of the dancers treat the songs and dance seriously, but not those who impersonate Aripi. Separating themselves from the other men, they perform a slow taunting dance a few feet from the women, displaying the wax genita-

lia. "This is your vagina, Ugly One," shout the men, pushing the model close to the women and pointing out its various features: "Here are your inner and outer labia; here is your 'vaginia's nose' (the clitoris). Why do you have sex with all the dirty penises from other tribes?"

Periodically the women lash out at their assailants, trying to rip away the wax genitals. Finally, several of the women simultaneously rush the men. The men's bodies are oiled and initially they slip away. But at last they are caught by the hair, thrown to the ground, and soundly beaten. The mood of the villagers is that of high carnival, and both men and women shriek with laughter. But those who are roughed up will bear their abrasions, scrapes, black and blue marks, and nail wounds for many days. For them and their comrades-at-arms in the gender war, the lesson is not lost: the women are a force to be reckoned with.

The final scene of Mapulawaja occurs the next day. The images of the spirits are fed a mash made of pequi, paraded on the plaza, and then taken to the orchards. Aripi's wax genitalia accompany the other pequi spirits, but now the mood has changed. Men and women dance together, carrying the images out of the village. In these last moments of the ritual, men and women are no longer antagonists, but partners within the natural cycle of sexuality and fertility.

SEVEN

Anxious Pleasures

Sex is not good.

—Kikyala

THERE IS A DARK SIDE TO THE RELATIONSHIP OF MEN AND WOMEN. THE myth of the toothed vagina, the aggressive component in the equation of eating and sex, and the sanctions that protect the men's house strike discordant notes in an otherwise harmonious interaction. This chapter explores some of the tensions and anxieties that shadow the relationship of the sexes.

Sexual Fears

THE CASTRATION COMPLEX

Many of the men's sexual concerns are linked to castration anxiety. Following Freud, this fear has its origin in the Oedipal stage of development (age three to five) when a boy's sexual longings toward his mother are repressed by the fear that his father will harm and even castrate him in jealous retaliation. Ideally, the boy experiences no more than enough anxiety to diminish his attachment to his mother and lay the groundwork for successful identification with the male role. More typically, however, the fear persists into adulthood. Anxieties associated with castration include both overt fears of harm to the genitals (as, for example, excessive concerns about venereal disease [see Sarnoff and Corwin 1978,216]) and more derivative fears of dismemberment, severing, phobias concerning harm to the body and death. Since male identity is anatomically based, castration fear is also symbolically linked to anxieties over loss of independence and self-assertion. Ultimately, castration symbolizes the diminished worth of the individual and the mutilation of the self. Taken together, these Oedipally derived anxieties are known as the castration complex.

Although theoretical questions remain about the nature of the Oedipal stage of development, the reality of castration-related fears is established in the psychoanalytic literature (see Klein 1948,13–61, for a compelling example) and in empirical tests of Freudian theory. In a particularly fair-minded review of fourteen investigations of castration fear (a few of which are elegantly designed experiments under laboratory conditions), Paul Kline (1972,116) finds "good evidence for the castration complex" in our own society. Among the Mehinaku, the evidence is even stronger. In the data that follows, we will examine the theme of castration in myths, theories of disease, and sexual practices and prohibitions. The motif is often overt and in sharp, unmistakable focus. Occasionally the theme is thinly veiled by humor and symbols, but the villagers' fear still shows through. It expresses, in ways that are alternately painful and funny, their all-too-fragile sense of being men.

CASTRATION ANXIETY: PUNISHMENT FOR SEXUAL WISHES

A large set of myths deals openly with the theme of castration and mutilation of the genitals. We begin with the most remarkable of these tales, the story of Katsi. Frequently the Mehinaku refer to this tale as that of Kapukwa, which is actually the name of Katsi's penis. To better appreciate the nature of Katsi's and Kapukwa's adventures, as well as the magnitude of their plight, the reader would do well to refer to their picture (fig. 22 below), which Kuyaparei has drawn for this book.

KATSI

This is really a myth. A myth of long ago, a story of sex with Kaitsapaneju, "Lizard Woman."

Kaitsapaneju looked like a beautufil woman, but she was really a spirit. She was forbidden for sex, no one dared have sex with her.

But there was one man, a real wise guy, named Katsi. He wanted to have sex with her. All the people warned him: "Don't do it! Her genitals are no good. Have sex with her and your penis will grow enormously long!"

"Is that really true?" asked Katsi. "Of course it's true," they said. "We wouldn't lie to you."

But Katsi looked at Kaitsapaneju and said, "I'm going to have sex with her anyway. I want to 'eat' her vagina."

One day, Kaitsapaneju went to get firewood. Oh, her

legs and thighs were so attractive. That joker Katsi saw her and grasped her by the wrist: "Ah, Kaitsapaneju, let's go have sex."

"Not me," she replied. "My genitals are so delicious, so voluptuous, they make your penis grow."

"Oh, but I want to have sex!" Ah, Katsi did have an erection.

"Wait a minute," said Kaitsapaneju, "I will get a clam shell and scrape out my vagina to make sex less sensual for you. Perhaps then it will be safe for you to have sex, and your penis will not grow."

"No, no," said that fool Katsi, "It's just fine as it is now. I want it to be really sensual."

"Well then, all right," said Kaitsapaneju, who was very angry with Katsi.

They sat down to have sex. Inside he went. He ate her, he ate her, he ate her. He thrust in and in and in and in: "*Ateke, ateke,* Kaitsapaneju, *ateke*!" he called. His semen arrived. He withdrew. His penis was as long as a snake.

"You see?" said Kaitsapaneju. "Ah, pity on you, Katsi."

Alas for Katsi. His penis grew and grew, all the way down to the river. He could not walk about with such a long penis, and so he wove large bags from palm fiber, "penis holders." Four great sacks he filled with his penis, which was coiled up in them like a snake. His penis was called Kapukwa. In this bag, Kapukwa. In that bag, Kapukwa. In this bag, kapukwa. And in that bag, Kapukwa. To go about, Katsi suspended his penis holders from the ends of his bow, which he carried slung over his shoulder.

Ah, Poor Katsi. He could hardly move about. He did not eat, he did not fish. But, Kapukwa ate *his* "food." At night, when everyone was asleep, Kapukwa woke up. He slithered out of his sacks and along the floor of the house. He opened the door, snaked across the plaza, and entered each of the village houses. He slid up the house poles, wound his way along the hammock cords, and slipped into the vaginas of the sleeping women. But none of the women knew that Kapukwa was having sex with them.

Finally, one man saw what Kapukwa was doing. He told his friends, and on the following night, they were ready with clubs. When Kapukwa emerged from his house, they attacked, beating him on the head with heavy sticks. With each blow he shrank back, until Katsi was left with a tiny, tiny penis.

Responding to my question, Ketepe, our narrator, explained the source of Katsi's difficulties. Since Katsi was copulating with Lizard Woman, he became like a male lizard, which in fact has a long penis. Of greater significance, however, was his sexual desire: "Katsi's penis grew because Katisapaneju was so delicious, because she was so

Fig. 22. Kapukwa. Burdened by his immensely long penis, Katsi wove baskets in which Kapukwa lay coiled. Watercolor by Kuyaparei.

attractive to him." At the end of the tale, Katsi's sexual desire gets him into further trouble. "The men clubbed Kapukwa because they held their wives dear; they did not want Kapukwa to have sex with them."

In its outline, the myth has some of the typical elements of castration fear that emerge from Oedipal conflict, since the damage to the penis comes in jealous retaliation for Katsi's sexual relationships. As is invariably the case of myths, however, alternative interpretations are possible. Despite warnings, Katsi cannnot resist having sex with Lizard Woman. His resulting enormous penis is an encumbrance that must be lugged around in unwieldy sacks. The penis then goes on uncontrollable sexual rampages. One of the messages of the myth is surely a warning against unfettered sexuality.[1] Nonetheless, as they tell the story, the Mehinaku men emphasize the castration motif. The narrator dramatically acts out each blow of the club and uses appropriate groans and body movements to mimic Katsi's agony. Finally, at the end of the tale, the narrator holds up a thumb and forefinger to frame a space of about one quarter of an inch—the size of Katsi's shriveled and mutilated penis.

Although undeniably a source of humor (and reminiscent of jokes in our own society), the story of Katsi and Lizard Woman suggests that a man's sexual impulses may lead to harm to his penis and even to castration. The next two frequently told tales, "Thatch" and "Eagle," support this interpretation. "Thatch" takes place just outside a house where a man is calling to his girlfriend to have sexual relations. All around him is a field of reeds used for thatching. As they emerge from the ground, the shoots of these red-tipped reeds are incredibly sharp, capable of causing a deep puncture wound for the villager unlucky enough to step on them.

THATCH

A man was calling to his girlfriend: "Come on," he said, making a kissing sound with his lips, "Let's have sex."

"Soon, soon," she replied. "Soon we will go have sex together."

"No, now. Come here."

"Soon, soon. I'm painting myself for you."

"Now?"

"Soon, soon. I'm putting on my belt for you."

Oh, the man had an erection like the log bench in front of the men's house. He rubbed his penis; it was so big. All around was the thatch grass, here, there, all

1. I am indebted to Waud Kracke for his suggestions regarding this myth and the story of the armadillo and the footprint that follows.

over. He rubbed and rubbed his penis. *Tssuk*! He pierced his penis on the thatch grass. "Aaaaah, . . ." he moaned, and died.

His girlfriend finally came outside. She looked all over for her lover. Then she saw him on the ground, dead. "Oooo," she called, "A man has died." Everyone came to see him. He died because the grass had pierced him.

Hawk

A man went to the house of his girlfriend. He lay down in her hammock and looked over to where she was sweeping the floor. Oh, but she was pretty, and the line where her labia met was very long.

"Come, come here. Get in the hammock," he said.

"Soon, soon. I'm sweeping now. Afterward we will have sex together."

Oh, the man had an erection, a big one, looking for its "food." "Come here, come here!" he said. "Come here quick and let's have sex. I'll make it really delicious for you."

"Soon, soon, very soon. I'm sweeping now. In just a second I'll come to you."

Oh, what an erection he had as he lay in his hammock. But just then his girlfriend's pet eagle saw him from its perch in the rafters of the house. It wanted to eat the man's penis, which was poking through a hole in the hammock.

"Come over here now!" the man said.

"Soon, soon. I just have to throw out the sweepings."

The hawk attacked the man's penis: *tak . . . tak . . . tak*! It ate the penis and flew off covered with blood.

Finally the girl came to her lover: "Wake up, wake up, we can have sex now." But it was too late. He was dead.

"Hawk" and "Thatch" are classified as myths (*aunaki*) by the Mehinaku, but they are really more in the nature of stories than serious myths. None of the characters is named, and the tales are quite brief and relatively spare in detail. Nevertheless, they are frequently told and have a role as "just so" stories that explain, for example, why hawks have red feathers and thatch grass has a bright red tip: "The redness," children are taught, "is men's blood from ancient times." To the villagers, the events are plausible and require no explanation. When we press for a fuller account, we are told that the protagonists came to grief because of their unfulfilled sexual desires: "The women did not have sex with them quickly enough."

The word used to express the men's vulnerable condition is *waritya*, which we have glossed as "frustrating and endangering." By postponing their sexual favors, the women in "Thatch" and "Hawk" made the men intensely amorous. And as in the story of Katsi, the men are punished for their strong sexual desire by injury to their genitals.

The Mehinaku find the tales amusing, and they occasion laughter even though they have been heard many times before. However, the laughter is edged with nervousness. I have even seen some of the men place a protective hand in front of their genitals as the stories reach their inevitable conclusion. The myths are nonetheless funny because they deal with a source of tension in a way that can be defined as nonserious. Gershon Legman, the author of two major compendiums of sexual humor in our own society, puts the matter like this: the joke can "absorb, control, even . . . slough off . . . the great anxiety that both teller and listener feel in connection with certain culturally determined themes" (1968, 13–14).

We have already recounted other Mehinaku myths with overt themes of castration, including the story of the toothed vagina, the tale of the man whose penis was severed by a jealous rival, and more symbolically, the myth of Patijai, whose hair was burned off in the garden. We will have occasion to cite other stories that make use of the same theme. Taken together, these myths are strongly suggestive of castration anxiety. Without additional evidence, however, the myths do not tell us how deep-seated and pervasive castration anxiety is among Mehinaku males. To take measure of this fear, we must move to more serious levels of Mehinaku culture, where we will deal with ideas about sexual dysfunction, disease, and the prohibitions that restrict male and female interaction. Because these concerns are all too real, the theme of emasculation is muted, disguised, or otherwise distorted. The message, however, is clear enough.

SEXUAL DYSFUNCTION: IMPOTENCE

We have already seen that masculine identity is closely associated with primary sexual characteristics, as expressed in the villagers' drawings and their knowledge of sexual anatomy. Because sexual function (erection and orgasm) is also a critical part of Mehinaku masculinity, the men have given considerable thought to a cure for impotence. The men's concern is augmented by the small size and openness of the community, where "kiss and tell" is the rule rather than the exception. A man's sexual failures are common knowledge, and his reputation as a lover rides precariously on the shifting currents of community gossip. Although the villagers have short memories and are perhaps more forgiving of occasional lapses than we Americans, the setting is fertile ground for "performance anxiety" and fear of sexual dysfunction.

Several of the myths reflect concerns regarding impotence. Among the most humorous and whimsical of these is the story "The Armadillo and the Footprint," a tail that intertwines themes of castration anxiety and fears of dysfunction. The protagonist of the story, Armadillo, is a notably witless animal in Mehinaku folklore.

THE ARMADILLO AND THE FOOTPRINT

> Armadillo left his house to wander about through the woods, leaving his penis in a basket suspended from the rafters. As he walked along the path, he saw a beautiful woman: "Hey! Come here, woman. Let's have sex."
>
> "Are you good to have sex with, Armadillo?" she asked.
>
> "I make it really delicious," he replied. Armadillo sat down on the ground in preparation for sex, looked down between his legs, and discovered that his penis wasn't there. "Oh! I forgot my penis," he said. "I'll get it."
>
> Returning to the house, Armadillo was greeted by his wife: "What's up?" she inquired.
>
> "Oh, nothing. I was just getting my bow to shoot a bird."
>
> Retrieving his penis, Armadillo left the house and returned to look for his girlfriend. "Hey, here I am!" he called. "I brought my penis with me this time. Wow, now I have an erection! Won't we have sex, woman?"
>
> Armadillo looked all over for the woman, but she had left. All he could find was her footprint, and he had sex with that. His penis "ate" the earth!

The image of the armadillo looking down to discover "that his penis was not there" strongly suggests fears of impotence. Armadillo has left his "penis" (for which we may well read "erection") at home, and he must return to retrieve it, sneak it past his wife, and go back to his girlfriend. In the fashion of a Mehinaku woman with an impotent lover, however, she has not wasted much time waiting around for him. More than likely, she is back in the village gossiping about him. The impotent male, much like Armadillo, is an oaf and an object of ridicule.

But there may be an even darker meaning to the myth. We have examined other tales of detachable genitals, including that of the wandering vagina, and we have seen that sexual feelings may be attributed to the genitalia themselves rather than to their possessors. The anatomical terms that label the genitalia also imply they have a life of their own, describing them as a kind of face with lips, foreheads, cheeks, and noses. The genitals of a lover may even be referred to as *nupuje*, a term that translates as my "pet" or "plaything." The motif of the detachability of the genitals and the separability of the individual and sexual feelings thereby restate a fear associated with the overt myths of castration: a man can lose his penis. Although we laugh along with the villagers over that fool-of-an-armadillo who absentmindedly leaves his penis in a basket, we will not be misled by the story's charm and whimsy. The jokes, the pratfalls, and the foolish antics of ancient times barely conceal emotional themes that have deep significance to the Mehinaku men.

Evidence for the seriousness of impotence to the men is the substantial effort they have invested in trying to understand its causes and find a cure. Terms for impotence include *maiyala eutɨ*, "the penis is tired"; the humorous *iaipiripyai eutɨ*, "the penis is ashamed"; and the grim *akama eutɨ*, "the penis dies," a term we have already encountered to signify orgasm. Whether "dead," "ashamed," or merely "tired," the penis must be "awakened." Fortunately, there are a number of effective cures known to virtually all men. As Ketepe put it, "My penis gets hard, but if yours does not, if it dies and does not wake up, there is a lot of good medicine." Ketepe then listed several procedures intended to "make the penis angry" (*japujate eutɨ*) by establishing a connection between the penis and an animal or plant that has phallic qualities. Table 4 lists these techniques along with others suggested by the villagers. In most cases, the phallic quality of the animal or plant is transferred to the penis through contagious magic—physical contact between the object and the penis.

Cures such as scarification of the penis may appear worse than the affliction to us, but some villagers think otherwise. The number of different treatments and the lengths men are willing to go to be cured should not, however, be taken as indication of mass impotence. Rather, it is a measure of fairly high concern about sexual dysfunction. Ultimately, this anxiety springs from fear of loss of masculine identity. As was true in the myths of castration, impotence is associated with sexual wishes and sexual activity. But in real life, as opposed to the unlikely hazards of ancient times, what is it about sexuality that arouses anxiety? The Mehinaku notions of sexual pollution and the dangers of intercourse move us toward an answer.

Sexual Relations and Sexual Pollution

Sexual relations are dangerous, according to the men, because women's genitals are frightening (*kowkapapai*). When pressed for an explanation of this fear, the men complain that women's vaginas are

Table 4. Cures for Impotence

Object	Application	Comments
Hejupi (needle fish and a number of related species)	Entire fish rubbed against penis, or fish oil similarly applied.	Long and hard, these fish are clearly phallic. Hejupi is the fish that invented human sexual relations.
Ipyu (turtle)	Neck and head of the turtle are rubbed against the penis.	In dream interpretation, the head and neck of a turtle are symbols of a penis.
Yanapi (bamboo)	Rubbed firmly on penis to the chant: "Yanapi, yanapi, go into the vagina, yanapi."	Yanapi is said to be unusually hard and strong. It's astonishingly rapid growth may also make it seem appropriate as a cure for impotence. Yanapi bamboo is used to make five-foot ceremonial flutes.
Ukalupeihi (sap from latex-producing plant)	White latex sap is rubbed on penis.	Sap is said to look like semen, and it is labeled by the same word, *yaki*. Latex sap produces a drawing sensation on the skin "like sexual feeling." It makes sexual relations more enjoyable and promotes conception. Women are said to be worn out by men who have used it and supposedly avoid them them as lovers.
Ukalu inyante (a plant called "Armadillo's erection")	Rubbed on the penis to the words "Eat your food, eat your food" (meaning, "have sexual relations").	Cure recollects the myth of Armadillo, who "left his penis at home" (was impotent) but subsequently recovered.
Piya (scarifier set with teeth from the dogfish)	The penis is scarified and a number of medicines are rubbed in.	An unpopular technique, said by some to have the opposite of its intended effect. Often used with *ejekeki*.
Ejekeki (breath magic)	An individual skilled in breath magic blows on the penis and chants.	Breath is the essence of life. Just as it can bring the dying embers of a fire to life, so it can also revive the sick, the dying, or the impotent.

"dark" in color, foul in smell, and otherwise "revolting." These aggressive comments mask a deeply seated insecurity; a vagina is disturbing for the men to think about. One villager, expressing his fear of the almost magical nature of the female genitalia, said, "the vagina is a spirit." When I asked him and other men to be more specific about their fears, they all mentioned menstruation. Above all else, women's genitals are dangerous because they are associated with menstrual blood.

UNDERSTANDING MEHINAKU MENSTRUAL TABOOS

In explaining Mehinaku menstrual taboos, we must take account of the fact that their beliefs are similar to those in other societies. William Stephens (1967) finds that all but fourteen of a sample of seventy-one tribal cultures have significant menstrual taboos. They believe that menstrual blood is dangerous and restrict women's sexual and domestic activities as a consequence. Nearly twenty-five percent of the societies in Stephen's sample went so far as to seclude women in special dwellings for the duration of their menstrual period.

A number of complementary theories explain the origins of menstrual taboos, including those of Young and Bacdayan (1967), who examine them as devices used by men to control women, and Montgomery (1974), who links them to men's symbolic participation in the reproductive process. The psychoanalytic theory of menstrual taboos is based on castration fear. In the distortion-prone thinking of the developing child, a bleeding vagina is like a wound and a menstruating woman resembles a mutilated male. Menstruation thereby arouses men's latent castration fear, which is reflected in the anxious practices that hedge and control women's menses. From this perspective, we can easily understand that the stated purpose of menstrual taboos is to protect men; only rarely are women thought to be at risk from menstrual contamination. Stephens (1967) provides substantial support for the psychoanalytic hypothesis by positively correlating the severity of menstrual taboos with antecedents of castration fear, such as punishment for masturbation, the overall severity of sex training, the strictness of the father's demands for obedience, and the importance of physical punishment as a technique of child discipline. Although all of these practices are only indirect indicators of castration anxiety, taken together their correlation with menstrual taboos makes a persuasive and statistically significant case for a Freudian approach.

The Mehinaku data support the psychoanalytic perspective on menstrual taboos. In fact, the villagers appear (as they do in their interpretations of other aspects of their sexual lives) to be amateur Freudians. Specifically, menstruation and the vagina are likened to a wound. Acusa, the Mehinaku chief and one of the oldest men in the village, explains how the first menstruation occurred in ancient times:

THE ORIGIN OF MENSTRUATION

> A long time ago, the Sun (Kama) wanted to have sex with Spirit Woman (Apapainyeineju). Oh, but her labia were long. The Sun took her by the wrist and said, "Let's have sex!" To which she replied, "Ah, not me. My vagina is very dangerous and frightening. Inside there is Stinging Ant, Mein. Inside there are snakes, such as Mekhe and others. Inside is Scorpion, Yucapanu. If it gets you, then you will really be sick. There are many of these between my labia too. I am really dangerous and frightening."
>
> The Sun then went into the forest and returned with fish poison and dredged it into Spirit Woman's vagina, just as he would have done into a pool. Out floated all of the dangerous animals. Out came the snakes, the the spiders, and the scorpions. All of these came out but one, a tiny piranha that remained lodged deep inside her.
>
> "This is good," said the Sun, and he gave tiny piranha to all the women. Each month the piranha bite the women and make them bleed. Sometimes, the women can feel the piranha bite, and tell their husbands, "Soon I am going to have my period."

A full appreciation of this story from the Mehinaku perspective requires a digression concerning the nature of the fauna found in Spirit Woman's vagina. Although the Mehinaku environment is a reasonably safe place to live, the villagers share it with a number of dangerous animals and insects. Mein, the giant tocandira ant (*Paraponera clarata*), measures up to two inches in length and can deliver such venemous stings that its victim may fall unconscious. A second ant sometimes mentioned in the tale, Kaipyalu, is so small that it is easily overlooked by the victim, who may sit down in a canoe only to find long columns of ants swarming over his feet and legs. In a matter of seconds (as I ruefully know from personal experience), he receives dozens of excrutiatingly painful stings, which burn and throb for hours after the ants have been frantically brushed away. Snakes are less frequently encountered than stinging ants, but they include some of the world's most aggressive and venomous, such as the rattler and the coral snake. Finally, the piranha, though seldom as voracious as its reputation suggests, can inflict very serious wounds.

To prevent accidents, the village fishermen routinely club these fish to death before taking them off the hook. Therefore, when stinging ants, poisonous snakes, and dangerous fish are included in a myth, we know that they are a serious matter for the Mehinaku. They are associated with mutilation, injury, pain, and death. Their presence in the tale of Spirit Woman recalls the *vagina dentata* motif of other myths and carries the implied fear of castration to a high level.

Thanks to Sun's application of fish poison, women's genitals are safer today than they were in ancient times. Nonetheless, the story is an anxious fantasy about women's anatomy. Menstrual blood is blood from a wound, and the female genitalia are associated with injury and danger. The capacity for harm persists to this day. A menstruating women is a hazard to all the villagers because her blood contaminates the food they eat.

FOOD AND MENSTRUATION

The moment a woman begins to menstruate, her blood "races" to water, stews, breads, and manioc drinks. Even if the woman has not touched the food or participated in its production, the blood "goes to" and "gets into" the food. "Strong" food produced by the men, such as fish and monkey, resist contamination. "Weak" food made by the women absorb the poison and must be discarded. On occasion, a whole day's supply of processed manioc flour is thrown into the bushes because one of the women of the house began to menstruate in the late afternoon. Menstrually contaminated foods cause chest pains and coughs. The illness is a minor one for women, but men, especially boys in adolescent seclusion, are supposed to have died from consuming such food. A woman who does not keep away from the house when she anticipates her period bears a heavy moral burden if any of her kinsmen fall sick. Some women are suspected of deliberately hiding their periods to harm men they dislike.

Once in a man's body, menstrual blood acts like a *kauki,* a term derived from the word for pain. A kauki is an intrusive, disease-causing object that is believed to be responsible for all illness. Usually it can be removed by a shaman, who then shows the object (typically a miniature arrow said to be made by a witch) to the victim. Menstrual kauki is particularly intractable and difficult to reach.

The mechanical imagery of an intrusive kauki as the source of menstrual contamination can take us only so far in understanding the taboo. When hard pressed for an explanation of what makes it so bad, the men may throw up their hands and conclude as did Ketepe: "I don't know why it is dangerous. The women don't know why it is dangerous. But somehow they make the blood revolting." At heart, the villagers' feelings about menstruation are magical and emotional in nature rather than part of an easily verbalized and consistent theory of disease.

Sexual Relations and Anxiety

In our earlier discussion of oral images of sex, we were introduced to an aggressive and destructive component of sexuality. The verb *aintya,* used for both eating and intercourse, also connotes injury and dismemberment. Although *aintya* is used reciprocally for either sex, it is the men who are more literally "consumed" during intercourse, and it is therefore the men who are most threatened. "Sex," says Kikyala, "is not good." Sex weakens a man, saps his strength and skill as a wrestler, stunts his growth, attracts malevolent spirits and animals, and exposes him to fatal diseases. Even thoughts about a woman can be dangerous. Let us examine each of these claims.

SEXUALITY AND GROWTH

In the course of evening speeches on the plaza, Mehinaku chiefs regularly point out that today's villagers are little more than pale "shadows" of their ancestors, the true Mehinaku. Not only were the ancestors harder working and longer lived, but they were taller and bigger. That size should be the measure of a man should come as no surprise to Americans. Our own prejudice against short men is built into courtship, the chances of finding a good job, and even language, where a rich vocabulary of abuse impugns the short man. Among the Mehinaku, the pattern is even more open and unabashed. No one is ashamed to say that he does not much care for undersized men. No father-in-law wants a runt for a son-in-law, and no man wants an undersized companion. As Ketepe puts it, "None of my friends are *peritsi,* 'twerps.'"

The ideal man is big and tall (*wekepei*). Such a man makes a strong wrestler, a powerful worker, and a prominent chief. He cuts a fine figure when he addresses the people from the center of the plaza, he is attractive to women, and he inspires fear and respect in his relationships with other men. Although body build, work skills, and political astuteness appear to be unrelated traits, a study of Mehinaku height and social position shows that they frequently go together (see Gregor 1977, 1979). On the average, tall men are more likely than short men to sponsor rituals, be wealthy, have many girlfriends, and become village chiefs. It is they, to the near exclusion of the short, who monopolize the positions of power and influence that are intertwined with the concept of masculinity. Height prejudice denies the short man an equal chance at realizing his manhood.

The connection of height to sexuality comes during adolescence, when, as we recall, Mehinaku boys are secluded for two to three years to achieve their full growth as adults. Enforcing the taboos associated with seclusion is the master of the medicines, an invisible being that lives alongside the boy in seclusion. What really stirs up the medicine spirit's wrath is sexual relations. A boy who slips out at night to have sexual relations with girls will grow up ridiculously stunted.

My informants were never able to spell out the precise mechanisms by which sex stunts growth, beyond angering the medicine spirit. Some said sex makes the bones hard and thereby prevents them from growing. Others pointed out that semen moves through the spine and therefore prevents the bones from reaching full size. This belief is related to a conviction that seminal fluid is debilitating. A sudden twinge of pain or inexplicable injury while walking through the woods, for example, may be attributed to semen left on the ground by a copulating couple. But no matter which theory my informants followed, all were in agreement that sex and a good physique do not go together. To reach full manhood, the temptation of female sexuality must be resisted.

WRESTLING AND STRENGTH

Wrestling, above all other expressions of masculinity, is the hallmark of an ideal man. Not surprisingly, sex and wrestling ability are antithetical. In seclusion, where young men assiduously direct their thoughts to wrestling, celibacy ensures the growth of powerful biceps and thighs as well as the development of wrestling skills. The best wrestlers are said to have sexual relations very infrequently and never before intertribal bouts. Traditionally, the responsibility of reminding the villagers about the hazards of excessive sex falls to the chief, who often touches on the subject in the course of his public speeches. I quote from his tape-recorded speech of 23 September 1968, in which he urged the men to avoid Tamalu, one of the more sexually active women in the village. As is characteristic of such speeches, it was delivered at dawn in the sing-song rhetorical style favored by Mehinaku chiefs.

> Soon we will have the ear-piercing festival. All of the Xinguanos will come here. All of you will wrestle. You must wrestle a lot in the coming days to get strong. But do not have sexual relations with Tamalu. Do not take her by the wrist if you want to be a wrestler!

The villagers are unanimous in their conviction that sexual relations weaken a man, but their certainty rests on analogy and magical thinking rather than logic. Kikyala puts the matter like this: "A woman's vagina is forbidden (*kanupa*) to a wrestler. He must avoid it.

It is like a clam, wet and soft. The vagina is not strong. And therefore a man must not come into contact with it or he will be weak too." We have already encountered similar deprecating descriptions of the vagina in which it is compared to soft, mushy objects such as clay and smelly fruit. Ketepe makes use of the same analogy, but from a slightly different perspective: "The vagina is soft, like a clam. It is enormously voluptuous, and you ejaculate quickly. Your penis becomes flaccid and dies (*akama*). And so you will be thrown quickly when you wrestle."

Both of these explanations see a similarity between an act of sexual relations and a wrestling match that we shall pursue further in our discussion of dreams. What is of interest at the moment is that Ketepe and Kikyala find the magical links between sex and wrestling satisfactory as explanations. Where we seek some kind of mechanical efficacy that would translate sex into defeat at wrestling, they are content with metaphor. When we press them for a causal link, the terms of the explanations are subtly shifted. Rather than elaborate on what to them seems self-evident, they provide us with a list of specific cases demonstrating that sex and wrestling ability do not mix. To a large extent, however, the villagers have already prejudged the matter. Let a celibate local champion fall to some well-known sex lover (*itsi nitsei*, literally, "genital lover"), and the men are still able to balance the equation by bringing in the factor of sexuality. In the fall of 1977, Kehe, a boy in seclusion, was thrown by a notoriously inept wrestler from a neighboring tribe. "You have been having sex!" shouted his father. When Kehe insisted that he was celibate, his father still interpreted his unexpected defeat in sexual terms. The winner, he argued, had recently had sex, and his contact with women "rubbed off" on Kehe when they wrestled, guaranteeing his defeat.

So strong is the belief in the debilitating effects of sex that the conviction becomes self-fulfilling. Kikyala, for example, is still a formidable opponent on the few occasions that he wrestles his fellow villagers. Though once a local champion, he now has five children and believes himself to have been weakened by many years of sexual relations. As a result, Kikyala no longer participates in intertribal bouts in which champions win their laurels.

In mythic times, female sexuality was as dangerous to wrestlers as it is today. Let us look at the myth of Kaluwana, one of the great champions of ancient times.

Kaluwana

Kaluwana was in adolescent seclusion. He wanted to be a champion wrestler and concentrated all of his thoughts on wresting. But at night, Kaluwana visited

> his girlfriends and had sex. In the afternoon, he visited them in their houses and lay in their hammocks.
>
> When Kaluwana wrestled, even the poorest wrestlers threw him to the ground. At the intertribal memorial festival (Ata Kaiyumain), the youngest boys easily beat him. Finally an old shaman approached him and said, "Kaluwana, you are weak. Let me look at you." The shaman felt Kaluwana's palm and suddenly removed a bit of fiber from a woman's pubic garment that had lodged beneath the skin. Kaluwana wrestled again and was much stronger, but still he was beaten. Then the shaman sucked at Kaluwana's hand and removed blood-soaked cotton used by women to wipe away menstrual blood. And now Kaluwana was much stronger, but still he was thrown by the other wrestlers. Finally, all the shamans in the village assembled around Kaluwana. They smoked and sucked at his body, removing many, many bits and pieces of pubic garments and menstrual cotton lodged in his shoulders, in his neck, in his chest, in his arms, in his legs, in his entire body. Then, Kaluwana went to an Ata Kaiyumain festival and beat all the great wrestlers from every Xingu village. He was a real wrestling champion.

SEX AND MEN'S WORK

A recurrent theme in the Mehinaku culture of sexuality is that intercourse jeopardizes masculine identity. Full growth, a good stature, wrestling ability, and health all depend on restraint. Even when these are achieved, however, continued success may require sexual abstinence. Men's work roles are especially vulnerable to sexual activity. We have already seen that prior to a group fishing expedition, the villagers refrain from sexual relations since sex reduces the size of the catch. A woman along on a major trip ensures its failure. Only preadolescent boys, who are presumably virgins, can participate in some phases of the work. "Women's genitals," the men explain, "are revolting to the fish." Other work roles besides fishing, such as housebuilding and monkey hunting, are also adversely affected by sex. A man who wants to be successful in his work does well to avoid excessive sexual contact with women.

SEXUALITY AND DISEASE: MAKATSIKI

To stunted growth, defeat in wrestling, and failure in work, we must add two more hazards of sexual relations: disease and death. The historical origin of all illness is sexual in nature. In mythic times, the Sun tweaked a few hairs from his wife's genitals and with these made the first disease-causing objects, or kauki. Although kauki are not usually said to be made of pubic hair today, sexual contact with women under the wrong circumstances remains dangerous.

The most dramatic of the sexually induced diseases is *makatsiki* (literally, "without legs"), a paralytic illness primarily afflicting young men who have sex while in seclusion. The first symptom of makatsiki paralysis is a numbness that begins in the hands and feet and spreads through the rest of the body. Gradually, the victim loses all power to care for himself. He withdraws into a fetal position in his hammock, elbows bent, hands together, knees up. He must be fed by his parents, the food prechewed and forced into his mouth. He is carried outside to urinate or defecate; otherwise he would foul his own hammock. As the disease progresses, the victims's jaws are clamped and his hands are clenched. He loses the ability to speak or understand and gradually slips into a coma. Striking without notice, often fatal, the disease is feared by all young men in seclusion.

According to medical personnel from the Escola de Medicina of São Paulo who have seen cases of makatsiki, the illness has several forms and causes. The most serious variant is caused by the root broths administered to boys in seclusion. Normally these potions are safe enough, but one called *kau*, "pain," contains a cyanide-related neurotoxin. When kau roots are harvested at the height of the dry season, the poison may be at its greatest concentration; broth made at this time can paralyze and kill. Far easier to treat are psychological forms of makatsiki. The Mehinaku, like other tribes of the area, appear to be subject to a host of illinesses of apparently hysterical origin. Many of the curing performances of the shamans take the Xinguanos' suggestibility into account and draw their power from the psychosomatic origins of the illness. The treatment preferred by Brazilian doctors who have handled psychologically induced makatsiki is to take the patient out of the Xingu park. Removed from the pressures that caused the illness and the supernatural explanations that might reinforce it, the patient quickly improves.

THINKING ABOUT WOMEN

The dangerous character of women and sex is not easily explained by the Mehinaku. Only rarely are their fears cast within larger, more rationally organized cultural systems, such as their intrusive-object theory of disease. More frequently, explanation rests on magical-emotional thinking, as in the methods of increasing strength in wrestling. These techniques are nonetheless rooted in physical action: one acquires strength by avoiding sexual relations. On occasion, the Mehinaku culture of sexuality moves to a more rarified plane, asserting that thought alone can influence events.

I first became aware of this possibility on trips with my friends and informants to distant lakes and rivers. Far from the cheery bustle of the village, my companions sometimes became somber. On such occasions, I was often asked if I missed my wife. "Such thoughts," my friends explained, "are dangerous." They are dangerous because thinking about a woman—a wife or a girlfriend—can attract a jaguar or a dangerous snake. A man who wanders through the forest on his own is in even greater danger, for his sexually tinged nostalgia can attract Japujaneju (Angry Woman Spirit). Appearing to him as a beautiful woman, sometimes even as the woman he misses, Japujaneju beckons and leads him deeper and deeper into the forest. What happens then, no one knows. For unlike Odysseus, who chained himself to the mast of his ship, no Mehinaku has ever returned from an encounter with this siren.

Conduct and Culture

The hazards of sexual relations include loss of health and strength, stunted growth, encounters with dangerous spirits, and inability to perform the masculine activities of wrestler or fisherman (see table 5). In examining this list, one may wonder why the men ever risk sexual relations at all, much less participate in the network of extramarital affairs. Sexual activity coexists with sexual fear because the men's anxiety is to a degree compartmentalized. Sex is hazardous in excessive quantities, with the wrong partners, and at prohibited times. However, the cautious man who honors all the taboos has relatively little to fear.

In practice, there are only a few villagers who completely encapsulate the diffuse anxieties associated with female sexuality. The most successful is surely Ketepe. He is enthusiastic about the pleasures of sex and women and maintains more affairs than any other man in the village. Undaunted by fear of contact with genitals, Ketepe engages in a variety of sexual activities, including kissing with tongue contact and manual and oral stimulation of his partner's genitalia. He does this "to make it sensual for the woman," but only when it is dark, since "she would be ashamed during the day." The women do not reciprocate, because "they are too ashamed." Ketepe also admits to having sex with menstruating women, but he prefers to do so while immersed in the stream, "so that the water cleans us." Even Ketepe, however, is not unrestrained in his sexual pleasure. He is careful to have an orgasm only in the midst of genital intercourse. To do otherwise, he explains, would "misuse my semen." Moreover, like other men, his pleasure in intercourse is sufficiently tainted with anxiety that he tries to avoid complete loss of control at the point of orgasm. "In ancient times," Ketepe explains, "men were foolish

Table 5. The Hazards of Sexual Relations

Sex is forbidden or restricted on the following occasions:	Consequence of violating prohibition:
1. During pregnancy	Twins or an oversized child. Parents or near kin bury such children alive.
2. For father, before the end of his child's first year	Child becomes sick. Shaman removes "semen."
3. Before adolescence	Unspecified pains and illnesses. In men, failure to grow to full height.
4. During seclusion	Makatsiki paralysis, stunted growth, poorly developed musculature, physical unattractiveness
5. While child is taking medicines in adolescent seclusion	Smell of parents' sexual fluids combines with food that they prepare for their child. Child may sicken or die.
6. Prior to important wrestling match or fishing expedition	Loss of match, reduced catch
7. During menstruation	Possible illness; a "disgusting" experience.
8. In excess, especially for men, at any stage of life	Weakness, defeat in wrestling, sickness, inability to hunt and fish successfully

when they had orgasms. They shouted and called out. They fell from their hammocks into the fire. Today, men should be like me, tough and contained."

Ketepe keeps his defenses up even though falling in the fire is not at all likely. He knows that the community is contemptuous of men who lose self-control, and he fears that a lapse during an evening's intimacies could become a choice tid-bit for village gossips by the next morning. "You know Maiyaku?" Ketepe asked me. "Well, he shouts when his semen 'arrives.' The women have told me. I don't want to be like Maiyaku. He is a 'trashyard man' and a fool." Ketepe regards Maiyaku as a fool because of his vulnerability to women. Women are so associated with danger that it is not really possible for Ketepe to relax and allow the experience to carry him along. Sex, even for this expert, is admittedly a little bit "frightening."

We should not underestimate the significance of these anxieties in an individual who is the most sexually adventurous and probably the most sexually healthy of the village men. Mature sexual relations require what Ketepe cannot offer: an abandonment of reserve and a willingness to experience a merging with the partner and a temporary loss of self-boundaries. It is unlikely that any of the village men are close to this ideal. Intercourse may be highly desired, but most sexual encounters are somewhat ritualized affairs in which there is a minimum of foreplay and interaction with the partner. Petala, for example, is appalled at the idea of oral sex and never touches the genitals of any of his girlfriends. "The vagina," he maintains, "is disgusting." For Petala, the sexual act is a brief occurrence, invariably in the standard Mehinaku sitting position. In explaining how he manages to have sexual relations without himself or his partner touching his genitals, he says, "The penis finds its own way." With his orgasm, the encounter is over, and he cleans himself off with some leaves. As Petala tells it, he loses little time in conversation or tender partings.

For Petala and many other Mehinaku men, the hazards of sexual relations are real. They evoke images of death, sickness, injury, and failure. Taken together with the castration fears expressed in mythology, they suggest that the men are insecure in their roles and conflicted in their feelings. To confirm this conclusion, however, we will want to examine evidence that bears more directly on individual personality. We find this evidence in dreams and dream interpretation.

EIGHT

Anxious Dreams

Tonight I will not sleep. . . . at night, there are dangerous dreams.
—Yuma, on the eve of an important wrestling match.

Mehinaku Dream Interpretation and Sexual Anxieties

"A TINY SOUL," SAYS KIKYALA, "LIVES WITHIN THE EYE OF EVERY PERSON. At night, the soul (*iyewku*) wanders about, returning before he wakes up. The dream is the wandering of the soul." Kikyala's soul theory of the dream is held by all of the Mehinaku. The soul, they say, is a tiny homunculus that looks exactly like its owner. One may get an occasional glimpse of this soul in the reflection of another's eye, but it remains with the owner until he falls asleep. Then the soul's expeditions and encounters with the souls of others are experienced as dreams. There is, in effect, a nocturnal village peopled by the souls of the sleeping Mehinaku. The events that occur there are real events but separate and apart from the waking world. Knowledge of this dream world is valued by the Mehinaku because it is a portent of the future.

The heart of the villagers' system of dream interpretation is the concept of the symbol, or patalapiri. Literally, patalapiri translates as "picture" or "representation," but the term may be used for more abstract symbols as well. A dream of flying ants, for example, foretells a possible death, since the short-lived flying ant is a symbol both for human life and the rain of tears that falls at the time of a funeral. But the dream symbol goes even further. Just as thoughts of Angry Woman Spirit can conjure her up, so may dream symbols change the future. Admittedly, only very special dreams (*jepuni waja*, literally, "true dreams") have this impact on events; more normally, dreams simply predict things to come. The villagers are uncertain as to how precisely their dream images intertwine with reality, but we see in their beliefs a clear example of the overvaluation of thought described by Freud. Dream symbols and their interpretation are not examples of reality-oriented thought, but projections of wishes and concerns. Let us examine those chapters in the Mehinaku dream book that bear on the question of sexuality. (A full treatment of Mehinaku dream symbolism may be found in Gregor 1981a.)

DREAMS OF GENITALIA AND SYMBOLS OF DANGER

The dangerous, harmful nature of female genitalia comes to the fore in dreams. According to the villagers, female genitals are symbols of wounds. A man unfortunate enough to dream of the genitalia would do well to leave his machete and ax at home in the morning since he risks a serious injury. The villagers' explanation of this omen is that a wound and female genitalia are similar in appearance. The edges of a clean wound come together, it is claimed, like the *labia majora* along the so-called genitals' path (*euti napu*).[1]

In making this equation, we note that the Mehinaku appear to have only slightly misread Freud's *The Interpretation of Dreams.* In the Freudian dream book, a wound is an unconscious symbol for a vagina and the fears of castration associated with physical injury. But for the Mehinaku, the female genitalia are symbols of wounds. The symbols are reversed, yet the interpretations are surprisingly psychoanalytic.[2] The basis of the villagers' insight may lie in the distancing nature of Mehinaku dream theory. Dreams are not so much threatening revelations about self as they are the curious adventures of a separable inner being. The meaning the villagers assign to these adventures need not, therefore, rely heavily on the distortions and censorship of the dream work to make them palatable.

The association of female sexuality with injury and danger continues in dreams in which epitsiri pigment is prominent. Used exclusively by the women, epitsiri is made from the waxy seeds of the annato tree (*Bixa orellana*). This yellow-red dye, which is used commercially in the United States as a food coloring, is employed by the Mehinaku women to adorn their hair and bodies in conventional patterns. Epitsiri pigment is sexually arousing. Men who scarcely notice a girl who is unadorned find themselves drawn to her after she has painted her body and face. But like a dream of female genitalia, a

1. Women are less concerned than men about dreams of female genitalia, but they are anxious about dreams of phalluses. An erect penis is a symbol of a snake, and a woman would do well to keep a wary eye on the path after such a dream lest she be bitten.

2. I am indebted to Waud Kracke for this observation.

dream of epitsiri portends danger and injury. According to the villagers, this pigment is a symbol of menstrual blood. Just like menstrual blood, epitsiri can "get into" the dreamer's skin, making him sickly and emaciated.

THE ANACONDA AND DREAMS OF SEXUAL RELATIONS

Mehinaku men welcome dreams of sexual intercourse with mixed emotions. Especially provocative of anxiety are dreams in which women initiate sexual relations. In waking life, a woman who would directly propose sex is considered the victim of *kuritsi* love magic. Supposedly such women are controlled by a magician known as "the master of kuritsi" (*kuritsi wekehe*), who applies an invisible wax to their bodies. Driven beyond reason by sexual desire, the women become frighteningly insatiable and solicit village men "as if they were men themselves." In truth, it is doubtful that there are any actual practitioners or victims of kuritsi. Love magic and sexually assertive women are male fantasies, albeit ones that are charged with anxiety as well as intense erotic feeling. In dream symbolism, the fantasy is dominated by fear. A woman who takes the initiative in sexual relations is the dream symbol for an attack by an anaconda.

At first, we are surprised by this association, since the anaconda has strong masculine associations. In a woman's dream, for example, the anaconda is a symbol of a phallus. To understand the female associations of the anaconda, we must make a brief detour through natural history of this unusual reptile. The villagers, who are astute practical zoologists, accompany us in their knowledge and observations.

The tropical anaconda (*Eunectes murinus*; Mehinaku, *walama*) is the largest of the American snakes, rivalling the reticulated python as the largest snake in the world. Unlike the other boas, the anaconda is a semiaquatic snake, at home in the swamp and meandering streams around the Mehinaku village. Occasionally surpassing twenty-five feet in length, three feet in girth, and weighing 600 pounds, this monstor is an awesome sight as it glides along the bottom of the riverbed, an undulating telegraph pole only a few feet below one's canoe. More commonly, however, the anaconda lies partly submerged and motionless in the muddy shallows. Only its eyes and nostrils show above the water as it awaits its prey: an alligator, a deer, occasionally a small child. In its devastating assault, we begin to see a basis for the men's anxious fantasies. It strikes without warning, anchoring itself to the victim's body. Casting its entire length over the prey in ever tightening and strangulating coils, the snake begins to squeeze and crush. At last the victim's ribs snap and break and it slowly suffocates to death. When there is no longer any movement or sign of struggle, the anaconda unhinges its lower jaw, clamps its widened maw over its prey, and gradually swallows it whole. Gorged, the snake slithers off to its hole where it lies sated as its gastric juices slowly digest its food. Hunger may not impel it to hunt again for several weeks.

For us, the anaconda is a grotesque curiosity, good for a momentary shiver as we edge past its glassed-in cage in the reptile house of the zoo. For the Mehinaku, walama is a real and frightening part of the environment. Even though the snake seldom attacks humans, we can empathize with the villagers' fear. The symbolic equation of the anaconda's mode of attack and human sexual relations may now be ready for solution.

The image of being eaten and swallowed offers few difficulties; it is in accord with the *vagina dentata* motif in mythology and the anxiety-charged oral imagery of sexual relations. The anaconda's crushing and strangling attack leads us in a different direction to the symbolism of wrestling. In the myths of ancient times, the anaconda was the best of all wrestlers. Today, a champion is likened to the anaconda in his muscular build and the quickness of his holds. He, like the reptile, ties up (*itsitya*) his opponents to defeat them. Traditionally, only champions sport the anaconda design (*walama yana*) body painting on their back and legs. Young men who want to become powerful wrestlers hunt the anaconda in the swamps around the village. Attacking smaller specimens with their bare hands, they haul them into their canoes and club them to death. The fat of the snake is then rendered in a ceramic pot and rubbed into shallow wounds opened by scarifiers. The tail of the animal is dried and becomes an ornament used for ritual dances (see figure 23). Like the unbeatable anaconda of the mythic past, the boy will grow up to be a future champion.

The anaconda is thus a nexus of symbols and associations that lead in one direction to women and sexual relations and in the other to

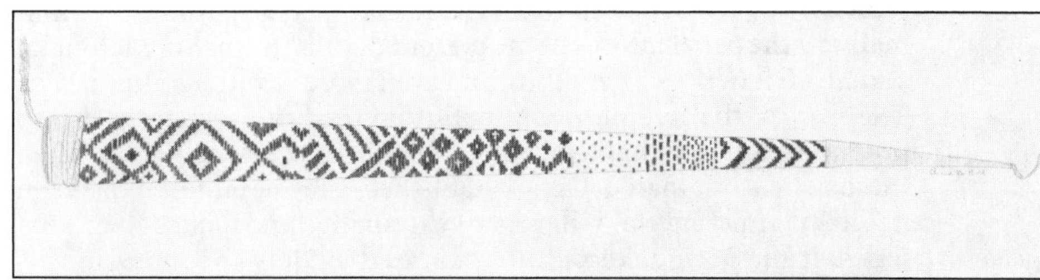

Fig. 23. Anaconda-tail dance ornament (actual size 37″). Young men weave imitation anaconda-tail ornaments from palm fiber. The ornament is worn suspended down the back during many rituals. Drawing by Anne Hill.

men and wrestling. But we have already discovered another link between wrestling and sexuality: a man who has sex before a wrestling match is bound to lose. Our informant Ketepe explained that "the vagina is soft, like a clam. It is enormously voluptuous, and you ejaculate quickly. Your penis becomes flaccid and dies. And so you will be thrown quickly." In response to my questions, Ketepe sees the implied equivalences: "Sex is like wrestling; a defeated wrestler is like a dead penis." An act of sex is dangerous because the man always loses. In the end, he is the losing "wrestler," the one with the "dead" penis.

We now close in on the meaning of the anaconda's assault as an image of sexual relations. The crushing, strangling attack of the snake is likened to both a woman and a winning wrestler. Sex is thereby equated with defeat in wrestling, which is the measure of a man's failure. The symbol of the anaconda condenses the multiple fears of assault, defeat, ingestion, and suffocation that are associated with sex. Walama is thus a powerful image for the villagers and a key link in the chain of associations and symbols that make up the culture of Mehinaku sexuality.

The Mehinaku have many fears associated with women and sexuality. These include castration, impotence, disease, stunted growth, failure, mutilation, and assault. The data suggesting these fears derive from the repertory of dream symbols, from language, from beliefs about diseases and their origins, and from mythology. Our informants have provided additional support for our interpretations with specific assertions about the frightening nature of sexuality. We recall Kikyala's comment, "A woman's genitals are a spirit."

However, we must take care. Cultural materials, and even informant statements, do not always directly reflect the motives and dynamics of individual personalities. Indeed, the links between custom and personality are often difficult to trace. Custom may be a reaction to personality conflicts and may appear in total opposition to the modal personality of the social group. Or custom may be molded primarily by historical and ecological circumstances and only minimally by the personalities of the present day. In the case of Mehinaku sexual anxieties, we face a third and even more vexatious alternative. The myths, the fear of sexual pollution, and the system of dream interpretation may have reflected Mehinaku social character when these beliefs originated. Once established, they became defensive in nature, permitting the villagers to externalize and defuse their anxieties. If the Mehinaku culture of sexual anxiety functions in this manner, it will be a most troublesome obstacle in the path of our efforts to trace the connection between social conduct and character.

Even though sexual concerns may be built into custom, we may find relatively little evidence for such fears on the individual level. Let us examine the dream life of individual Mehinaku to see if we can find reflections of the anxieties that are so abundant in the culture.

Sexual Anxieties in Dreams

DREAM RESEARCH AMONG THE MEHINAKU

The Mehinaku are interested in their dreams and make an active effort to recall them. Unlike Westerners, who arise each morning in a cloud of forgetfulness, the Mehinaku remember their dreams in considerable detail. They are skilled in dream recall because they often narrate their dreams to their housemates upon awakening and because of their habit of getting up several times during the night to stoke the fires. This pattern of interrupted sleep and immediate verbalization is precisely the one recommended by psychologists in our own society to those who wish to remember their dreams (see Casiday 1974).

During two field sessions (summer 1976 and 1977), I took advantage of the villagers' aptitude for dream recall and systematically collected 385 dreams from all but a few of the adults in the village. Reflecting my interest in masculine psychology, 276 of the dreams in my sample were men's. As a field task, dream collecting among the Mehinaku turned out to be a surprisingly easy and productive form of research. Once I had explained my interest in dreams and dream symbolism, the villagers were for the most part helpful participants. Each morning, as I moved from house to house harvesting the previous night's crop of dreams, I would be summoned across the plaza by an enthusiastic collaborator: "Come here Tommy! I have a dream for you." Told without shame or hesitation, the dreams were well worth listening to. Embarrassing or frightening dreams were seen, not as revelations of the narrator's true nature, but rather as the strange conduct of the soul over which no one has control. In narrating dreams, the villagers made it quite clear where the responsibility for dream action lay: "Not me," they assured me while they recounted a particularly bizarre dream, "It was my soul that did these things."

The self-distancing of Mehinaku dreams parallels that of myths. Much as there is a separate and distant world of ancient time upon which the Mehinaku can project concerns and fantasies, there is a dream world that is distanced from individual responsibility. The effect of the separation of self and dream is that there seems to be little conscious dream censorship. The villagers provide the researcher with an opportunity that is normally afforded only the therapist who has reached full rapport with his client: a view of dream life free from deliberate distortion.

CASTRATION ANXIETY AND OTHER SEXUAL CONCERNS

One of the more important themes to emerge from the cultural material we have examined is castration anxiety. Indeed, from a psychoanalytic perspective, many of the other anxieties we have documented derive from this fear. Paradoxically, however, we should not expect to find many overt dreams of castration in our sample. The distancing nature of Mehinaku dream theory notwithstanding, such nightmares are onslaughts to the personality and are likely to be unconsciously censored or distorted. In my sample of 276 men's dreams, I have only two unambiguous examples of castration dreams, one of which was told to me by a young man in his mid twenties.

> I—my soul, in my dream, really—went to the post and saw an attractive Brazilian girl. She said, "Come and let's have sex." I wanted her. She took off her clothes and we had sex in the water. I wanted to do it on the land. I asked her if she had a sore (veneral disease). I was frightened of her vagina. She said, "No, this is the first time I have had sex. I have never had sex with a Brazilian before." She lay down, but I did not go inside her because I was afraid of her vagina. I saw her vagina and her pubic hair, and I was frightened. I looked at my penis. It had a little blood on it. I pulled my penis off in my hand and washed it off in the water. When it was clean—all the blood was off—I put it back on. I did it to prevent the disease from getting me.

The detachability of the genitals, the association of sexual relations with disease, and the frightening character of women's genitals that we saw in Mehinaku myths and cultural beliefs are all repeated in this narrative. In discussing the dream, our informant was profoundly disturbed: "This was a bad dream," he admits.

Dreams of castration will more typically be distorted by the anxiety they generate so that their content is disguised. Fears of harm to the genitals, for example, may be deflected onto another part of the body in dreams of injury, dismemberment, or of being bitten, stabbed, or clawed. Fear of loss of the genitalia or their function may be similarly transformed into dreams about loss of an object or animal closely associated with the dreamer or into inability to use an object that is phallic in nature, such as a gun or a bow and arrow.

Screening a large sample of American dreams for instances of latent castration anxiety, the psychologists Calvin Hall and Robert Van de

Castle (1966) have found that they appear in twenty percent of men's dreams. As would be predicted from the authors' psychoanalytic perspective, far fewer womens' dreams (nine percent) incorporate these motifs. These results are of special interest to us because they make it possible to compare Mehinaku dream life along the dimension of castration anxiety with Americans'. Following Hall and Van de Castle's methods (1966), I have calculated comparable figures for the Mehinaku dreams: thirty-five percent of men's dreams and thirteen percent of women's dreams reveal latent castration fear. The Mehinaku men apparently exhibit seventy-five percent more latent castration anxiety in their dreams than do the Americans in Hall's sample.[3]

Together with the cultural evidence, these psychological data are a compelling argument for the reality of fairly intense castration anxiety among Mehinaku men. The lingering doubt remaining about this diagnosis concerns the connection between latent castration fear and the manifest dreams of injury, dismemberment, and loss. After all, could not these dreams simply reflect the anxieties they appear to describe? The answer to this question hinges on the outcome of a much larger debate concerning the validity of dynamic psychology, which is beyond the scope of this case study. Nonetheless, I must point out that the manifest concerns expressed in the men's anxious dreams are for the most part unrealistic. Our description of dangerous fauna notwithstanding, the Mehinaku environment is reasonably free from physical aggression. Certainly it seems no more exposed than our lives amid frequent personal crime, carnage on the highways, vicarious violence in the media, and the omnipresent threat of atomic destruction. The stabbings, dismemberments, and violent encounters measured by the Mehinaku index of castration anxiety must therefore be explained by deeper psychological processes than fear of a dangerous environment. Admittedly, our interpretation of these processes rests on the foundation of psychoanalytic theory, but we can find additional evidence for our case by narrowing our focus to the anxiety-charged dreams in the sample that deal openly with sex.

Overt dreams of sex occurred in thirty-five (fifteen percent) of the men's dreams, a figure that is virtually identical to Hall and Van de Castle's study of American men (1966, 181). Half of the Mehinaku's sexual dreams were perceived by the dreamers as distressing. Among these anxious dreams were virtually all of those whose content was

3. We post one note of caution in comparing Mehinaku and American norms. Hall and Van de Castle's sample consisted of 500 men attending college. Ours included adult men of all ages. From a theoretical perspective, however, this difference should minimize the contrast of Mehinaku and American data since sexual insecurities tend to peak in early years and decline with maturity (Lynn 1966,469).

highly bizarre by our standards or those of the Mehinaku. Here we find dreams in which the narrator has sexual relations with a woman whose rotting flesh bursts open during intercourse, in which he is called by a girl to have sex but has no eyes to see her, or in which he removes his own penis, as in the dream narration above. The intensely surreal quality of many sexual dreams is unmatched by any other category of dreams in my study, suggesting that sexuality is associated with deeply seated conflicts and fears. When we examine the content of these disturbing sexual dreams, we are reminded of the anxious themes that emerged in the myths, disease theories, and attitudes that make up the Mehinaku culture of sexuality.

INJURY

According to the Mehinaku dream book, dreams of sex portend maiming, assault, and defeat. The narratives of sexual dreams often include these themes as part of the dream itself. Usually the motivation for assault within the dream is sexual jealousy. Hence the dreamers are struck by clubs and machetes of jealous husbands or, on occasion, by their own betrayed wives. The narrators of these dreams often found their dream experience intensely frightening, reporting that they called out in fear and pain until they were awakened by their kin. Many of the dreams of injury bear a striking resemblance to Mehinaku myths in which men are punished by dismemberment, death, blindness or castration for their sexual adventures. From a psychoanalytic point of view, the myths and the dreams reflect fantasies of the Oedipal stage of development in which the child fears harm at the hands of his father in jealous retaliation for sexual wishes about the mother. The convergence of both myth and dream around this motif is evidence that the culture of sexual anxieties is expressing the actual fears of individuals.

THE SEXUALLY AGGRESSIVE WOMAN

Dreams of sexually aggressive women, as suggested by the symbolism of the anaconda, are anxious experiences for the Mehinaku. In every such dream in my sample, the woman who initiated sex was too old, too unattractive, or otherwise unwanted by the dreamer. When she was rejected, she assaulted the dreamer, striking him with her fists and pulling his hair. In one instance, the sexual attack reminds us of the anaconda: the narrator reports he was crushed by the weight of a woman who lay on top of him. In waking life, this position is all but unknown, suggesting a full role-reversal in the dreamer's sexual fantasy.

It is important to add that women are also overtly threatening in nonsexual dreams. In 78 of the 276 dreams in our sample, the dreamer was the victim of physical violence. A woman was the aggressor in 15 (nineteen percent) of these dreams. In daily life, however, women almost never injure men. Moreover, we find that women figure as aggressors in only three percent of American men's dreams of being attacked. (Hall and Van de Castle 1966,174). This contrast is in accord with the previous data on latent castration anxiety and the generally threatening nature of women to the Mehinaku men.

THE FRIGHTENING NATURE OF FEMALE GENITALIA

Our narrators' accounts often mention that seeing women's genitals in a dream is frightening (*kowkapapai*). In a few profoundly disturbing dreams, the sight of the genitalia is the only anxiety-arousing stimulus recalled by the narrator. One dream links the theme of impotence to fear of genitalia: "I tried to have sex but saw her genitals. And therefore my penis 'died.'" In narrating these experiences, most of the men mentioned that their dreams were omens of an ax wound or machete cut. This symbolic association brings us full circle to the maiming, injurious character of female genitalia.

The content of men's dreams replicates the culture of sexuality in its message about the dangers of sex. Fear of assault, impotence, and being maimed and crushed are closely linked to sexual wishes and fantasies. Were it not for the highly threatening nature of the castration theme, it too would probably be a frequent part of the manifest dream. Insofar as our sample of dreams measures a modal character, Mehinaku culture and personality express the same masculine insecurity. In the following chapters, we shall try to explain the origins of this insecurity and at the same time frame our data within the structure of modern personality theory.

NINE

Tapir Woman: Socialization and Personality Theory

> Make children and they will help you later. They will get fish for you when they grow up and you are old.
>
> —The chief, in a public speech.

MEHINAKU MEN VALUE THE AFFECTION OF THEIR WIVES, THE CONTRIBUTION of woman within the division of labor, and the pleasures of sexual relations. But at the same time, women arouse fears that permeate virtually every level of masculine culture. Religion, mythology, codes of hygiene, dream life, and theories of disease and physical development are all infused with anxieties and taboos that betray male insecurity. Our purpose in this chapter is to describe the life experiences that lead to this ambivalence and the cultural institutions that express it. We begin by examining our data within the context of the psychology of gender development.

The Origin of Gender Differences

The critical period in the formation of gender is when a child is between eighteen and thirty-six months of age. Prior to eighteen months, as the unplanned experiments produced by medical malpractice and hormonal abnormalities have taught us, gender socialization is reversible. Children who are surgically assigned a sex before this age can be raised in their altered identity relatively easily (Money and Erhardt 1972, 188ff.). After three years, however, normal children have crossed the sexual Rubicon and are committed to their identity as male or female.

What has happened in the year and a half between eighteen months and three years that accounts for the formation of gender identity? Despite the narrowly bracketed span of years in which gender differences emerge, and despite heavy investment in research, we still have no sure answers. Instead, we have a set of partly overlapping developmental models, all of which have some support in laboratory and field data. These models include the Freudian, which is articulated by Parsons and Bales in a way that recognizes the importance of social influences (1955); the social learning theories of Bandura (Bandura and Walters 1963) and Mischel (1966); and the cognitive development theories of Kohlberg (1969) and his followers. What emerges from these models of gender development are mechanisms by which socially androgynous infants come to think of themselves as boys or girls. These include emotional attachment to the parents, imitative behavior, rational and self-reflective thought about gender, and ultimately, self-identification with the sex-appropriate parent.

Despite the diversity of models and mechanisms, recent work in two widely different traditions in psychology has converged to produce a view of masculine gender development that is of great interest to our understanding of the Mehinaku data. The first perspective is that of Robert Lynn (1966), a psychologist whose major orientation to gender development is in the areas of cognition and social learning. Lynn's theory is structured in terms of thirteen developmental principles, all of which reflect a universal fact of growing up: In every society, the primary caretakers of infants and small children are women. For girls, the path toward gender identity is therefore smooth and unbroken. They imitate, feel close to, and appropriately, come to identify with their mothers. For boys, however, the road to manhood is circuitous and strewn with obstacles. They, like their sisters, are initially closer to and identify with their mothers. Hence, as they grow up, both they and their sisters will resemble their mothers more than their fathers in basic values, speech, and anxieties (Lynn 1966,467ff.).

A boy's association with his mother establishes an incipiently feminine identification that he must overcome. The task is difficult, however, for "being a man" in most societies is a highly diffuse role that is not clearly spelled out. In practice, the role is negatively defined by sanctions that state the limits of acceptable behavior ("sissy stuff"). Little boys must stumble about in search of masculinity relatively unaided by a close male socializer and guided largely by the reprimands of their parents and the taunts of their peers when they err. Thus, Ruth Hartley's eight-year-old informants in her now classic study (1959) of male socialization pressures show considerable uncertainty about what is expected of boys, other than such thoughts as "not to be softies" and "to make a lot of noise."

The relative absence of a close male socializer and the haziness of male stereotypes produce anxiety about masculinity and errors in role taking that exceed similar problems for women. Homosexuals are primarily men (by a ratio of approximately four to one in the United States), male transvestites and transexuals vastly outnumber their female counterparts, and fetishistic preoccupation with women's garments is almost exclusively a male deviation (Greenson 1968, 370–71; Stoller 1974). Anxiety about being male and its correlate, hostility toward women, also seem characteristic of men in Western society. Men are concerned about feminine characteristics in other men and in their own offspring and are intensely distressed by homosexuality (Maccoby and Jacklin 1974, 328; Lehne 1976). Women, on the other hand, are far less threatened by homosexuality and show considerably more flexibility about gender "appropriate" activities.

Ethnographic data is less conclusive than the sexual statistics from our own society, but here too sexual deviations and cross-sex behavior such as the couvade are far more characteristic of men than of women (Munroe and Munroe 1975,129). Men's errors in role taking and their antagonism and fear of women suggest an underlying insecurity and a latent feminine identification. Because of the sanctions that enforce conformity to the masculine stereotype, however, the insecurity is seldom directly expressed, and the feminine component of the masculine self remains hidden and frustrated.

Lynn's emphasis on the impact of the mother on masculine development finds unexpected support in recent psychoanalytic research. We would not have anticipated confirmation from this quarter, since classical Freudian theory has a very different model of masculine growth. According to Freud, masculinity has its roots in the boy's sexual desire for the mother, which eventually brings the boy into real or fantasized conflict with the father. His jealousy and resentment of the more powerful father are translated into an unbearable anxiety about castration. In a successful resolution of this Oedipal stage of development, fear forces the boy to suppress his forbidden sexual desires for the mother and to identify with his father and the male role.

Since Freud, however, psychoanalysis has partly shifted the direction of inquiry from the ambivalent father-son interaction to the relationship of mother and child. During the first months of infancy, the child perceives the mother and his environment as an appendage of himself: "The boundaries between ego and external reality develop out of an original state where, psychologically, there are no boundaries and therefore there is no distinction between the two" (Loewald 1951, 14). Lacking control over the presence of the mother, however, the infant faces issues of "individuation and separation" through which he begins to discover the limits of his body and the frontiers of the external world (Mahler, Pine, and Bergman 1975). At nine months, he is well along in this process. Like many babies of his age, he may take a small bit of food and place it in his mother's mouth. She fondly interprets this "gift" as her child's first altruistic gesture, but it may actually be an experiment that tests the limits of self: will baby taste the food when mother chews it?

All minimally normal children learn the lesson of these experiments fairly quickly.[1] A little boy, however, must go farther than his sister in the process of self-differentiation. He must discover not only that he is separate from his mother but fundamentally different from her as well. The task is not an easy one, since the early months of basking in maternal intimacy and physical gratification have established an incipiently feminine identity. To become masculine, the child must "disidentify" from the mother. He must "renounce the pleasure and security-giving closeness that identification with the mothering person affords, and he must form an identification with the less accessible father" (Greenson 1968, 373).

Disidentification with the mother is now widely accepted in psychoanalysis as part of a developmental path that leads to mature gender identity (see Tyson 1982 for a recent statement). One of the best lines of evidence for the importance of this process is the price paid by those who cannot make the transition. Under normal circumstances, the mother facilitates her son's growth by rewarding the boy's efforts at masculinity and admiring the father who serves as his role model. When, however, the relationship with the mother is exceptionally intimate and she smothers her son's sense of differentness, his own identity may merge with hers. According to Robert J. Stoller (1974), when this pattern is reinforced by a weak or absent father and a number of other serious (and uncommon) pathological factors, the boy will grow up with an inner conviction that he is really a woman.

Stoller, who has worked extensively with transexuals, labels the merging with the mother "maternal symbiosis." Only overwhelmingly intimate mothering ("lush" is the term preferred by Stoller) lays

1. But fascination with the body's boundaries persists into adulthood. In a perceptive essay (1964), Edmund Leach points out that magic and ritual make heavy use of symbols that are associated with the "edge" of the self and the environment. Thus hair clippings, nail pairings, urine, feces, tears, and blood have more than ordinary significance for ceremony and witchcraft.

the groundwork for transexualism, but separation versus symbiosis is a serious issue for all boys. The mother is at once a source of nurturance, security, and physical pleasure, but she must be left behind if development is to move forward. Maternal symbiosis, the merging with the mother and the loss of male self-identity, is a frightening temptation against which the boy struggles in the course of normal growth. But even in adulthood, the fear of symbiosis can manifest itself in character traits and phobias that are symbolic of defeat in the battle of masculine self-differentiation. These may include the fear of taking the initiative, the fear of competition, and the fear of one's own aggression, as well as more specifically focused anxieties that incorporate elements of being confined and crushed (claustrophobia).

The quintessential expression of loss of male identity, however, is castration fear. Castration not only is emasculation, but it is also symbolic of the loss of difference between the child and his mother and total defeat in the struggle for self-differentiation. "Above all," writes Robert Murphy, castration anxiety "bespeaks the frailty of the masculine sense of power and the uncertainty of male identity. The masculinity project, a treacherous venture, is fraught with the apprehension that one will lose his autonomy, slip back into passivity, and be swallowed up in the ambivalent fantasies that spring from mother love" (1979,50). In normal development, expedited by a rewarding relationship with the father, the boy largely overcomes symbiosis anxiety, differentiates himself from his mother and the world of women, and comes to think of himself as a man. In many cases, however, the path back to maternal symbiosis remains partly open, and the adult must struggle against an underlying feminine orientation. The signs of incomplete identification with the male role are the same as those identified by Lynn: transvestism and homosexuality, fear of women, or an exaggerated pattern of compensatory masculinity.

The covergence of the cognitive-developmental and psychoanalytic models of masculine psychology provides us with a new perspective on the Mehinaku data. The castration anxiety evident in myths and the crushing, smothering anaconda in dream symbols begin to look like pieces of a puzzle that will eventually fit neatly. Before assembling each element of the jigsaw, however, we must return to the villagers to follow the course of socialization that produces Mehinaku men. Guided by our formulations of gender development, our major focus is on the early years of childhood, when boys must discover that they are different from their mothers, that they are in fact men.

Mehinaku Mothers and Sons

Among the Mehinaku, as among Western peoples, the first three years of life are critical in shaping gender identity. Our account, however, begins prior to birth, since conception and pregnancy link offspring to parents, frame the villagers' beliefs about the origins of sex differences, and set the stage for gender development.

CONCEPTION, PREGNANCY, BIRTH

The Mehinaku theory of conception is male centered. Children are accumulations of semen and may even be referred to by their fathers as "my former semen" (*nuyakiyein*). While it is believed that the men's semen has its origin in female-produced foods, Mehinaku "ethnoembryology" denies an active maternal role in procreation.[2] A few of the women stress the key role of Grandmother Spirit (Atsikuma) in determining the child's sex, but most others look to the father's thoughts and dreams. His preference for an infant daughter during the gestation of a son, for example, can produce a transvestite male, like so called Slightly a Woman."

Whatever the sex of the baby, most women greet pregnancy with ambivalent feelings. Pregnancy is uncomfortable, birth is dangerous and painful, and children are burdensome. Yet any woman who is barren is intensely ashamed of her status and would welcome a child as a symbol of her maturity and fulfillment as a woman. Indeed, the purpose of sexual relations is to create children. "Worthless intercourse" is sex that does not lead to conception.

From a woman's perspective, there are even stronger practical reasons for having children, especially girls. From age seven, little girls are an economic asset, helping to produce manioc flour, fetching water, weaving hammocks, and taking care of younger siblings. In old age, sons and daughters assure their parents' economic security and provide them with a circle of kin who will support their interests within the community. The chief, in an evening speech in June of 1972, offered some public advice to one of his kinsmen that underscores some of the practical advantages of children:

> My son, Kupate, make more children. Like a copulating frog, thrust your semen deep inside. Look at yourself all alone with no kinsmen. Make children and they will help you later. They will get fish for you when they grow up and you are old.

Children are valued for their energy, charm, and promise for the future as well as for self-interested reasons. Nonetheless, they are in

2. I derive this useful term from Robert L. Carneiro's "The Concept of Multiple Paternity among the Kuikuru: A Step toward the New Study of Ethnoembryology."

their early years very burdensome, and many women of the village, especially those who already had several children, were not happy about the prospect of yet another pregnancy. These women, a few of whom had undergone dangerous self-induced abortions, often questioned my wife and me about the white man's methods of birth control.

"Only men create new life," says the villagers' official theory of conception, but the woman's physical connection to her child is difficult to deny. It is visible for all to see during pregnancy; the father's link to the child is a matter of conjecture. Indeed, given the theory of multiple paternity, the identity of a particular father is highly problematic. When at last the baby is born, all men, fathers or otherwise, are excluded from the mysteries of parturition. The mother, surrounded by her closest female kin, lies in her hammock while they assist in the birth and provide emotional support. Only in extremely difficult births when the services of a shaman are required do the women admit a man to the proceedings. And even then, his assistance is limited to singing and chanting rather than direct treatment of the mother; that is left to the women. For their part, the men do not resent the exclusion. They regard birth, and especially the postpartum blood that accompanies it, as unsavory and even defiling: "I'm not going to go over there" was Kikyala's somewhat disgusted reply to my suggestion that he visit his sister's newly born son. Birth is a woman's secret, but unlike the more tantalizing mysteries of the men's sacred flutes, there are few who wish to penetrate it.

EARLY YEARS: PERIODS OF INTIMACY AND SEPARATION

A newborn child is a *howka,* an "infant," and for the first year of his life being a howka is a total identity. Only at the end of his first year, when he has just begun to walk, does he receive a "real" name, one that identifies him with his family. Prior to that time, he is called by affectionately descriptive nicknames, such as "Fat Bellied One" or "Laughter."

During the first year of life, the child is almost exclusively associated with his mother. It is she who nurses him, cleans him when he soils, and sleeps with him in her hammock. It is the mother, say the villagers, not the father, who is charged with the child's general welfare. She both "raises" (*ipyeitsa*) and "takes care of" (*akajata*) her infant. When questioned about the reasons for the mother's primary responsibility, the men point out that they cannot supply food for the baby. He drinks only his mother's milk, which is produced in the breast from the same feminine foods that manufacture semen. The men are under special obligation to supply their wives with fish and monkey meat during this period of infancy, but this "masculine food" does not nourish their offspring.

At the end of a year, the child receives his first haircut and his first set of "real" names—those of his grandparents when they were his age. Gradually he becomes a public figure, seeing his village world from his mother's hip. She carries him everywhere; to the gardens, to work, to dance on the plaza when she participates in a ritual, and to travel along forest trails when she visits other tribes with her husband. It is a tribute to the dexterity of Mehinaku mothers to watch a woman returning from the bathing area with a large ceramic cauldron of water balanced on her head, a bucket of water in her hand, and her baby riding on her hip.

The intimate association of mother and child continues during the second year of life. As in the first year, the toddler is never far from his mother. At the first sign of discomfort or tears, he is offered the breast. At night, he and his mother sleep together in the same hammock. Lying unclothed and closely embraced, they rock gently back and forth. She quietly sings a lullaby as he slowly drifts off to sleep. Fires on each side of the hammock keep them warm; the house is quiet and dark. Later in the night, he may awaken, nurse briefly, and doze off to sleep once more. From his perspective, the world is a safe

Fig. 24. Kuya-Kuya bathes her son. Kuya-Kuya has gone down to the river to get water for processing manioc. After bathing her eighteen-month-old toddler, she will return with a bucket of water on her head and her son on her hip.

Fig. 25. Sisters. Once little girls reach the age "when they no longer gurgle, and can walk and talk a little," they begin to learn a fundamental rule of Mehinaku gender. Men and women each have their place. A woman's place is in and around the houses and away from the men's house and the center of the village. Here two sisters, the older assigned as the babysitter, sit in the back yard of their house. The older child has already begun to assume some of the responsibilities of woman and works several hours each day making manioc flour as well as taking care of her siblings.

maternal place that envelopes him in the warmth of his mother's body, the firm support of the hammock, and the secure presence of kinsmen sleeping nearby.

The third year of life begins a period of maternal separation that will have a powerful impact on the child's personality. The groundwork for this separation has already been laid during the second year, when the mother occasionally assigns the child to the care of an older sister. It is a common and charming sight to see a seven-year-old girl leaning far over to the side to balance her stocky two-year-old brother on her hip. The child, however, is never too far from his mother. Whether carried about by his siblings, or conducting his own toddling explorations of his environment, he is almost always a willing participant in these adventures away from home. Much more painful are the separations occasioned by a new pregnancy and the arrival of a younger sibling, an event that occurs in the first child's second or third year.[3] Even when handled with gentleness, the separation will be a struggle. The most intense battles will be fought in the two most desired and gratifying areas of mother-child contact: sleeping arrangements and nursing.

Shortly before a sibling is born, the mother weaves her child's first hammock. Suspending it near her own, she allows the child to play in it. At night, however, she takes him to her hammock and rocks and nurses him to sleep as usual. As soon as he is sound asleep, she gently moves him to his own hammock. Later in the evening, when he discovers that he is alone and bursts into tears, she picks him up and cradles him in her arms. But as soon as he falls asleep, he is once more returned to his own hammock. Before morning, his mother may have repeated this procedure several times. With near endless patience, she will continue to do so until parturition, when the older sibling is finally and permanently displaced from his mother's hammock.

Weaning is handled gradually. Once a child is in his third year, he is eating the same foods as his parents. Nonetheless, he is not weaned and often returns to his mother's lap to nurse. With the arrival of a new sibling, this relationship is all but severed. Many displaced children, however, will not accept the inevitable and stage angry tantrums at their mothers' rejection. The mothers of these children resort to a variety of rough methods to wean their offspring, including smearing the nipple with an infusion made form hot peppers. But this weaning technique is regarded unfavorably, and only a few make use of it. Most mothers simply put up with their children's anger and give them the breast when they can no longer bear their cries. The result is that there is no clean break in weaning. Children continue to nurse sporadically into their fifth year, and on occasion I have even seen an older child playfully take his mother's breast as she leans over to pick something up. By this time, the child is aware that nursing is babyish, and the matter is something of a joke. Nonetheless, this intimate contact between mother and child presists far beyond the norm in many other small-scale societies, where the arrival of a new sibling marks the definitive end of nursing.

The displacement from the center of the mother's affection and intimacies is an extraordinarily painful experience for many children, and they react with tantrums and tears. By age three, the issue goes well beyond nursing and sleeping with the mother. Now the battleground has enlarged to include experiences that are symbolic of separation and rejection. Let a mother decide to leave her three-year-

3. This ample spacing of children is a consequence of a year-long postpartum taboo on sexual relations and of extended nursing, a practice that significantly reduces fertility.

old son at home while she goes to the river, and she must brave a storm of protest. The boy shouts, cries, and clutches at her legs as she tries to leave. The same child, to his parents' irritation, cannot be pried away from the house when his mother is home no matter what the inducements or threats. His place is outdoors with his friends and siblings, but the "little house stayer," as his parents jeeringly describe him, prefers to remain at home.

Parents differ in the ways they react to their childrens' clutching and clinging. Some, by our standards, are heroically accepting, willing to acquiesce to ever-escalating demands. On a casual stroll through the village, we can easily identify such parents. They are the ones who gamely hoist their pudgy three-year-olds onto their shoulders or hips for a walk down to the stream. It is they who select the oiliest and most desirable fish, the beefiest cut of monkey meat, and the largest share of honey as a sop for their children's tears. But all of their pacifiers are stop-gap measures that do not meet the child's deeper needs. His demands spiral ever upward, his tears flow more copiously, and the struggle enlarges to include new issues. At last a limit is reached. Enough is enough, and there comes a time when even the most patient of parents resort to punishment. Let us listen in as Maiyako disciplines her cranky three-year-old son, Kana, who has been hanging about the house all evening. She begins with name calling, the bottom rung on the ladder of punishments.

"Outside, go outside. That is your place. Are you a little girl, is that why you hang about the house all day? A little girl, a little girl, that's what you are!" Kana responds to this stinging taunt with more tears and whines, and his mother escalates to threats: "Get out or the medicine spirit will get you. If you don't get out, I will hit you. Get out now or I will scrape you with a jagged-edged scarifier!" Kana leaves the house, whimpering and crying, but soon returns crying more than ever. It is dark now, the shamans have returned to their houses from the smokers' circle, the village is quiet. Kana is still in tears, but now the issue has been raised to a level that concerns the house as a whole. No one can sleep. In fury, Kana's mother inflicts what for the three-year-old is the ultimate punishment. Slapping him heavily on the back, she grabs him by the arm, drags him to the door, and tosses him bodily out of the house: "Yukweikwityuma Spirit will get you in the dark," she says as she ties the door shut. Fifteen minutes later, after Kana's screams and tears of terror and rage have died down to a tolerable whimper, he is allowed back in the house.

The punishment is extreme because the house is a nurturant feminine area. Within the house, women work, socialize, give birth, and care for their children. Within the house are all the accoutrements of maternal love: hammocks, hearths, cookpots, and warm fires. A woman who expels her child from the house severs him from his base of security and recreates the anxieties of abandonment occasioned by loss of intimacy with the mother.[4] Like parents everywhere, Mehinaku mothers and fathers have an intuitive sense of what will be the greatest deprivation for their children. But as is ironically also true of parents everywhere, the Mehinaku cannot escape the anxieties of their own childhood. For them, the most dangerous spirits are the ones that carry the souls of their victims far from home to distant and unknown places. For them, the most disturbing myths are those that draw their power from the same fear of maternal abandonment that parents inflict on their own children. The terrors of childhood live on within the fantasies of adult culture.

SIBLING RIVALRY

A baby is a wedge that forces his older sibling out of the center of the family. Mehinaku children are quick to grasp the implications of a new infant and react to their diminished status with tears and anger. Parents, for the most part, cope as best they can with little understanding of what their children are experiencing. If a child cries too much, he is punished, scarified, or administered a magical cure for tears, which in one instance consists of forcing his nose into the fumes of a burning mouse. It is no accident that one of the age-coded names for children in this period of life is "Tears."

Sibling rivalry among the Mehinaku is inhibited and probably rechanneled by parents, who severely punish open hostility among their children. Nonetheless, we can find traces of it in culture and behavior. Kinship terms of address, for example, reflect age differences between siblings. Older siblings always command more respect and a greater share of family resources. Normally, only the oldest son of a chief will be inaugurated as a chief, though all sons could claim the right to the office by virtue of descent. The justification for this practice is that younger sons are less serious and deserving. As one older man put it in explaining why he had been bypassed as chief, "I was the worthless younger brother." Mehinaku kinship thereby provides an older sibling with a justification for devaluing his younger brothers.

A second line of evidence for sibling rivalry is more speculative. From time to time, children playing near the village capture a small animal, such as an armadillo or an agouti (a large rodent). Their

4. In the context of one ritual, that of the anteater (see Gender Wars essay following page 117), the doorway to a house is a conscious symbol of a vagina. A Freudian-oriented psychologist might speculate that the child's violent expulsion from the house awakens memories of deprivation experiences that go back to his own birth.

shouts quickly attract a pack of youngsters armed with sticks, clods of earth, and toy bows and arrows. The hapless animal races from one side of the village to the other, hemmed in by shrieking children. At last it is stunned by a stick or a potsherd, and the children gradually finish the job with clubs and arrows. I have watched with considerable distress as a small rodent was tormented in this fashion for half an hour before its lifeless body was tossed into the bushes. I interpret this treatment of animals as displaced sibling aggression.[5] The children who participate most gleefully are those youngsters who are in the throes of adjusting to their secondary role in the family. Older children and parents look on in an amused and patronizing fashion. The identity of the victims also persuades me that we are witnessing the retaliatory anger of recently displaced siblings. For the most part, the victims are the kinds of animals that most closely resemble human babies in their appearance, movements, and agonized groans and shrieks. Large rodents and other small mammals do very well in this role. The armadillo, whose swaying, stumbling run resembles that of a toddler, seems to make the ideal victim. Snakes, birds, and lizards are another matter. They are fun for target practice but are seldom tortured by the village children.

The content of dreams provides us with a final line of evidence for sibling aggression. I have no examples of dreamed hostility between siblings, perhaps because there are powerful sanctions against such violent behavior. Brothers are expected to maintain a respectful relationship in which they refrain from sexual joking and treat each other's wives "as their own sisters." There are, however, frequent dreams of witnessed hostility in which the dreamer's sibling is the victim of assault from another quarter. Among my sample of dreams are those in which brothers and sisters come to violent ends at the hands of Brazilians, wild Indians, jaguars, and other dangerous animals. In some instances the dreamer heroically tries to intervene. In other cases, he remains a passive observer. A reasonable interpretation of such dreams is that they are expressive of the dreamer's own forbidden aggression. The projection of this hostility onto a third party satisfies the hateful wish, but leaves the dreamer guiltless.

THE FATHER AND THE PEER GROUP AS ROLE MODELS AND CARETAKERS

By age five, a Mehinaku boy has been substantially separated from maternal intimacy. The separation is painful and he continues to struggle, but there is no turning back. In theory, the period of intense

5. In this interpretation, I follow Yolanda and Robert Murphy, who write of a similar pattern among the Mundurucu Indians of Brazil: "We saw little ones try to hurt infant siblings, and the exquisite cruelties commonly inflicted on household pets by Mundurucu children probably have the same source" (1974,168).

attachment with the mother could have laid the groundwork for rivalry with the father for the mother's affections and the formation of a full-blown Oedipus complex. Certainly older Mehinaku children are aware of their parents' sexual activity, as is clear from the "Song of the Cricket" (see Gender Wars illustrations following page 117). But despite the openness of sexual behavior, the father never emerges as a strongly antagonistic figure. Far from being the punitive and authoritarian father of Freud's Victorian Vienna, he is often a warm and occasionally adoring parent. It is he who will enhance his son's security and make further growth possible. Fathers frequently hold their children, play with them, and care for them when the mother is unavailable (see figures 26–28). Although a father's formal obligations to his son are described by the villagers in primarily educational and economic terms (getting fish for his son, teaching him how to make baskets), he is emotionally supportive as well. Injured or crying children can count on the father for sympathy and assistance.

By the time a boy is nine or ten, he is spending a substantial portion of each day with his father, often accompanying him on long fishing trips away from home. Although it is difficult to make quantitative judgments on the basis of my data, the father appears to be a far more salient figure in the socialization of children of this age group than in

Fig. 26. Father and daughter. With the help of a stamping tube and a discarded gasoline can, Pitsa drums the rhythm from the Kaiyapa ritual, a frequent ceremony. He is also taking care of his daughter while her mother is absent from the village.

Fig. 27 and 28. Fathers and sons. Most men do not relish the job of babysitting. "It is a nuisance to take care of children," they complain. But it is also clear that fathers can be caring and affectionate parents. The children are comfortable on their laps and trusting when held up high. Here, in their fathers' arms, they are introduced to the men's house and the bustle of the plaza. Until the age of two, even little girls can accompany their fathers into the men's house. As soon as mother returns, however, these adventures are over. It is she who is the principal caretaker of the young child.

the United States, where "the old man" may hardly see his children except on weekends. Even as an adult, a Mehinaku may nostalgically recall his long-dead father's attention and instruction, and he looks forward to the coming paradisical afterlife when he will be reunited with his father in the Village in the Sky.

The rewarding relationship with the father and interaction with peers provides a boy with desirable models of masculine behavior. In the peer group, which becomes increasingly sex-segregated at about eight years of age, a boy becomes engaged in the patriarchal nature of Mehinaku culture. In the security of his mother's hammock, he was

at the axis of a warm and protective feminine world. Now he learns that the real center of the society is held by men. It is they who plan rituals and make decisions. It is they who control the men's house, the political and religious nexus of Mehinaku culture. Women, a boy comes to realize, are physically weak, mentally deficient, morally inferior, and dangerous. They cannot recall the basic myths ("the words will not stay in their stomachs"), they are frightened to walk through the forest alone, and they are given to invidious and incessant gossip. One of the pejorative terms for a gossip is *tenejukanatɨ*, "woman mouth," whether the gossiper is male or female. A man's place is with other men, in the men's house. A man who spends too much time at home with the women is like a woman himself, and that is what he may be called by jeering village gossips.

Symbiosis

The path of socialization for Mehinaku men has a series of sharp bends and reversals. We begin with a "lush" period of physically intimate contact with the mother during the first two-and-a-half to three years of life; move through a phase of rejection and separation until approximately age six; and then go on to masculinity, with its somewhat hostile and anxious separation from the feminine world. It is a simple task to find cultural evidence that justifies our characterization of the final stage of male socialization. This material, presented in chapters 6 through 8 on the men's house and sexual anxieties, is the official culture of Mehinaku masculinity. Can we find any survival in Mehinaku culture of the earlier periods of socialization, those of maternal symbiosis and separation? Although the anxieties concerning castration fear documented in previous chapters are suggestive, we would like evidence that spells out the symbiotic union with the mother and the trauma of separation from her. But here our research penetrates a region that the men must defend. The path back to fusion with the mother and the pleasures of infancy is symbolic of regression and emasculation. Any lingering temptations to return to this period will be distorted and deflected by the anxieties it awakens. We have, nonetheless, two myths from ancient times that express the hidden desire and flag warnings to those who would succumb.

The first tale is that of Temeneju, Tapir Woman. The tapir is a distant cousin of the horse and the rhinoceros, a hoofed water-loving ungulate living in a tropical habitat. Several characteristics of the tapir make it an appropriate choice for its role in Tapir Woman. These include its habit of blindly running through the forest no matter what obstacles may be in its way and its prodigious production of dung, a characteristic that figures in many Mehinaku myths and scatological jokes. Most significant, however, are the tapir's hairless buttocks, which more than any other animal's in the Mehinaku environment resemble those of a human being.

Tapir Woman

> A child was alone in the house. His mother had left him there alone. He cried and cried for his mother, but no one came. But then Tapir Woman heard his crying, and she came to comfort him. "Don't you know me?" she asked. "I am just like your mother. Don't cry."
>
> Bending over, Tapir Woman said, "Put your arm into my rectum." "No!" replied the child. "I won't do that."
>
> But Tapir Woman urged and begged and urged and begged, and at last the child slid his entire arm inside her, up to his shoulder. Tapir Woman tightened herself around the arm and raced off, dragging the little boy behind her. The little boy tried to pull himself free, but he could not; his arm was squeezed and crushed, tight inside. Tapir Woman dragged him through the forest,

> through the swamp, day after day. He was cut with thorns and bloodied. He was covered with the tapir's ticks and biting insects.[6] But then Tapir Woman come to a grove of fruit trees and ate and ate and ate. She filled herself with fruit. She ate more and more fruit. Later that day, she defecated the fruit. Out came all the fruit. Out came the arm of the little boy. But the arm came out shriveled and tiny. Too tiny, too shrunken for the boy to use it at all.

"Tapir Woman" is an unusual myth for the Mehinaku in that it directly reflects thought processes and fantasies from a very early period of life, perhaps that of a two- or three-year-old child. At the outset, Tapir Woman makes it plain who she is: "I am just like your mother," she informs the child. Her invitation to the boy to place his arm in her rectum appeals to a childhood theory of sexuality and birth: the anus is the route to the womb (Freud 1963, 279; Jaffe 1968, 525–27). What makes Tapir Woman's urgings so attractive is the fusion with the mother and a return to the passivity and warmth that were until recently the child's everyday privilege. Moreover, the entry into the mother may be regarded as a symbol of sexual relations, distorted by the child's lack of comprehension of adult intercourse. "Tapir Woman," along with the tale of Araukuni below, is the closest the Mehinaku will come to a myth of maternal incest.

Like all Oedipal tales, there can be no happy ending. As soon as the boy gives in, his arm is swallowed up. Abruptly, Tapir Woman reveals her identity as an animal. Squeezing and crushing the boy's arm (an attack reminiscent of the fantasy of the anaconda), she leaves him with a withered, useless limb. Symbolically, the child is castrated and emasculated, a victim of his mother's seduction. The lesson of the tale is that the road from symbiosis to separation can go only in one direction. Those who attempt to return lose their manhood. The next myth, that of Araukuni, makes the same point, but from a different perspective.

In chapter 4, we described an actual case of father-daughter incest and told the tale of Tuluma, the woodpecker who tricked his daughter into incestuous relations. To judge from the lighthearted tone of "Tuluma," and from Eweje's success in living with his daughter, father-daughter incest is not traumatic, at least not for the father. Other forms of incest, such as between brother and sister, are no laughing matter. In the tale of Araukuni, a young Mehinaku boy is in seclusion. His sister is a seclusion girl, or literally, "little female house stayer." Like all secluded girls, her skin has lightened from the

6. Tapir are said to swarm with ticks, which are sometimes referred to as "the tapir necklace" (*teme nete*).

lack of sun, and her hair has grown until it covers her eyes and face in a way that men find erotic and myterious. Time hangs heavy on the hands of Araukuni and his sister, and sex in the privacy of their seclusion barrier provides exciting relief from the tedium. Unlike parents of today who, as one father explained, do not want their children "ending up like Araukuni," parents in ancient times secluded brother and sister behind the same partition. It is in this setting that the tale begins.

Araukuni

Araukuni was in seclusion with his sister, a beautiful girl. Her thighs and calves were big and firm, and for that reason he wanted to have sex with her. Finally he did. He had sex with her, he had sex with her, he had sex with her. No one knew. But then Araukuni's sister became pregnant. "Who has been having sex with you?" said her mother. "I have seen no one coming to visit you."

"My brother has given me a child," she replied.

Oh, the mother was angry. She struck Araukuni and beat him with a club. She cut down his hammock and burned it. She burned his bow, his arm bands, and his belt. All of these she burned. She would not make bread for him. She would not give him manioc porridge or fish stew. All she would do was beat him, beat him, beat him. All the time she beat him.

Araukuni grew sad. He went off into the forest and wove a great canoe of bark fiber, bigger than a house. It could fly through the air like a plane, and it made frightening sounds like a shaman's rattle as it moved through the sky. In his village, Araukuni's family and friends said it was so much better that he had gone. "Good riddance," said the father. "He had sex with his sister."

But they came to miss him. They went to find him in a place where the waters were so deep that the sun could not be seen on the bottom. Araukuni lived deep in these waters. He ate birds that came near the water.

His sister came to him. "I want to be your wife," she said.

"No," replied Araukuni. I don't want you. I don't want my mother or my father. They have misused me."

Then some of Araukuni's friends came to him. They saw that fur was beginning to grow all over his body, on his arms and legs. A long beard came down to his lap. His hair grew to his waist. He was changing into a spirit.

> "If you come here again I will kill you and eat you," he said.
>
> All of Araukuni's friends left and warned everyone else to stay far off. None came back. And Araukuni went off to a distant place, far away in the north.

"Araukuni" is a disturbing story for the Mehinaku. In contrast to "Tuluma," it is told in dead earnest, and the narrator uses dramatic timing and extensive repetition to impress the frightening nature of the tale on his listeners. Moreover, "Araukuni" has a central place in Mehinaku knowledge of ancient times. All the villagers know the story and it is told (in slightly different versions) by the other Xingu tribes.[7] A song that Araukuni chants under the waters is sung during one of the major intertribal festivals, and the decorative pattern (*Araukuni yana*, literally, "Araukuni design") on his woven aircraft is reproduced on baskets, in body paintings, and in other ornamental designs.

Unlike "Tapir Woman," whose origins arise out of the conflicts of early childhood, the story of Araukuni seems to spring from the psychological stresses of adolescence. During this period, boys and girls are secluded for several years to promote their growth and development. A boy at this age is well along the path to masculine maturity, having aligned himself with his father and the view of the feminine world promulgated by the culture of the men's house. At this time, he enters seclusion "to make him grow into a man," but in many respects, he returns to an earlier stage of development, in which his parents provide for all of his physical needs and place severe restrictions on his movements and conduct.

This period of extreme dependency, in which the adolescent is separated from his comrades and isolated for the entire day in the half-light of the seclusion space, is ideally suited for the reawakening of the anxieties and struggles of symbiosis and separation. Incest with one's sister at this point is, like Araukuni himself at the end of the myth, highly atavistic. To commit incest is to surrender in the battle for self-differentiation and to succumb to the temptations of family dependency. Moreover, the sister's close association with the mother (the sister is regarded as the mother's "former self") evokes the possibility of sexual union with the mother. Maternal incest, however, cannot be contemplated. Unlike other "family romances," it is never overtly mentioned in mythology, it is beyond discussion for my informants, and it is absent in my study of dreams. Nonetheless, the mother in "Araukuni" overshadows the sister herself. To the villag-

7. One version is found in Harald Schultz's compilation of Waura myths (1965, 76–80).

ers, the primary theme is that of maternal rejection. To my question "Why did Araukuni turn into a spirit?" I had expected an answer that hinged on punishment for incest. Instead, the narrator explains, "He turned into a spirit because his mother did not give him manioc bread. Because she did not make him fish stew and porridge. Because she beat him and beat him all the time. Therefore, he was unhappy and went far off."

We now begin to see the story of Araukuni as an anxious memory of the conflicts of symbiosis and separation. Unlike "Tapir Woman," which is a warning against symbiosis "Araukuni" is the self-justifying fantasy of the child who has been punished for it. Rejected by his mother and family, he goes off to a distant place. His parents' efforts to reestablish contact and his sister's offer to become his wife are an apology for their rejection and an acceptance of his conduct. But the offer comes too late, and Araukuni metamorphoses into a spirit.

In contrast to some of the matter-of-fact and even humorous myths we have narrated, "Araukuni" is surreal and dreamlike. With its unexplained shifts from land to air and then to water, the story resembles a nightmare rather than waking thought. Like "Tapir Woman," it draws its power form a deeply seated conflict in Mehinaku male psychology, the struggle of separation and symbiosis. On the distant screen of ancient times, each villager projects images of fear and temptation. Thanks to this mythic world, we begin to discern the core of Mehinaku masculinity and to make out the conflict hidden in the darkness of each villager's forgotten childhood.

Mehinaku Masculinity

The key to Mehinaku masculinity is the extraordinarily intense and sensual period of intimacy with the mother during the first years of life. At a time when male children in most cultures have discovered the differences between themselves and their mothers, a Mehinaku boy is still basking in an undiminished maternal warmth. With the arrival of a new sibling, he is evicted from the mother's hammock, and given (at best) second place at the breast. His conflicting feelings of anger and dependency are generalized to all women and become the basis for devaluing women and accepting the culture of masculinity. The boy's transition to manhood, however, is dearly bought. A part of him, as "Tapir Woman" suggests, continues to yearn for the lost union with the mother. He must, however, be vigilant against such regressive and forbidden urges. Sexual desire is especially dangerous because it is symbolic of both dependence upon and physical union with women. The purported hazards of sex, such as stunted growth and castration, are warnings: Women emasculate men. Women who are hard to resist sexually are the most dangerous of all. We recall the special hazards of the three women who in Mehinaku belief are almost irresistible. Give in to sex with Angry Woman Spirit, and you never return home. Succumb to the temptations of Lizard Woman, and you risk near castration. Dream of a woman who takes the sexual initiative, and you are attacked by an anaconda.

The most frightening of these possibilities is the anaconda, since unlike the other dangers, anacondas are real. Moreover, the symbolism of the anaconda's assault leads directly to the darkest of men's sexual fears. The anaconda smothers and crushes its victims, incorporating them into its body. Tapir Woman makes use of the same methods, squeezing and crushing a little boy's arm as she draws it inside her.[8] With but few changes, these fearful images of destruction and engulfment could be those of the sexually conflicted individuals seen in psychoanalytic practice. Intercourse is described by these patients as "being drowned, sucked in, overpowered" (Loewald 1951,15) or as "a hot blackness enveloping and threatening to overwhelm and destroy, . . . an all-encompassing force which [sucks] one in like a whirlpool, irrisistable, but dirty" (Jaffe 1968,535–36). The fears voiced in both the myths and the clinical data are those of maternal symbiosis. What was so highly prized in early childhood as warmth and closeness is feared in adulthood as a crushing attack. The path back to maternal symbiosis is closed; the memories of union with the mother are tinged with fearful meaning. Temptations of sexuality arouse fears of a destroying and negating parent, a mother who smothers and crushes her son's efforts to be a man.

The other sexual fears we have documented, including those linked to disease, stunted growth, failure in work roles, impotence, menstruation, and thoughts about women, are derivative anxieties. Each reminds the men that women are destructive to manhood. Women emasculate men and propel them back to a beginning they can no longer face. In a hidden corner of the Mehinaku masculine psyche, all women are anacondas.

8. Conceivably, some of the images of being crushed and smothered are memories of actual experiences of being pushed and squeezed in the hammock by the sleeping mother.

TEN

Ears, Eclipses, and Menstruating Men: The Feminine Self in Masculine Culture

> Dionysus, the god of eternal youth, of initiation and of secret societies was the twice born: Zeus destroyed his earthly mother by fire, and caught the baby to his thigh saying: "Come, enter this my male womb."
>
> —Norman O. Brown, *Love's Body*

By the time a Mehinaku boy becomes a man, he accepts and participates in the prevailing culture of masculinity. Women are necessary, pleasure giving and nurturing. But they are also dangerous and repulsive. The origins of this ambivalence lie in the intense relationship with the mother and the relative absence of the father during the first three years of life. But this same crucial period of maternal symbiosis also lays the groundwork for a conflict in identity even more profound. A boy brought up in a feminine world will to a degree model himself after his caretakers and come to think of himself as being like them. As he begins to take part in the culture of masculinity, however, he discovers that women are held in very low esteem and are regarded as being wholly unlike men. A man who admits to even a hint of femininity repudiates his own nature. His identification with women must be distanced, so that it can be obliquely expressed and yet denied. Mehinaku myth and ritual are ideal vehicles for handling this conflict.

Mehinaku Rituals and Myths as Social Fantasies

Both myths and long-established rituals are believed to be creations of ancient times, ordained by the spirits and culture heroes of the distant past. A participant in a ritual or a teller of a myth need be no more personally identified with his production than an actor in a play. Both have their lines; neither is equated with the character portrayed. Ritual and myth may thereby serve as screens upon which the Mehinaku can comfortably project their inner lives. There are, however, a number of differences between myths and rituals as projective fantasies. A myth is a transient verbal product, involving little outlay or commitment on the part of the teller or listener. But a Mehinaku ritual often initiates lifelong relationships between the participants and demands complex and voluminous exchanges of food, goods, and services (see Gregor 1977, 321–24). Structured by the requirements of broadly based economic and social interaction, rituals may not leave quite as much room for the impress of the personality as the more flexible myth.

Nonetheless, Mehinaku rituals are linked to individuals. The villagers believe that many illnesses are caused by the loss of the soul to a well-known spirit, such as Kauka, the spirit of the sacred flutes. Dances, music, and food propitiate the spirit and induce it to return the soul to the owner. But on rare occasions, a shaman or the patient himself will diagnose an illness caused by a spirit hitherto unknown in the Mehinaku pantheon. I was present when Kikyala realized that his soul had been taken by the spirit of the deer. Kikyala's knee had been severely strained when he tried to capture a deer by wrestling it to the ground. The unusual circumstances surrounding his injury, the failure of his knee to mend as expected, and above all, his week-long isolation in the semidarkness of his household stimulated a rich series of dreams and semiconscious fantasies about the deer spirit. Kikyala told his kinsmen what he had seen and instructed them in the costumes, dances, and flutes that were needed to appease the spirit. Several villagers impersonating the deer spirit entered the village and were fed ceremonial food. Should another villager lose his soul to the deer spirit, the Mehinaku now have a ritual with which to respond to the challenge.

I am convinced that all Mehinaku rituals are like Kikyala's in that they have their inception in the creative fantasies of individuals. As such, they are expressive vehicles that may carry the desires and inner conflicts of their creators. To endure and become part of the villagers' ceremonial repertory, however, the ritual must strike a chord in the other Mehinaku. The outlandish and the idiosyncratic will fall by the wayside. Since the ritual creators and evaluators are nearly always men, the ceremonies that survive provide us with a rough measure of masculine psychology. Admittedly, these rituals will not tap the extremes of the collective psyche as well as the more expressive myths, but they are likely to be better measures of the mode.

Ears, Eclipses, and Menstruating Men

THE RITUAL OF EAR PIERCING

For the Mehinaku, menstruation is the most anxiety-charged of the physiological characteristics of women. Caused by deadly fauna living in the vagina, menstrual blood is associated with wounds, castration, poison, disease, stunted growth, and enfeeblement. Yet there are a number of occasions in which the men symbolically menstruate, the most significant of which is the ritual of ear piercing.

Pɨhɨka ("piercing") is one of the major intertribal rituals (*kaiyumain*) put on by the Xingu tribes. The purpose of the ritual is to pierce the ears of the young men of the community and ceremonially confer upon them their first pair of earrings, one of the hallmarks of Xingu masculine status. At the start of the ceremony, a group of boys who will refer to each other through life by the special term *jatsa* are paired with ceremonial sponsors who supervise their initiation. Every few days, for a full year prior to the final ritual, the sponsors awaken their charges at two or three in the morning for a dance that goes on until dawn. Sleep is for dogs and "hammock lovers," not for boys who would be men. The privations of the ritual give the boys a sense of going through a difficult but worthwhile experience. They abstain from food and drink "so that they will become strong." They swallow noxious medicines designed to promote their growth and then force themselves to vomit. Above all, they courageously face the perforation of their ears.

The sharpened wooden and jaguar bone dowels used for the ear-piercing operation are not likely to cause serious pain, but the boys fear that they will. The songs sung during the year of preparation for the ceremony are intended to reduce the pain and staunch the flow of blood. Special medicines imported from the Kamaiyura tribe are regularly swabbed onto the earlobes to soften the flesh and facilitate the penetration of the dowel. On the day of the operation, the terrified boys lie silently in their hammocks. Carried out to the bench in front of the men's house, they are held tightly on their sponsors' laps. Suddenly, the men performing the operation leap toward the boys and rapidly pierce their ears. The children are then carried by their sponsors into one of the houses, where their hammocks are tied to a common pole and a large seclusion partition is erected around them. Most of the boys will remain in seclusion for a month, honoring a variety of food taboos and other regulations that bring favorable dreams.

The boys in "piercing seclusion" are expected to have a special relationship that will endure the rest of their lives. When one dies, the rest serve as his pallbearers. The passing of the last of these jatsa has a special poignancy, since it marks the demise of a group of men who have gone through the life cycle together. While in seclusion, the boys are constantly reminded of the importance of the ritual and the worthwhile nature of the hardship. Occasionally, however, morale begins to falter, as happened in October 1967 when two initiates slipped out of isolation to show up shamefàcedly in their parents' houses. Ketepe's pep talk to the remaining boys gives a good sense of the ethos of piercing seclusion:

> When I had my ears pierced I stayed in seclusion a long time. But there were three jatsa who left early. Now they are all dead. The ones who stayed with me are all alive. You must not be homesick for your father or you will get sick and die. You will have a bad dream in which you see a wasp, a jaguar, or a witch, and then you will die. Kano just went back to his house. Well, Kano will die shortly. He does not have long to live.
>
> Tomorrow you will eat manioc porridge, your fast will end. Your fathers will go hunting and bring back birds and monkeys for you to eat. When I was in piercing seclusion there were no shotguns or rifles. My father went to hunt for me and shot an arrow at a bird and missed. For you there will be plenty of food.

Ketepe's lecture had its intended effect. Kano's father returned his son and there were no further defections.

The solidarity of the boys in seclusion is further reinforced by their separation from women. Women are excluded from crucial phases of the ritual, including the ear piercing itself, and the men are at special pains to make sure the boys are free from the contaminating presence of menstruating women. The boys' comradery is also buttressed by aggression toward women. As soon as the most stringent phases of fasting associated with the ritual are over, the boys set to work making large numbers of wax-tipped arrows. When the arrows are ready, one of the boys keeps watch from a small slit window in the wall of the house. "Now!" he calls, and suddenly a volley of arrows descends upon a group of women unlucky enough to be caught on the plaza. Women are fair game during piercing seclusion and shooting at them is the boys' principal sport. To protect themselves, the village women set up large woven mats as shields so that they can sit outdoors to watch the afternoon wrestling matches. The moment a village girl stands up, archery practice begins anew.

Thus far, Pɨhɨka resembles many rites of initiation whose chief function is to identify young men with the masculine values of their fathers. Amid the comradery of the ritual and the boys' high jinks, however, we note conduct and beliefs that nearly reverse this interpretation. We start with a set of correspondences between ear piercing and menstruation.

EAR PIERCING AND MENSTRUATION

According to the Mehinaku, the ear-piercing ceremony is the male equivalent of the ritual that occurs at the onset of a girl's first menses. Both ceremonies focus on blood and seek to staunch its flow as rapidly as possible with various medicines. A girl who is menstruating and a boy who has had his ears pierced are immediately carried to their hammocks so that their feet do not touch the "weakening" ground. That night, they will have a dream that will predict their future life. To favorably influence the dream, their parents tie a frond from the cotton plant to the hammock cords. The first plant to emerge from a burned over field and said to be the plant that "never dies," cotton produces dreams that augur long and productive lives (see Gregor 1981a).

The list of correspondences between the ear-piercing and menstrual rituals can be extended further, as outlined in table 6. What should be emphasized is that the parallel is perceived by the Mehinaku. "Ear piercing," as Ketepe puts it, "is menstruation. The Pɨhɨka ceremony is like a girl's first menses." When pressed further, Ketepe recognizes that menstrual blood and blood from the boys' incisions are not precisely identical: "The boy's kid a little when they menstruate. It's not real menstrual blood." Nonetheless, the term *iyumekepei*, "menstruating," describes both the condition of women at the time of their monthly period and of boys whose ears have been pierced.

THE SEXUAL SYMBOLISM OF FEATHER EARRINGS AND HEADDRESS

With the conferral of feather earrings, the boys of the tribe are privileged to display a major symbol of masculine status. But like the ear-piercing ritual itself, the earrings are an ambivalent symbol of masculinity. Mythology links them to female sexual anatomy. Kikyala is our narrator for the story of the origins of the first feather earrings.

> All of the men were on a fishing trip. The village was emptied of people. The Sun's wife was sweeping the plaza. But Kɨje (the toucan, *Rhamphastos*) had not gone fishing. He saw the Sun's wife. Oh, but she had a great deal of long hair on her vagina. Kɨje wanted the hair since his feathers were very short. "May I take some of your hair for my earrings?" he asked.

Table 6. Parallels of the Ear-Piercing Ceremony and Ritual of First Menses

1. At the moment blood flows, both boys and girls are carried to their hammocks. Highly vulnerable to witches and spirits, they are safe only inside their houses.
2. Girls hold a cotton spindle in their navel "to keep it from closing up." Boys hold the dowel used to pierce their ears clenched between their teeth.
3. Leaves from the cotton plant, the plant that "never dies," induce a favorable dream, which boys and girls interpret with a similar set of symbolic equations.
4. Both boys and girls must lie quietly and speak only in whispers.
5. Both boys and girls must follow certain food taboos to ensure the rapid cessation of the flow of blood and a favorable dream. Initially, the children are subject to a fast; they are allowed to drink water after twenty-four hours.
6. Following the fast, they may eat all foods but fish, which would prolong the blood flow. "Fish," it is said, "eat other fish and therefore are filled with blood." Monkeys and birds eat only fruit and have a "different kind of blood" and are therefore acceptable to "menstruating" boys and girls.
7. With the total cessation of the flow of blood, a ceremony reintroduces fish to the diet. The boys are led outside, taste a small amount of fish, and spit it onto a fiber mat. The girls follow the same ritual inside the house.
8. Fish are now permissible, but food labeled as "sweet" (*puya*) and "salty" (*kaki*) are forbidden to both boys and girls (see Gregor 1977, 235, for a fuller description of food taboos and seclusion).

> "Oh, no. You can't do that. My hair is very dear to the chief," she replied.
>
> "Oh, but I'll just take a few," he said.
>
> *Tsuk! Tsuk! Tsuk!* He plucked out all of the hairs. Just one here and there he left. He then cut and tied all the hair into earrings.
>
> Later in the afternoon the Sun returned home and saw his wife. "What has happened to your genital hair?" he asked.
>
> "Oh, I decided I didn't like it, so I plucked it out," she replied.
>
> But then a man said to the Sun, "That man over there. He is the one who plucked your wife's genital hair to make his earrings. There he is over there, wearing them."
>
> Oh, the Sun was angry!

Kikyala adds: "Those were the first earrings. They were red and black because they are 'pictures' of the Sun's wife's genital hair, tipped with her blood."

Kikyala's myth complements the ritual of ear piercing. If the blood of ear piercing is menstrual blood, it is reasonable that earrings are female pubic hair. Although the Mehinaku do not consciously conclude that pierced ears are like female genitals, it is clear that the masculine imagery of the earrings is alloyed with a strong element of feminine symbolism. Another myth, that of the bat, restates this theme and firmly connects masculine garments, ear piercing, and female sexual anatomy.

In reading the story of Bat, it is well to keep in mind that one of the strictest rules of Mehinaku kinship is an avoidance taboo between mother- and son-in-law. Bat's guile in violating the taboo is in line with Mehinaku prejudices against this animal. Bats are said to be stealthy and aggressive creatures with razor-sharp teeth. A man unlucky enough to sleep out of doors unprotected may awaken with a vampire bat clinging to his body and sucking his blood. The chickens and roosters that the villagers keep as alarm clocks often fall victim to vampires, which gradually drain their strength and energy.

Fig. 29. Portrait of a villager. Akanai's watercolor depicts a well-adorned Mehinaku. The earrings receive detailed treatment, allowing us to see their three bands of feathers.

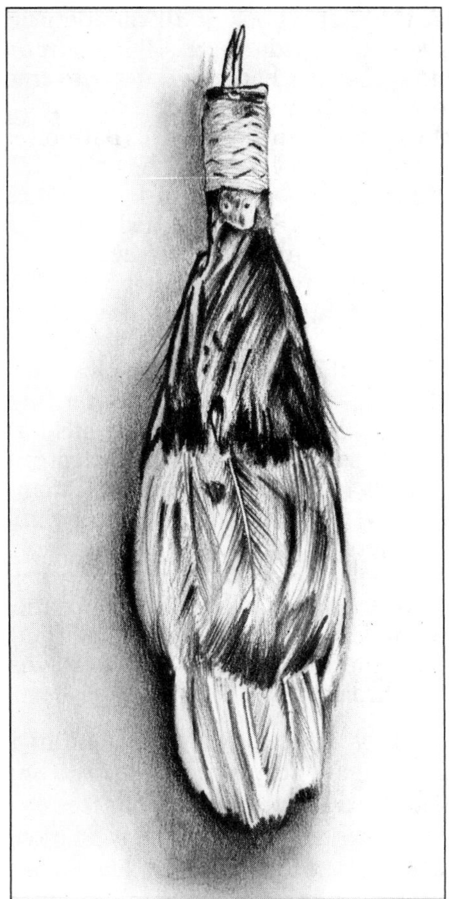

Fig. 30. An earring. Drawing by Marshall Capps.

Whenever the narrator of the story speaks as Bat, he emphasizes the animal's deviousness and cruelty by making his voice high-pitched and thin, much like the audible portion of a real bat's sonar.

Bat (*Alua*)

In the village of the vultures, the birds were holding the ear-piercing festival for their sons. They were sad, since they had no headdresses with which the boys could dance on the plaza. But then Vulture looked at Bat's mother-in-law, and he saw that her labia were enormous. "There," he said, "are the headdresses we need."

Bat decided that he would get the headdresses for the birds and lured his mother-in-law to a distant village where there was only one house. "You will not be

> alone", Bat told her. "Look at all the footprints on the trail. Everyone is already there." But the mother-in-law did not know that Bat had previously covered the trail with his own footprints.
>
> When they arrived in the village, Bat pretended to be surprised: "Where is everyone?" he asked. There is no one here!" Bat and his mother-in-law went into the one shabby house in the village and tied their hammocks at opposite ends. Suddenly, a bird screeched in the night, and the mother-in-law called to Bat: "What is it saying?" "It is saying you should move closer to me," Bat replied.
>
> And so the mother-in-law moved closer each time an animal called in the night.[1] Finally, after the jaguar growled, the mother-in-law got into Bat's hammock. There they had sexual relations. Bat then cut away his mother-in-law's labia with a clam-shell manioc scraper and filled many, many baskets with her genitals.[2]
>
> All the baskets he carried to the village of the vultures. There the ear-piercing ceremony was still underway. Bat gave the labia as headdresses to the ducks and the turkeys and all the other birds. And that is how the birds first got their headdresses, their crowns, their crests, their throat folds.

The myth of Bat is an extremely rich one in its reflections on Mehinaku kinship and concepts of sexuality. The mother-in-law is punished for her sexual interest in Bat, but it is clear that Bat, egged on by his vulture friends, had previously marked her for assault: "There are the headdresses we need." He lures his unsuspecting victim to the empty village and deliberately mistranslates the calls of the animals. In another version of the story, Bat even forces fishbones down his mother-in-law's throat to make it look as if she accidentally choked to death.

The sexual assault on the mother-in-law, which is the myth's principal motif, is compounded by the cruel joke of comparing a bird's crown and throat folds to female genitalia. A glance at a turkey is enough to make one appreciate the aggressive intent of this caricature. But even though it is a woman who is assaulted, mutilated, and ridiculed, the myth inevitably reflects upon the men and the symbolism of being male. Thus the headdress, ostensibly a crown of masculine adornment, caps an altogether different view of a well-dressed

1. In the full version of the myth, this sequence is repeated with many different animals, each more dangerous and menacing than the one before.

2. Note the continued association of the clam and the implements of manioc processing with female sexuality.

Mehinaku man. His earrings are conferred in a ritual in which he "menstruates." The feathers for his earrings were in mythic times taken from the vagina of the Sun's wife. And his prominent headdress is symbolically associated with a woman's labia. Fully adorned, the Mehinaku male is an ikon of female sexual anatomy.

THE ECLIPSE

On 24 December 1973, I was startled by a tremendous shout from the men of the village. They had just noticed that the sun was gradually being eclipsed. Dropping all their activities they rushed back to the village in a state of genuine fear and alarm, for Kama (Sun), one of the important male spirits and culture heroes, was "menstruating." As Kama's "menstrual blood" covered more and more of his face, he "reddened" and darkened (during a full eclipse, the sun and moon actually appear deep coppery red in color). The heat of the sun fading, a chill wind sprang up, rustling the leaves in the forest around the village. Kama's blood, the villagers said, was falling to earth and rattling the leaves.

Blood from the sun, like menstrual blood, is very dangerous. Each drop can penetrate the skin, causing sickness and leaving moles and blemishes. Quickly the villagers smeared themselves with ashes and manioc flour to ward off the blood. Carrying pots of porridge and stacks of manioc bread, the women threw large quantities of food into the bushes. Contaminated by the blood of the sun, just as a house's food may be contaminated by a menstruating woman, it was no longer fit for human consumption. The men gathered in the center of the village to watch the progress of the eclipse and speculate nervously about its meaning. They erected a tripod of arrows over the community burial ground in front of the men's house, so that the souls of the dead could rise up to their home in the Village in the Sky. Within the men's house, the village shamans sang, rattled, and sucked at the body of one of the men to remove the bits of menstrual blood that the sun had shed upon him. The most powerful village shaman, the *yakapa* (see Gregor 1977, 340), fell into a trance to "look at" the sun. Returning to consciousness, he reported what he had seen to the assembled men:

> The menstrual blood is drooling from his mouth. He showed me his teeth and rolled his eyes so that only the whites showed. I saw the souls of murdered witches rising from the ground. I saw souls turning into snakes, bats and birds.

This description articulated the men's fears, for an eclipse is a frightening occurrence, a Last Judgment during which graves yawn open, the spirits of the dead ascend to the paradisical Village in the Sky, and the souls of animals and men freely transform themselves into one another.

In the late afternoon of the day of the eclipse, the villagers scarified themselves with scrapers (*piya*) set with dogfish teeth. Opening long shallow cuts on their bodies, they "menstruated" so that the sun's blood could flow out of their bodies and leave them free of contagion. Some of the children had to be chased and held down by their parents, but by late afternoon, nearly everyone had been scraped and bled, and the villagers finally returned to their normal routines.[3]

Eclipses are rare but inherently disturbing events. They therefore take on greater psychological significance to the Mehinaku than their frequency or status as realistic threats would warrant. Like other frightening natural occurrences, such as sickness or attacks by snakes and jaguars, eclipses are ascribed to female sexuality. Sexual fears thus form a broad resevoir of anxiety that may be tapped by many stressful experiences. The tension-reducing remedy in the case of the eclipse is to imitate female physiology and act out the feminine portion of the personality. The ritual is successful in that this facet of the personality is under control and only briefly expressed. But in one instance, that of the couvade, the pattern of feminine imitation breaks out to dominate daily life.

THE COUVADE

Deriving from the French *couver*, "to hatch or incubate," the couvade is an institution that requires a father to imitate some of the behavior of his wife at the time of childbirth. In South America, which has a disproportionate number of couvade-practicing societies, it varies from literal acting out of the woman's labor to relatively informal observances of food taboos. Although a Mehinaku man does not imitate the act of childbirth, he enters what is surely one of the longer and more intensive couvades thus far recorded in the ethnographic literature.

As soon as the child is born, the father enters seclusion with his wife and infant. Called "the infant's father" (*hauka enɨja*; a similar term is used to describe the period of seclusion), he is said to "resemble" the mother. In fact, the taboos and restrictions honored by the father appear to have been generalized from the mother to him. Like the mother, he lives behind a palmwood barrier, refrains from sexual relations and avoids those foods that are taboo to a woman who is experiencing postpartum blood flow. Specifically, he avoids fish, but he may eat monkey and bird meat brought to him by close kin. When

3. Vera Penteado Coelho (1983) describes a similar sequence of events during a solar eclipse among the Waura, a tribe with a language and culture similar to that of the Mehinaku.

the mother's postpartum bleeding ends, both husband and wife sit on benches within the house and, in a ritual identical to that of boys in the ear-piercing ceremony, chew a small morsel of fish. The mother then leaves seclusion, symbolized by her going out of the house by the front door, bathing, and frequenting the central plaza. But the father does not "go out." His food taboos change to reflect a "non-bleeding status," similar to boys whose ears have healed and girls in seclusion after their first menses. These food taboos and numerous other restrictions on sex and on the kind of work he may perform (see Gregor 1977, 272, for a list of seventeen prohibitions) are honored in the interest of the child. Were the father to eat fish or to thatch a roof, for example, the bones of the fish or the sharp ends of the thatch would injure the child.

The father's period of seclusion lasts until the infant assumes the status of a child. According to the villagers, an infant "lies around, gurgles, crawls on the ground, and does not talk." A child "walks and talks." By these criteria, seclusion lasts approximately a year, though some of the villagers claim that in past times a new father spent as long as three years in isolation. With the birth of subsequent children, the couvade is reimposed, but in an attenuated form. The father is no longer confined behind an isolation barrier, but he must still honor many of the prohibitions on sexuality, physical activity, and diet that he followed with the birth of his first child. When fathers violate the rules—and many do—they put both their children and their own good names at risk. If an infant becomes sick, the village shamans are likely to ascribe the illness to the father's irresponsibility. Tabooed sexual relations, said to attract the spirit of the bull-roarer, is the most frequent of the shamans' diagnoses. But I have also seen fathers tear down fences and rip the thatch off the family house in order to "undo" the harm they have done to their child.

The Mehinaku couvade serves many of the functions that have been attributed to the institution in other societies, such as dramatizing paternity (Bachofen 1961; Young 1965) and dampening the expression of resentment toward the newborn child (Spiro 1961). The most striking feature of Mehinaku couvade symbolism, however, is the feminine nature of a father's connection to his offspring. Like mother and child prior to birth, the link is direct. The father's movements are restricted, much like a woman in an advanced stage of pregnancy; all of his activities have an impact on the well-being of his child; and, analogous to a woman who has recently given birth, he assumes the taboos appropriate for the postpartum flow of blood.

Bruno Bettleheim and Ruth and Lee Munroe and John Whiting have proposed a theory of the couvade that centers on its sexual implications. Bettleheim maintains that the couvade is an expression of a hidden but universal male desire "to find out how it feels to give birth" (1954, 211). The Munroes and Whiting trace this wish to the father's latent feminine identity. Examining a sample of thirty-one societies, they show that the couvade appears where the father is absent from the household, where mother and son sleep separately from the father, and where a husband moves to his wife's house at the time of marriage (1973; 1981, 618). In each of these instances, the father may be perceived as an interloper in the mother-infant relationship. The son's initial identification is with the mother rather than the absent or shadowy father. Mehinaku mother-son sleeping arrangements and the general course of socialization fit the pattern described by the Munroes. These practices promote a maternal identification, and relegate the father to second place as a role model in infancy and early childhood. The couvade, like the imagery of the headdress and the symbolic menstruation of ear piercing and the eclipse, is an expression of fundamental ambivalence in Mehinaku male sexual identity.

SEX CHANGE

There are limits to the men's mimicry of female biology. The facts of life and antagonism toward femininity constrain how far the men will go in their ritual imitations of women. In the more expressive and less committed world of myths, however, the concept of men as women can be played out to its most extreme conclusions. Thus a few Mehinaku myths relate how in ancient times, men's and women's roles were the reverse of what they are today. The most developed of these stories is an alternate version of "The Women Discover the Songs of the Flute," the story of the origin of the men's house. The tale opens in a scrambled world in which gender and biology are turned topsy-turvy.

> In ancient times, a long time ago, the women were the ones who could go in the men's house. They were just like men and had a lot of long pubic hair. A woman's clitoris was as big as a man's penis. The women had sex with each other.
>
> The men were the "house stayers" then. They took care of the children, spun cotton, and processed great heaps of manioc flour. They were the ones who worked hard in those times. When the children cried, it was the men who picked them up. They took their children to their breasts and nursed them, though they gave only a little milk . . .

From this point, the myth continues much like "The Women Discover the Songs of the Flute." Under the leadership of the chief, the men used the bullroarer to frighten the women and take over the men's house. After smearing the women's masculine paints and tearing off their ornaments, the men lecture the women in the family residences: "You in there. Just keep still. Make manioc bread and take care of the children. Nurse the children and never again come back to the men's house."

This myth is of interest because it suggests the mutability of both gender and sex for the Mehinaku. Not only are the roles of the sexes changeable, but even human biology is open to occasional reorganization. Being masculine is not forged, as it is in our own society, of a cast-iron belief in the inevitability of sex-linked genes. Rather, the myth says, gender and biology intermesh with politics and human will. Although this perspective could be the groundwork for a liberating feminist ideology, it is more an expression of the men's fears. Just as the men in ancient times wrested maleness from the women, so the men of today must be vigilant against the insidious woman within. In unusual circumstances, such as those provided by myth telling and ritual, she can be given free rein in ways that are nonthreatening. But in everyday life, she must be held at bay with taboos, antagonism, health rules, and other anxious precautions.

Sex, Gender, and the Imitation of Women

Table 7 summarizes the ways in which Mehinaku ritual and mythology express identification with women. A look at the symbolic meaning of the rituals and legends shows that the men are especially drawn to imitate female sexual biology. The women's place in the division of labor, ornamentation, and other aspects of gender roles are represented but appear far less compelling of male imitation. This pattern is surprising since the men claim that female sexuality, especially menstruation and the female genitalia, is defiling and repulsive, associated with stunted growth, loss of strength, dangerous fauna, and castration. The men seem to be attracted to the characteristics of women they hold in lowest esteem.

To understand this paradox, we return to the processes of socialization that form the Mehinaku masculine personality. We recall that the child's initial intense relationship with the mother is transformed by his expulsion from her hammock and hearth in the third year of life. The anxiety that this experience engenders is later expressed in the fear of magical contamination by women and antagonism toward them. The hostile and fearful elements of Mehinaku men's culture reflect this transformation of anxiety and suggest the use of many of the standard defense mechanisms known to clinical psychology, such as projection, reaction formation, and denial. In the pattern of feminine behavior, however, we find a psychologically more primitive method of coping with anxiety: identification with

Table 7. Feminine Symbolism in Mehinaku Ritual and Mythology

Myth, Ritual, Adornment	Interpretation
Ear-piercing ritual and ritual at time of eclipse	"Menstruation" from ear and from scarification. Male initiates equated with girls at first menses.
Feather earrings	Said to have been made from Sun's wife's pubic hair
Headdresses	Said to have been made from Bat's mother-in-law's labia
Couvade	Symbolic participation of men in some phases of childbirth, linking them to their offspring. Men "bleed" after childbirth.
Female origins of men's house	Men act women's roles and nurse babies.
Aripi dancers in Mapulawaja make grotesque wax imitations of women's vaginas	Hostile imitation of female sexuality
Husband/wife roles in rituals	Spirits perceived as male or female. In many rituals, men represent both male and female spirits, addressing each other as "husband" and "wife." The "husband" provides food; the "wife" serves it to the other men.

the source of fear. According to Freud, this process occurs in normal masculine development, when a boy identifies himself with a somewhat threatening father. The same principle is also at work in unusually stressful situations (see, for example, Bettelheim's [1943] descriptions of prisoners accepting Gestapo values in German concentration camps), and it is intuitively exploited by fraternities that practice hazing, bosses who bully their subordinates and terrorists who seize hostages. In all these situations, the victims gain some control of their anxieties by identifying with their tormentors.

In the case of the Mehinaku, the mother is the perceived aggressor. It is she who rejects her son after the arrival of a younger sibling. The displaced child controls his fears by partially identifying himself with the mother, and especially with those aspects of her that he finds most frightening. It is thus the threatening nature of menstruation and female genitalia that compels imitation. By their partial incorporation into the masculine self-image, they are mastered and defused of some of their mystery and terror. Yet there remains a great deal of ambivalence about the feminine component of the male self. There is no comfortable way to remain in touch with the anxieties associated with feminine identification. Ritual and myth resolve the problem by separating this aspect of self from the individual. The stories of ancient times, the rituals of the eclipse, the couvade, and ear piercing are a view through the large end of the telescope. In their distancing lens, we see a feminized masculine self that is normally deeply recessed and hidden.

ELEVEN

The Universal Male

> Only in the clubby warmth of the all-male retreat, where there is no doubt that men are men, can "real" men behave like women.

GANG RAPE. SYMBOLIC MENSTRUATION FROM THE EARS. WANDERING vaginas and detachable penises. Lizard woman. Bullroarers. Tepu, the worm. Dreams of sex and the anaconda. Tapir Woman and matriarchy . . . Our recollection of the Mehinaku culture of sexuality is compellingly drawn to the exotic and the bizarre. Even when we recall those aspects of the villagers' lives with which we comfortably identify, such as the cooperation of men and women in work and the affection between husbands and wives, we are left with an uneasy sense that the Mehinaku live in a very different sexual universe from ourselves. In part, our reaction derives from the foreignness of Mehinaku life. The symbols that express their sexual ideas are, like the vocabulary of their language, different from our own. But this does not mean that the fundamental meaning of sexuality is different in the two cultures. Beneath the veneer of cultural differences, there are striking similarities of sexual desires, fears, and defensive reactions.

The Imbalance of Desire and Gratification

In one respect, Mehinaku society comes as close to a stereotypical male sexual utopia as is possible in a functioning family-based community. Married men are able to have noninvolving sexual relationships with many women with little risk to their reputation or community standing. Even in this setting, however, male libido expands beyond the boundaries of available sex. The men complain that "women are stingy with their genitals." They condemn some of the women as "persons who do not like sex" and speak ill of others who are only reluctantly compliant. When masculine charms and importuning are insufficient, the men turn to gifts and verbal coercion to obtain sexual services. The imbalance of gratification and desire is perceived by the villagers as a powerful force. Men are assumed to be perpetually sexual. There is no such thing as a "professional" or platonic relationship between male and female. Their interaction is charged with potential sexuality unless it is explicitly ruled out by the incest taboo. Even in that event, the men are able to make exceptions to the rules. The impact of male libido extends beyond male-female interaction to same-sex relationships. Men who do not get along explain their hostility in terms of sexual jealousy. Men may even seek revenge against thieves and gossips by having sex with the culprit's wife. Allegations of witchcraft often derive from the tension of competing for the same women. Few Mehinaku relationships or institutions escape the tensions generated by sexual desire and frustration.

The same imbalance of male and female sexual interest characterizes our own culture. Whether these differences in libido are innate (as seems probable) or culturally patterned is beyond the scope of our investigation. But it is plain enough that the American sexual marketplace is one-sided. Courtship and dating reflect the fact that sex is a service that women provide for men in exchange for financial or social commitment. Coarser transactions in sexuality meter the value of the service more precisely. That is, the going rate for intercourse with a prostitute (apparently \$50–\$150 in large American cities) measures the extent that male sexual demand exceeds the supply of freely given female sexual services.

Men's chronic sexual frustration is addressed directly in the *Hite Report on Male Sexuality*, which is based on a large representative sample of American men. According to Hite, the major male sexual dissatisfaction is that "women do not want sex often enough." As expressed by one of her informants, "More. I just want *more*." Only eleven percent of those who participated in the survey were satisfied with the frequency of sex (1981,599). Insofar as masturbation represents a less valued substitute for sex, Hite provides us with a way of measuring just how much more the average male wants. Virtually all men, it seems, practice masturbation even when intercourse is available on a regular basis. The median incidence of masturbation is about two-to-three times per week regardless of the frequency of sexual contacts with partners (1981,1104–6). Like the Mehinaku, we conclude, American men are kept on short rations and evince high levels of sexual frustration and dissatisfaction. The result is a reservoir of sexual preoccupation that spills over into everyday life. Our culture is an eroticized culture that derives its energy from the pressure of pent-up male libido.

Sexual Anxiety

The Mehinaku believe that sexual wishes and contact with women may lead to failure in work, weakness, stunted growth, sickness, and death. Women, in the culture of Mehinaku sexuality, emasculate men. Admittedly, our own society does not institutionalize these ideas to the same extent. In the culture of our all-male groups, however, there are enough vestiges of such fears to show that the Mehinaku beliefs are not completely foreign. The most lurid examples are found in fantasy products marketed to adolescent males. Boys of this age are struggling with the same sexual issues that we attribute to the Mehinaku. Women are alluring, but they arouse primitive fears of dependence and loss of male identity.

In a series of articles on comic books that appeal to boys, Kenneth Adams examines story lines in which sexually enticing women destroy the men who succumb to them. At their most garish, these fantasies of women bear striking resemblances to Tapir Woman in Mehinaku mythology or the anaconda in the villagers' dream symbolism. Men who give in to their sexual urges are engulfed and swallowed up. In a typical episode, Conan the Barbarian embraces a beautiful woman who suddenly turns into an octopus-like creature with "snakelike tentacles pulling him down, downward," into her hideous maw (Adams 1983b,428). This image of woman-as-monster is fairly common in the comics, where alluring human females metamorphose into giant spiders (Adams 1981), medusaes, or other fantasy horrors. Even when the female monster theme is less overt, as in Superman or the all-time best-selling Captain Marvel series, women are portrayed as simultaneously attractive and threatening to the male protagonist (Adams 1983a). Ultimately, the tensions from which the comic book dramas draw their energy are also those that preoccupy the Mehinaku: separation from the mother and the definition of a masculine identity (c.f. Adams 1981).

Comic books and much of the expressive culture of youth is partly hidden from us by the age-segmented structure of American society. Nonetheless, when the boys grow up, their sexual anxieties linger on. Thus construction workers, submarine crews, tunnel sandhogs, and football coaches all agree: women must be kept at a distance if the mission is to succeed. The solidarity of these groups is linked to the exclusion of women. Masculine cohesiveness is fertile ground for emotional ideas that characterize women as threatening and emasculating. Such thinking is also subtly present in advertising directed toward men, and it is encountered on a daily basis by psychoanalysts and others in the therapeutic professions.

One of the better indicators of the prevalence of sexual anxieties in the general population is our attitude toward menstruation. We recall that among the Mehinaku, menstruation is a central symbol of sexual fear. Said to be caused by the bite of a piranha, menstrual bleeding is linked to death, disease, injury, and castration. The villagers separate menstruating women from men who are sick or otherwise vulnerable and take precautions to make sure the blood does not magically contaminate food. We would hardly expect these anxious ideas and practices to emerge in our own culture. In fact, however, the Western folk traditions regarding menstruation have always been extremely negative. From Frazer's *The Golden Bough*, we learn of the following European folk taboos:

> The touch of a menstruous woman turned wine to vinegar, blighted crops, killed seedlings, blasted gardens, brought down the fruit from trees, dimmed mirrors, blunted razors, rusted iron and brass (especially at the waning of the moon), killed bees, or at least drove them from the hives, caused mares to miscarry, and so forth. Similarly, in various parts of Europe, it is still believed that if a woman in her courses enters a brewery the beer will turn sour; if she touches beer, wine, vinegar, or milk, it will go bad; if she makes jam, it will not keep; if she mounts a mare, it will miscarry; if she touches buds, they will wither; if she climbs a cherry tree, it will die. (1951,702).

Through most of the nineteenth and early twentieth centuries these magical ideas were replaced with pseudoscientific beliefs about menstruation that justified restrictions on women for medical reasons. As recently as 1934, the "Voice of Experience" in *The Notebook of Intimate Problems* urged that girls avoid exercise, cold or hot baths, arduous household duties, and high-heeled shoes. During the winter, girls were advised to wear tight-fitting bloomers. These precautions would help prevent a "catarrhal condition" of the vaginal tissues, fallen organs, irregular menstruation, and a "critical menopause" (in Delaney, Lupton, Toth 1976,94).

Expanding medical knowledge has largely replaced the folk traditions and health warnings, but the anxiety they expressed lingers on. Menstruation is still a taboo subject, so that twenty percent of adolescent girls reach their first menses with no idea of what is happening to them (ibid., 66). Those girls who are better informed are taught to use products that will "cover up" so that "nothing will show" and "your secret will be safe." The word "menstruation" is itself anxiety-laden, and is covered up with euphemisms ("time," "time of month," "period").

The potency of our current menstrual taboo is revealed in our reaction to its violation. Thus in *The Curse,* a study of menstrual taboos, Delaney, Lupton, and Toth cite with approval the work *Red Flag* by artist Judy Chicago, which depicts a woman removing a menstrual tampon: "Chicago has made an enormous contribution to freeing women artists" (p. 238). In addition, the authors, "feeling the need of a female ritual to inspire us" conducted a "Bleed-In" in which menstrual paraphenalia and evidence of bleed-throughs were used as decorations (p. 241). What is of interest in these antics is not the act of violation, but our own reaction upon learning of it. To the extent that our feelings stray from the neutral—toward shock, disgust, or irritation—we reveal the degree to which the taboo is still a part of us.

In 1981 the Tampax corporation conducted one thousand interviews designed to reveal attitudes toward menstruation among a subject population that statistically profiled the general population of the United States. Two-thirds of the survey's respondents felt uncomfortable with the subject and maintained that a woman should make an effort to conceal menstruation from others at work or in social situations. Over a quarter believed that menstruation should also be hidden from family members. Approximately the same number were convinced that menstruation affected a woman's ability to think, changed her appearance, and interfered with her work. Eight percent of the survey population believed that women should make an effort to stay away from other people while they are menstruating. Although this last figure appears small, it represents fourteen million adult Americans.

While the survey does not reveal the psychological nature of the respondents' concerns, it certainly suggests that menstruation is an emotionally loaded issue for Americans as well as for Mehinaku. Like the villagers, we construct a mythology of this natural process that hedges it with evasions, restrictions, and apparent anxiety. Moreover, as among the Mehinaku and as predicted by psychological theory, it is the men who have the most intensely negative feelings about menstruation. Thus twelve percent of the men surveyed and only five percent of the women believed that a menstruating woman should stay away from other people.

But we are also struck by the differences between Americans and Mehinaku revealed by the Tampax survey. Most Americans, both male and female, feel that menstruation does not impair a woman's ability to function normally. Substantial minorities (approximately one third of the sample) feel that a woman need not conceal the topic at work or in social situations. To a degree, similar variation is found among the Mehinaku (we recall that some of the men will risk intercourse with menstruating women), but it is clear that American concern about menstruation is more limited in scope and muted in intensity; by and large, our scientifically oriented society does not promote such ideas. In the setting of the tribal society, they support the social and economic division of men and women. They fit well with prevailing ideas of disease causation, hygiene, and religion. That concern about menstruation exists at all in our complex technological culture is evidence in favor of an underlying similarity in gender psychology.

SEXUAL ANTAGONISM

The psychological flip side of fear of women is antagonism toward them. Among the Mehinaku, there is abundant evidence of masculine hostility. It is built into ritual, myth, and informal jokes, and it is institutionalized in the men's house with its bullroarers and sacred flutes. For us, the most shocking facet of this pattern of intimidation is gang rape. Yet rape in American society is very common. There were 72,452 reported rapes in the United States in 1982 (F.B.I. 1984), making it one of the most common crimes of personal violence. The actual number of cases may be more than five times this figure (Brownmiller 1975,190). What makes the Mehinaku pattern so much more morally distressing to us, however, is that for them rape is a sanctioned political act in which men as a group assault the women. In America, the rapist violates our laws and risks community condemnation. However, this point admitted, there is some evidence that the rapist in our society is motivated by hostility toward his victims and the desire to humiliate them. Even when he meets little resistance, the rapist often savagely beats the women he assaults. The effect of the pattern is that women in our society may be fearful of men and must avoid "unsafe" areas of their community—much as do their sisters-in-spirit among the Mehinaku. Rape thereby assumes some of the dimensions of a political act in both societies.

Among the Mehinaku, rape and aggression toward women are closely associated with the men's house. Although American men's clubs are primarily organized to support their members' financial and social interests, there are points of correspondence between these groups and the Mehinaku men's organization. American clubs bar women from participation in all but peripheral events and conceal secret objects and ritual knowledge from outsiders. The secrets, sometimes known as "mystics," are usually no more than the details of initiation rites. Like the Mehinaku secrets of the sacred flutes, they function to mystify those who are excluded rather than to hide strategic information. Nonetheless, American men's organizations, in parallel with their tribal equivalents, are almost invariably near the center of their communities' political and economic power. Amid the high jinks of masculine comradery, the members exchange information, angle for position, and conclude business deals. The impact of their organizations is substantial, since the membership is large. There are nearly seven million members of men-only organizations—Elks, Moose, Lions, Rotarians, Eagles, Jaycees, and Kiwanis. The membership rolls of the smaller, more elite clubs comprise the directorate of the nation's largest corporations, banks, universities, and public institutions (see Domhoff 1974). As a congressman recently confided to columnist Jack Anderson regarding the swank Bohemian Club, whose membership includes three past American presidents and the incumbent, "If I were to run for the Senate, I can think of no place where I could spend time more productively" (1980,19).

Men's clubs, whether Mehinaku or American, encourage boisterous comradery among the members and promote a hostile yet anxious image of women. Jokes and banter, which are nearly inevitable in all-male settings, effectively serve both of these ends. William Fry (1972) has shown that all-male settings foster patterned jokes about women that denigrate them as sexually insatiable, "dumb blondes," and exploitative of men. Gershon Legman, who has cataloged more than 6,000 American and British "dirty jokes" and 2,000 sexually oriented limericks (1968, 1972, 1977) finds many of the themes we detect in the Mehinaku view of sexuality. The sections of Legman's compendia have such titles as "the sadistic concept," "male motherhood," "sex-hatred and rejection," "fear of the female genitals," and "rape and rape by animals." An entire chapter is devoted to jokes about castration and the *vagina dentata* motif. Legman persuasively argues that the jokes should be taken seriously, that they are in effect a "helpless unveiling of the joketeller's sacredest guts . . . nothing less than his blitz psychoanalysis or diagnostic, performed by and on himself" (1977,000). The jokes Legman records, both in theme and underlying psychological content, are strikingly like the banter and some of the aggressive myths associated with the Mehinaku men's house.

The potential for shared sexuality is also characteristic of men's organizations. In America, gang rape is primarily committed by adolescent youth gangs (see Blanchard 1959 for an interpretation of this behavior in terms of homosexual solidarity), but sex as a group activity is present in more elite groups, including the most prestigious. The major event of the year at the Bohemian Club is a retreat in a redwood forest in Sonoma County, California, where the members attend theatrical and cultural activities. Much informal time, however, is spent talking about sex. "The topic is outranked as a subject for light conversation," notes sociologist William Domhoff, "only by remarks about drinking enormous quantities of alcohol and urinating on redwoods" (1974,27). A few of the Bohemians provide some substance for the gossip. They "jump the river" to join prostitutes who reportedly used to set up operations near the Bohemian retreat. According to newspaper accounts, a madam who organized such a group claimed to have entertained the Bohemians in a house near the encampment: "I'd tell the girls to bring all their fancy underclothing so they could do the [erotic] shows, and the gentlemen just loved it. [We would] have a little thing we called the 'Final Jinx' in which the last customer from the encampment got to be the 'Jinx'. The gentleman who got to be the 'Jinx' could never believe his good fortune. . . . Oh, the Bohemian was fun" (Cheshire 1981,C6).

MASCULINITY AND IDENTIFICATION WITH WOMEN

The pattern of shared sexuality, masculine comradery, and hostility toward women appears to be built into both American and Mehinaku men's organizations. American men, however, seem to lack the anxious identification with women that is implicit in Mehinaku ritual and myth. Bohemians do not trace their origins to a founding ancestress, and no American man "menstruates." We do have transvestite and homosexual subcultures that engage in blatant imitations of feminity, but these, unlike men's clubs, are decidedly outside the cultural mainstream. Nonetheless, I contend that within the emotional center of our society, we may eoncouter ideas and conduct that recollect the myths and rites of the Mehinaku.

Once again, we return to the Bohemians as an example of an Establishment men's organization. Recently, the club has had to defend itself against allegations of sex discrimination both in hiring practices and in club admissions policies. The basis of its defense has been that admission of women would alter the character of the organization. Club member and California's former governor, Edmund Brown explained that the Bohemians would feel inhibited from telling off-color jokes and that they would no longer be willing to wear women's clothes for the comic reviews staged by the members. In a separate account, a club attorney reportedly described his own stage appearance as a wood nymph: "we wore wings and body-stockings."

Although it boggles the mind to imagine the well-heeled Bohemians in nylons and high heels, female impersonations are staple fare in the theatrical presentations that are the highlight of each year's encampment. Other men's organizations, whether at the elite level of the Bohemians or that of soldiers in the barracks, often stage similar though less elaborate productions. Frequently, the characterizations of women are hostile parodies depicting them with exaggerated breasts, in an advanced stage of pregnancy, or in some other way grotesquely overfeminized. The audiences regard these characterizations as extremely funny, but we may well ask why. After all, the clubs, with their strongly masculine ethos, would appear to be the last place to find imitations of feminine behavior.

In the absence of psychologically oriented ethnographies of American men's clubs, the nearest approach we can make to the problem is a series of studies of hypermasculine behavior in male adolescents. The burden of the research is that hypermasculine conduct is compensation for an unconscious feminine identification (see especially Harrington 1970, but also Joseph Pleck's criticisms [1982,95ff]). I would suggest that men's clubs' theatrical presentations function to express precisely the same kind of ambivalence in sexual identity. Admittedly, the motives of the participants will vary. Some will be in the chorus simply because their boss is directing the show. But for many, imitating women gives vent to a feminine side of the personality within a safe, masculine setting. Just as a Mehinaku may encapsulate his mimicry of female physiology within the limbo-land of myth and ritual, so the member of the men's club discharges his identification with women within the circle of the theatrical spotlight.

None of this is to say that the participants in our men's club's transvestite reviews are different from "normal" men. On the contrary, my point is that they are normal. Our society, like that of the Mehinaku, creates a masculine personality type that is composed of an amalgam of masculine and feminine traits. Psychoanalysts have long been aware of the ambiguity of sexual identity and social psychologists are now beginning to measure it. From the work of Sandra Bem (1974), we know that approximately one third of the male population is "androgynous" in that the men regard themselves as possessing an equal number of stereotypically masculine and feminine personality characteristics. The fact that such traits are not neatly segregated between male and female reflects the complexity of sex identity and the fact that our society is not fully sexually divided. Boys especially grow up in a world that is dominated by the opposite sex and in which men are somewhat remote role models. Time-budget studies reveal that fathers spend less than two hours per week in caring for their children (Vanek 1973), and according to one study, less than fifteen minutes per day even when there is a child of under four years in the household (Szalai 1973). Given the feminine environment of socialization, it is not surprising to find men who are uneasy within the confines of the masculine role. But given our expectations of male behavior, there is no comfortable way to express the feminine side of the masculine self, or even to be aware of it. Only in the clubby warmth of the all-male retreat, where there is no doubt that men are men, can "real" men behave like women.

The similarity of male frustration, fear, insecurity, and antagonism in different societies persuades me that there are continuities of masculinity that transcend cultural differences. To the American visitor, the Mehinaku men's house is in some ways a familiar place. But I would also admit that the Mehinaku pattern of masculinity is more exaggerated than our own, more central to the villagers' culture, and in many respects more extreme. This raises a fundamental question. If masculine psychology is fundamentally similar in both cultures, how can we account for the differences? "Why are we not," as Robert Murphy puts it, "all swinging bull-roarers?" (1969,96).

Murphy answers this question by pointing to structural differences between societies like that of the Mehinaku and our own, differences that promote men's culture in tribal communities and dampen it in large-scale societies. Tribal societies with men's institutions tend to be culturally homogeneous, unstratified, and above all, marked by a division of labor that separates men and women into different work groups. Yolanda and Robert Murphy provide ample support for this position in their study of the Mundurucu Indians (1974), and the Mehinaku data may be regarded as additional confirmation. We recall that Mehinaku women work collectively processing manioc, while together the men fish and farm. The sexual division of labor thereby supports division at every other level in the community: the use of space, the organization of kinship, the structure of religion and mythology.

Comparative studies of societies with men's organizations (for example, Allen 1967) further demonstrate that the intensity of the men's house pattern is directly related to the structural features that unify the men in opposition to the women. Where the men are united to defend the community, and where residence is patrilocal, males are joined together as blood kinsmen and warriors. Women represent foreign communities, some of which may actually be at war with those of their husbands. In such societies, of which the "Sambia" (Herdt 1981) are a good example, the division of men and women and the ethos of sexual fears and antagonism reach heights even beyond those of the Mehinaku.

In contrast to a tribal community, the mass society conceals sexual themes by virtue of its very complexity. Thus male adolescent sexual conflicts are easily overlooked in an age-segregated culture such as ours, while they are an organizing theme in the rituals of a small society. Our society blurs the unity of same-sex groups by all the other ways in which it joins and separates its adult members. We are unified and divided by race, religion, ethnicity, class, vocation, education, and geography. The opposition of the sexes and the pervasiveness of sexual ideas that emerge so sharply among the Mehinaku are blunted. Men's clubs, army barracks, and construction crews are islands and promontories of pure masculine ethos in a society that is primarily organized by the production line and the profit motive.

It therefore seems that we have come a long way from societies like the Mehinaku, and possibly from our own tribal past. But in truth we have not come so far as we think. Masculine sexual frustrations, anxieties, and defensive reactions persist within individual personalities, even if they are not always manifest within our institutions. Between us and the Mehinaku there remains the common bond of masculine gender with all of its uncertainty and ambivalence.

References

Abraham, Karl. 1908. "Dreams and Myths." *Journal of Nervous and Mental Disease*. Monograph no. 15 (1913).

Adams, Kenneth Alan. 1981. "Arachnophobia: Love American Style." *The Journal of Psychoanalytic Anthropology*. 4:157–97.

———. 1983a. "The Greatest American Hero: Ego Ideals and Familial Experiences." *Journal of Psychoanalytic Anthropology* 6:345–414.

———. 1983b. "Love American Style II: 'Octopoid' Genitality and the Medusal Madonna." *Journal of Psychohistory* 10:409–62.

Allen, M. R. 1967. *Male Cults and Secret Initiations in Melanesia*. Melbourne: Melbourne University Press.

Anderson, Jack. 1980. "Trouble Brewing for the Paradise of the Rich?" *Parade*, 22 February, 16–20.

Arlow, Jacob A. 1961. "Ego Psychology and the Study of Mythology." *Journal of the American Psychoanalytic Association* 9:371–93.

Bachofen, Johann J. 1961. *Das Mutterrecht*. Basel: Benno Schwabe.

Bamberger, Joan. 1974. "The Myth of Matriarchy: Why Men Rule in Primitive Society." In *Women, Culture, and Society*, ed. M. Z. Rosaldo and L. Lamphere, 263–80. California: Stanford University Press.

Bandura, Albert, and Robert H. Walters. 1963. *Social Learning and Personality Development*. New York: Holt, Rinehart and Winston.

Becker, George. 1984. "The Social Regulation of Sexuality." In *Current Perspectives in Social Theory*, vol. 5, ed. Scott McNall. Greenwich, Conn.: JAI Press.

Bem, Sandra M. 1974. "The Measurement of Psychological Androgyny." *Journal of Consulting and Clinical Psychology* 42:155–62.

Bettelheim, Bruno. 1943. "Individual and Mass Behavior in Extreme Situations." *Journal of Abnormal and Social Psychology* 38:417–52.

———. 1954. *Symbolic Wounds*. New York: Free Press.

Blanchard, William. 1959. "The Group Process in Gang Rape." *Journal of Social Psychology* 28:512–26.

Blau, Peter M. 1964. *Exchange and Power in Social Life*. New York: John Wiley and Sons.

Broude, Gwen J. 1981. "The Cultural Management of Sexuality." In *Handbook of Cross-Cultural Human Development*, ed. Ruth H. Munroe, Robert L. Munroe, and Beatrice B. Whiting, 633–73. New York: Garland STPM Press.

Brown, Norman O. 1966. *Love's Body*. New York: Random house.

Brownmiller, Susan. 1975. *Against Our Will: Men, Women, and Rape*. New York: Bantam Books.

Bruner, J. S. 1960. "Myths and Identity. "In *Myths and Mythmaking*, ed. H. A. Murray. 276–87. New York: George Braziller.

Carneiro, Robert L. 1957. *Subsistence and Social Structure: An Ecological Study of the Kuikuru Indians*.. Ann Arbor, Michigan: University Microfilms.

———. 1958. "Extra-marital Sex Freedom among the Kuikuru Indians of Mato Grosso." *Revista do Museu Paulista (São Paulo) 10:135–42.*

———. *"The Concept of Multiple Paternity among the Kuikuru: A Step toward the New Study of Ethnoembryology." Typescript.*

Casiday, Margie. 1974. "Dream Catching: A Few Easy Steps to Remembering Dreams." Psychology Today 7:54.

Cheshire, Maxine. 1981. "VIP: Lobbyist and a Madam Prepare to Tell All. *Washington Post* 6 March, C1,6.

Coelho, Vera Penteado. 1983. "Un Eclipse do Sol na Aldeia Waura." *Journal de la Societe des Americanistes* 69:149–67.

Cowan, John. 1980. "Science of a New Life." In *Human Sexuality*, ed. Sam Wilson, Bryan Strong, Mina Robbins, and Thomas Johns. St. Paul, Minn.: West Publishing.

Da Silva, Pedro Agostinho. 1978. "Upper Xingu Basin Cultural History: Some Methodological Suggestions." Paper presented at the Meeting of the American Anthropological Association, Los Angeles, California, November 1978.

Delaney, Janice, Mary Jane Lupton, and Emily Toth. 1976. *The Curse: A Cultural History of Menstruation*. New York: E. P. Dutton and Co.

Dole, Gertrude. 1978. "The Use of Manioc among the Kuikuru: Some Interpretations." In *The Nature and Status of Ethnobotany*, ed. R. Ford, 212–47. Anthropology Museum Paper no. 67. University of Michigan.

Domhoff, G. William. 1974. *The Bohemian Grove and Other Retreats: A Study in Ruling Class Cohesiveness*. New York: Harper and Row.

Dundes, Alan. 1976. "A Psychoanalytic Study of the Bullroarer." *Man* 11:220–38.

Dwyer, Daisy H. 1978. *Images and Self-Images: Male and Female in Morocco*. New York: Columbia University Press.

Federal Bureau of Investigation. 1984. "1982 Uniform Crime Reports." In *The World Almanac, 1984*. New York: Newspaper Enterprise Association.

Ford, Clelan S., and Frank A. Beach. 1951. *Patterns of Sexual Behavior*. New York: Harper.

Frazer, James George. 1951. *The Golden Bough*. New York: Macmillan.

Freud, Sigmund. 1950. *Totem and Taboo*. New York: W. W. Norton.

———. 1957. "Three Essays on Sexuality." In The Complete Psychological Works of Sigmund Freud, ed. J. Strachey, 125–245. London: Hogarth.

———. 1963. *A General Introduction to Psychoanalysis.* New York: Simon and Schuster.

Fry, William F. 1972. "Psychodynamics of Sexual Humor: Women's View of Sex" *Medical Aspects of Human Sexuality* 6(4):124–139.

Garfinkel, Harold. 1967. "Passing and the Managed Achievement of Sex Status in an 'Intersexed' Person." In *Studies in Ethnomethodology.* Englewood Cliffs, N.J.: Prentice-Hall.

Gay, Peter. 1984. *The Bourgeois Experience: Victoria to Freud.* Vol. 1. New York: Oxford University Press.

Gist, Noel P. 1940. *Societies: A Cultural Study of Fraternalism in the United States.* Columbia: University of Missouri Press.

Goulding, Michael. 1980. *The Fishes and the Forest.* Berkley: University of California Press.

Greenson, Ralph R. 1968. "Dis-Identifying from Mother: Its Special Importance for the Boy." *International Journal of Psycho-Analysis* 49:370–74.

Gregor, Thomas. 1977. *Mehinaku: The Drama of Daily Life in a Brazilian Indian Village.* Chicago: University of Chicago Press.

———. 1979. "Short People." *Natural History* 88(2):14–23.

———. 1981a. "Far, Far Away, My Shadow Wandered . . .": Dream Symbolism and Dream Theories of the Mehinaku Indians of Brazil." *American Ethnologist* 8:709–2.

———. 1981b. "A Content Analysis of Mehinaku Dreams." *Ethos* 9:353–90.

Hall, Calvin S., and Robert L. Van de Castle. 1966. *The Content Analysis of Dreams.* New York: Appleton-Century-Crofts.

Harrington, Charles. 1970. *Errors in Sex-Role Behavior in Teen-age Boys.* New York: Teachers College Press.

Hartley, Ruth E. 1959. "Sex-Role Pressures and the Socialization of the Male Child." *Psychological Reports* 5:457–68.

Hayes, Rose Oldfield. 1975. "Female Genital Mutilation, Fertility Control, Women's Roles, and the Patrilineage in Modern Sudan: A Functional Analysis." *American Ethnologist* 2:617–48.

Heider, Karl G. 1976. "Dani Sexuality: A Low Energy System." *Man* 11: 188–201.

Herdt, Gilbert. 1981. *Guardians of the Flutes: Idioms of Masculinity.* New York: McGraw Hill.

Hite, Shere. 1981. *The Hite Report on Male Sexuality.* New York: Alfred A. Knopf.

Hoyenga, Katherine Blick, and Kermit T. Hoyenga. 1979. *The Question of Sex Differences.* Boston: Little Brown and Co.

Hunt, Martin M. 1974. *Sexual Behavior in the 1970s.* Chicago: Playboy Press.

Jaffe, Daniel S. 1968. "The Masculine Envy of Woman's Procreative Function." *Journal of the American Psychoanalytic Association* 16:521–48.

Kinsey, Alfred C., William B. Pomeroy, and Charles E. Martin. 1948. *Sexual Behavior in the Human Male.* Philadelphia: W. B. Saunders.

Klein, Melanie, 1948. *Contributions to Psycho-Analysis, 1921–1945.* London: Hogarth.

Kline, Paul. 1972. *Fact and Fantasy in Freudian Theory*. London: Methuen.

Kohlberg, Lawrence. 1969. "Stage and Sequence: The Cognitive-Development Approach to Socialization." In *Handbook of Socialization Theory and Research*, ed. D. A. Goslin, 347–480. Chicago: Rand McNally.

Leach, Edmund R. 1964. "Anthropological Aspects of Language: Animal Categories and Verbal Abuse." In *New Directions in the Study of Language*, ed. Eric H. Lenneberg, 23–63. Cambridge, Mass.: M.I.T. Press.

Legman, Gershon. 1968. *Rationale of the Dirty Joke: An Analysis of Sexual Humor*. Vol. 1. New York: Grove Press.

———. 1972. *Rationale of the Dirty Joke: An Analysis of Sexual Humor*. Vol. 2. St. Albans: Panther Books.

———. 1977. *The New Limerick*. New York: Crown Publishers.

Lehne, Gregory K. 1976. "Homophobia among Men." In *The Forty-Nine Percent Majority*, ed. Deborah S. David and Robert Brannon, 66–88. Reading Mass.: Addison-Wesley.

Lidz, Ruth, and Theodore Lidz. 1977. "Male Menstruation: A Ritual Alternative to the Oedipal Transition." *International Journal of Psycho-Analysis* 58:17–31.

Loewald, Hans W. 1951. "Ego and Reality." *International Journal of Psycho-Analysis* 32:10–18.

Lowie, Robert H. 1920. *Primitive Society*. New York: Boni and Liveright.

Lynn, David B. 1966. "The Process of Learning Parental and Sex-Role Identification." *Journal of Marriage and the Family* 28:466–70.

Maccoby, Eleanor E., and Carol N. Jacklin. 1974. *The Psychology of Sex Differences*. Stanford: Standord University Press.

Mahler, Margaret S., Fred Pine, and Anni Bergman. 1975. *The Psychological Birth of the Human Infant*. New York: Basic Books.

Malinowski, Bronislaw. 1929. *The Sexual Life of Savages*. New York: Harcourt, Brace and World.

Marshall, Donald S. 1972. "Sexual Behavior on Mangaia." In *Human Sexual Behavior: Variations in Ethnographic Spectrum*, ed. D. S. Marshall and R. C. Suggs, 103–62. Englewood Cliffs, N.J.: Prentice-Hall.

Martin, M. Key, and Barbara Voorhies. 1975. *Female of the Species*. New York: Columbia University Press.

Messenger, John C. 1972. "Sex and Repression in an Irish Folk Community." In *Human Sexual Behavior: Variations in Ethnographic Spectrum*, ed. D. S. Marshall and R. C. Suggs, 3–37. Englewood Cliffs, N.J.: Prentice-Hall.

Meigs, Anna S. 1984. *Food, Sex, and Pollution: A New Guinea Religion*. New Brunswick: Rutgers University Press.

Mischel, William. 1966. "A Social Learning View of Sex Differences in Behavior." In *The Development of Sex Differences*, ed. E. E. Maccoby, 56–81. Stanford, Cal.: Stanford University Press.

Money, John, and A. A. Erhardt. 1972. *Man and Woman, Boy and Girl*. Baltimore: Johns Hopkins University Press.

Montgomery, Rita E. 1974. "A Cross-Cultural Study of Menstruation, Menstrual Taboos, and Related Social Variables." *Ethos* 2:137–70.

Munroe, Robert L., and Ruth H. Munroe. 1975. *Cross-Cultural Human Development*. Monterey, Cal.: Brooks/Cole Publishing Company.

Munroe, Robert L., Ruth H. Monroe, and John W. M. Whiting. 1973. "The Couvade: A Psychological Analysis." *Ethos* 1:28–74.

———. 1981. "Male Sex-Role Resolutions." In *Handbook of Cross-Cultural Human Development*, ed. R. H. Munroe, R. L. Munroe, and B. B. Whiting, 611–32. New York: Garland STPM Press.

Murdock, George Peter. 1949. *Social Structure*. New York: Macmillan.

———. 1964. "Cultural Correlates of the Regulation of Premarital Sexual Behavior." In *Process and Pattern in Culture: Essays in Honor of Julian H. Steward*, ed. Robert A. Manners, 339–410. Chicago: Aldine.

Murphy, Robert F. 1959. "Social Structure and Sex Antagonism." *Southwestern Journal of Anthropology* 15:89–98.

———. 1974. "Deviance and Social Control II: Borai." In *Native South Americans*, ed. Patricia J. Lyon, 202–8. Boston: Little Brown.

———. 1977. "Man's Culture and Woman's Nature. *Annals of the New York Academy of Sciences* 293:15–24.

———. 1979. *Overture to Social Anthropology*. Englewood Cliffs, N.J.: Prentice-Hall.

Murphy, Yolanda, and Robert F. Murphy. 1974. *Women of the Forest*. New York: Columbia University Press.

Ortner, Sherry B., and Harriet Whitehead. 1975. *Sexual Meanings: The Cultural Construction of Gender and Sexuality*. New York: Cambridge.

Parsons, Talcott, and Robert F. Bales. 1955. *Family Socialization and Interaction Process*. New York: Free Press.

Pleck, Joseph H. 1982. *The Myth of Masculinity*. Cambridge, Mass.: MIT Press.

Pontius, A. 1977. "Dani Sexuality." *Man* 12: 166–67.

Prescott, James W. 1975. "Body Pleasure and the Origins of Violence." *Bulletin of the Atomic Scientists* 31:10–20.

Sarnoff, Irving, and Seth M. Corwin. 1959. "Castration Anxiety and the Fear of Death." *Journal of Personality* 27:374–85.

Schultz, Harald. 1965. "Lendas Waura." *Revista do Museu Paulista* (São Paulo) 16:21–149.

Simmel, Georg. 1950. "The Secret and the Secret Society." In *The Sociology of Georg Simmel*, ed. Kurt H. Wolff, 307–76. Glencoe, Ill.: Free Press.

Siskind, Janet. 1973. "Tropical Forest Hunters and the Economy of Sex." In *Peoples and Cultures of South America*, ed. Daniel R. Gross, 226–40. New York: Natural History Press.

Spiro, Melford. 1961. "An Overview and a Suggested Reorientation. In *Psychological Anthropology*, ed. F. L. K. Hsu, 459–92. Homewood, Ill.: Dorsey Press.

Steinen, Karl von den. 1940. "Entre os Aborigenes do Brasil Central." *Separata da Revista do Arquivo*, nos. 34–58. Departamento de Cultura. São Paulo, Brazil.

Stephens, William N. 1967. "A Cross-Cultural Study of Menstrual Taboos." In *Cross-Cultural Approaches*, ed. Clellan S. Ford, 67–94. New Haven: HRAF Press.

———. 1972. "A Cross-Cultural Study of Modesty. "*Behavior Science Notes* 7:1–28.

Stoller, Robert J. 1974. "Symbiosis Anxiety and the Development of Masculinity. *Archives of General Psychiatry* 30:164–72.

Stoller, Robert J., and Gilbert H. Herdt. 1982. "The Development of Masculinity: A Cross-Cultural Contribution." *Journal of the American Psychoanalytic Association* 30:29–59.

Symons, Donald. 1979. *The Evolution of Human Sexuality*. New York: Oxford University Press.

Szalai, Alexander. 1973. *The Use of Time: Daily Activities of Urban and Suburban Populations in Twelve Countries*. The Hague: Mouton.

Tampax Corporation. 1981. *The Tampax Report*. New York: Research and Forecasts, Inc.

Tyson, Phyllis. 1982. "A Development Line of Gender Identity, Gender Role, and Choice of Love Object." *Journal of the American Psychoanalytic Association* 30:61–86.

Valentine, Charles A. 1961. *Masks and Men in Melanesian Society*. Lawrence: University of Kansas Press.

Vanek, Joann. 1973. *Keeping Busy: Time Spent in Housework, U.S. 1920–1970*. Ann Arbor: University of Michigan Microfilms.

Wikan, Unni. 1977. "Man Becomes Woman: Transexualism in Oman as a Key to Gender Roles." *Man* 12:304–19.

Willey, Gordon R. 1971. *An Introduction to American Archaeology*. Vol. 1. Englewood Cliffs, N.J.: Prentice-Hall.

Young, Frank W. 1965. *Initiation Ceremonies*. Indianapolis: Bobbs-Merrill.

Young, Frank W., and Albert Bacdayan. 1967. "Menstrual Taboos and Social Rigidity." In *Cross-Cultural Approaches*, ed. Clellan S. Ford, 95–110. New Haven: HRAF Press.

Zarur, George. 1975. "Parentesco." *Ritual e Economia no Alto Xingu*. Brasilia: Fundação Nacional do Indio.

Zerries, Otto. 1942. "The Bull-Roarer among South American Indians." *Revista do Museu Paulista* (São Paulo) 7:275–309.

Index